THE
NEXT
BIG
THING

THE
NEXT
BIG
THING

How Football's Wonderkids
Lose Their Way

R Y A N   B A L D I

First published by Pitch Publishing, 2019

Pitch Publishing
A2 Yeoman Gate
Yeoman Way
Worthing
Sussex
BN13 3QZ
www.pitchpublishing.co.uk
info@pitchpublishing.co.uk

ISBN 978-1-78531-501-5

Typesetting and origination by Pitch Publishing

Printed and bound in India by Replika Press Pvt. Ltd.

Contents

Introduction 9

Acknowledgements 13

Just Getting Started 15

A Different World 33

Shattered 51

Such Great Heights 77

Fixed 91

From Club to Club 104

Chaos Theory 117

The Long Goodbye 135

Worn-Out Tools 151

A Tale of Two Strikers 166

Virtual Reality Bites 182

Price Tag 193

Degree of Separation 202

Keeping the Faith 215

The Weight 232

Epilogue 249

For Sophie and Dylan, my world

Introduction

NOTHING captures the imagination of the football fan in quite the same way as the emergence of a prodigious young player. Whether it's a home-grown prospect moulded within the club's academy, a rough diamond plucked from obscurity overseas, or a fearless teen talent making fools of experienced pros, it has the power to get bums out of seats, hairs stood on end and spines tingling in anticipation of what this intrepid new hero might do next.

No matter how young or old the supporter, we live vicariously through these nascent superstars as they act out every fan's fantasy. We forgive their shortcomings and plot their career paths, forecasting at which point they will be ready for landmarks such as regular first-team involvement, international caps and big-money transfers.

The success stories are well known, subsequently making these early steps real 'I-was-there' moments. Who could forget, for example, Wayne Rooney's stunning strike for Everton against Arsenal as a 16-year-old in 2002, or his debut hat-trick for Manchester United two years later? Those inside the Camp Nou on 1 May 2005 will forever remember the day they saw Lionel Messi lob his first-ever senior goal for Barcelona over the head of the helpless Espanyol goalkeeper. Likewise, the story of a 17-year-old Brazilian forward named Pelé lighting up the 1958 World Cup in Sweden has been passed down the generations by those old enough, and fortunate enough, to have witnessed it first-hand.

The young players who burn brightly and fade quickly, though, are remembered less vividly. Every football fan will be able to list a handful of names of players who burst on to the scene and promised great things with their initial performances before falling from view. The eyes glint at the memory of those exciting early outings, but a shrug often accompanies any remembrance of what came next, with little known of how or why these players were unable to fulfil their potential; more often than not, it is simply assumed that they were never quite as good as first believed, or that for all their talent they were held back by a lack of professionalism or a bad attitude.

But the connection these players made at the very beginning, the intrigue they sparked when they appeared to have the world at their feet, often endures. For many, there remains a certain curiosity about the meandering, out-of-view paths these young players' careers ended up following. And it is the same curiosity around which the idea for this book was formed.

I set out with the intention of tracking down and interviewing players who were all tipped for the top as youngsters, but whose careers never reached the heights expected. By speaking to them, hearing their stories in their own words, with further context provided by former team-mates, coaches and journalists who covered their careers, I learned not only how best-laid plans fell apart for these individuals, but also the strain it placed on them, emotionally and physically. Through these honest accounts of their setbacks, struggles and disappointments, I came to understand how these young men were forced to grow up quickly and reconcile with a faded dream.

The 15 players kind enough to share their time and experiences for this book have many things in common. All, at some stage of their careers, were developmentally ahead of the curve, supremely talented outliers in the ultra-competitive and demanding world of professional football. They played for major clubs – such as Manchester United, Liverpool, Tottenham Hotspur and Internazionale – and were youth or senior internationals. And all suffered setbacks – some of their own making, many beyond their control – which ultimately left their potential unfulfilled.

But each player's experience differs greatly. Some reached the highest level before their fall, playing Champions League football, featuring in major international tournaments and commanding large transfer fees, while others were tripped by hurdles much sooner. And the 15 players featured are not presented as a definitive list of football's great unfulfilled talents, they are simply the players I approached who were willing to share their journeys, most of whom enjoyed enough success to look back on their time in the game with pride, while some are still playing and working towards realising their vast potential.

The reasons for their struggles differ, too. Exploring the myriad of factors that can affect a young footballer's development became my primary aim as the process of putting this book together went on. As I travelled from city to city, country to country, to speak to these players and those they've worked closely with, I grew to appreciate just how tenuous a grasp any sportsperson has on their career.

Injuries, of course, are a recurring theme here, but in reading this book you will learn how injuries can affect players in different ways. For example, Ally Dick, the precocious Scottish winger who is the subject of Chapter 1, was a high achiever at an early age but reconciled with the fact that, by 23, knee and ankle problems meant he would never play at the highest level again. Dick's experience was different to Matt Murray's (Chapter 8), with the Wolverhampton Wanderers and England under-21 goalkeeper spending more than a decade battling back from injury after injury, each time recovering peak form before agonisingly being cut down. And then there is the case of Lionel Morgan (Chapter 9), the highly coveted Wimbledon winger who admitted that by 19 he knew his body was not going to allow him a prolonged career in the game.

Injuries are just one potential stumbling block aspiring young players have to contend with, though. Some of the other factors that can derail a budding career you'll find detailed in this book include off-field substance problems, the snowball effect of seemingly innocuous decisions, strained relationships with managers – such as the one Giuliano Maiorana (Chapter 2) had with Manchester United boss Sir Alex Ferguson – and how regime change at a club can see even the brightest talents forgotten about.

With each chapter dedicated to one player's career and personal journey, *The Next Big Thing* is, in effect, a collection of case studies into some of the different ways a promising young footballer can be derailed.

By virtue of the age range of the players featured, with the oldest in his mid-50s and the youngest a 24-year-old still making his way in the game, this book's timeline also traces the advances in medical science, with injuries such as cruciate knee ligament ruptures going from a genuine threat to a career to a painful inconvenience that can be fully overcome within nine months. The formation and growth of the Premier League, and the ever-expanding river of cash it flooded football with, runs alongside the book's progression, too, with the rewards on offer to young footballers growing steadily throughout, and likewise the pressure to perform.

More than anything else, what you will learn from reading this book is that so much more goes into the making of a top-level football career than simply talent and desire. I hope that each player's story will give context to the contrasting trajectories of their contemporaries who 'made it', showing just how slippery a slope must be navigated in order to reach football's summit, and why it is important for the game and its followers to afford the proper care and compassion to those it leaves behind.

These forgotten, misunderstood or previously untold stories are important, eye-opening and illuminating. They deserve to be heard.

Acknowledgements

FIRSTLY, I'd like to sincerely thank every player who so kindly shared their time and their story with me for this book; without them, this literally would not have been possible. Thanks also to all the team-mates, coaches, managers, administrators, journalists and writers whose input helped provide crucial background and context for each chapter.

Thank you, too, to everybody who aided my efforts in contacting the players featured and helped set up the interviews around which the book is based: James Bain, Stuart Brown, Jamie Hall, Karen Shotbolt, Darren Bentley, Paul Rogers, David Winner, David Endt, Paul Edwards, Kevin Watson, Paul Dews, Florent Nyanga, Alan Redmond, Matt Lorenzo, Matt Paddock, Greg Gordon, Ally Palmer and Alex Kay-Jelski.

Thanks to Sarah Winterburn and the team at *Football365*, who helped publicise the project by kindly publishing multiple extracts, and to Will Denny, my ever-reliable soundboard. And thank you to my colleagues at *Football Whispers*, who showed support and offered helpful insight and suggestions along the way.

A special thank you to my wonderfully supportive parents, Mark and Diane, and the family and friends whose interest, enthusiasm and tireless support has helped drive this project.

Above all, thank you to the love of my life, my beautiful fiancée, my Sophie. Without your love, support and encouragement, I would still be bouncing between unfulfilling jobs I have little interest in. I will be forever grateful for how you drove me to pursue my passion and remained not only tolerant but encouraging of this project despite it coinciding with pregnancy and the birth of our first child.

And to Dylan, our beautiful little boy, whose arrival in June 2018 ensures this book can only ever aspire to be my second-proudest creation.

Just Getting Started

EVERY football-loving 15-year-old has had a version of the same dream: the pristine turf of a packed-out Wembley Stadium, the stands awash with flags and banners as the oldest rivalry in football resumes in front of a television audience of millions. A nine-goal thriller ensues as you, stationed on the wing, put in a virtuoso display of skill and invention, capped by a goal that sees the ball fired high into the crisp, taut net. The instant the referee brings his whistle to his lips to signal full time, the biggest clubs from around the land are falling over themselves to court your services.

Ally Dick lived this dream. When Scotland under-16s travelled to London to take on their English counterparts on 7 June 1980, it was standing room only as 69,000 flooded into Wembley, while the game was broadcast live on ITV. It was an era in which televised live football was a rarity, before satellite TV brought 24-hour, sport-dedicated channels.

Sponsors Halls Hudnut, makers of Dentyne chewing gum, provided the victors' prize: the Dentyne Trophy. But above all else, pride was at stake; England were looking to avenge a Victory Shield defeat to the Scots suffered months earlier.

Dick was the star of the show when Scotland beat England in their Victory Shield meeting in Motherwell, scoring both his side's goals in a 2-1 win. At Wembley, he once again marked himself out as an exceptional talent.

'It was a laugh, that game,' Dick begins, recounting the schoolboy fixture played before a scarcely believable audience. 'I was the youngest in the team; I was a year below everybody else. That was a game that every man and his dog came to watch

– all the scouts. You're just a wee schoolboy, you're not expecting that. You think maybe some people will turn up, but not like that. Someone said there'd be 50,000 people – 50,000 people? Come on.

'I already had tons of clubs after me, but because I hadn't signed any S-forms [a schoolboy contract with a professional club] – I was the only one on the park who hadn't – I was available. The phone didn't stop ringing the next morning.'

No wonder. The fact that Dick was not affiliated to a professional club was not down to any lack of interest in him, rather he possessed the clarity of thought as a teenager to keep his options open while still in school, allowing the buzz around him to grow. Distinctive gliding along the Wembley pitch thanks to an upright running style and the kind of flowing blond locks that would have seen him endorsing the highest-bidding shampoo brand in a different era, you didn't need a scout's trained eye to see that here was a player a cut above his peers.

Before the game, Ted Austin, the English Schools FA chairman, went into the away dressing room and told the Scotland boys he didn't mind them winning, so long as it was by a 5-4 scoreline, 'for the cameras'. They didn't disappoint. Two goals for future Celtic legend Paul McStay helped ensure a hat-trick for Paul Rideout (whose career would reach its zenith when he headed an FA Cup Final winner for Everton against Manchester United on the same ground 15 years later) didn't prevent Scotland triumphing 5-4. You're welcome, Ted.

Dick, scorer of a sublime, left-footed effort, direct creator of one of McStay's strikes and whose mesmerising wing play was the catalyst for most of Scotland's attacking success, revelled in the limelight. Calm under pressure, he was a born entertainer.

'That was my thing: the bigger the better, for me. I knew everybody else would be nervous. I liked the fact that it didn't affect me that much. I was quite calm and never got overawed. The bigger the game, the bigger the crowd, the better I was.

'It was when we'd play reserve-team games away at Wycombe Wanderers, on a Wednesday night in pouring rain, that's when I struggled. I thought I was there to entertain. I was never one of these players who'd play it backwards, keep it simple.'

The Wembley match was the first time journalist Graham Hunter saw Dick in action. Like the 69,000 in attendance and the millions watching on TV, he was struck by the young winger's skill and sense of adventure.

'I didn't know any of the other players that day, but Ally stood out,' Hunter says. 'I'd grown up seeing wingers at my club, Aberdeen, with Arthur Graham and Ian Scanlon. Wingers were a big thing. I'm not old enough to have lived in the golden generation of Jimmy Johnstone and Willie Henderson, but I loved, at national level, Willie Morgan and Tommy Hutchison and Eddie Gray and John Robertson, who'd already won two consecutive European Cups [with Nottingham Forest] by the time I saw Ally play, so wingers were really *en vogue*.'

I met Dick at the Colessio Hotel in Stirling, the city in which he was born and bred. The 'Gateway to the Highlands', Stirling is a city rich in history, its vistas dominated by the picturesque Stirling Castle. But it is not a big city, home to just 36,142 people, according to a 2011 census. Still, Hunter believes geography had a part to play in Dick's footballing aptitude.

'He comes from a particular part of Stirling where there was a real bedrock of successful Scottish footballers,' Hunter says. 'He comes from the area where Billy Bremner was born and brought up, but also John Colquhoun, who went on to play for Celtic and Hearts, Brian Grant went on to play for Aberdeen, Gary Gillespie played for Liverpool, Willie Garner won cups with Aberdeen.

'He was growing up in an area where being a football star, being a professional, was quite commonplace. That changes your aspirations. I would never say it was expected, but there was a pride in the area that if you were from that part of Stirling and you could kick a ball the least you'd end up doing was playing for Stirling Albion. And once an area begins to produce footballers, scouts just go back there.'

Dick never did play for Stirling Albion, although he did spend some time coaching the club's academy players in 2011; with respect to the Scottish League Two side, his aspirations were much higher.

After his performance at Wembley, Dick's stock was higher than ever. He'd already been courted by Scotland's biggest clubs, even spending time training with Celtic, but his virtuoso display against the English, coupled with his lack of ties to any professional club, made him hot property. Within days of the game, he claims, 42 clubs made their interest known. Shortly after returning home from the London excursion, the *Daily Record* dispatched a reporter to Dick's house for a feature on the 15-year-old. In the short time the journalist spent at the Dick family home, an offer from Arsenal arrived in the post and a phone call came in from Tottenham Hotspur, the club the winger elected to join the following year.

'I had 42 clubs offering me contracts, whereas if I'd had an S-form,' Dick suggests, 'I'd have been tied to one club that whole time.

'On the weekends, when I finished school on a Friday, me and my dad would fly down to London – or Manchester, or Birmingham – and I'd play with Tottenham Hotspur or Queens Park Rangers' youth teams.

'I'd play under an assumed name, because you weren't allowed to play at under-16s. Everybody knew who I was, but technically I was "Joe Bloggs". My school gave me permission to do that for three weeks out of a year. When it became clear that this could be my career, they gave me an extra three weeks' holiday at the start of the year.'

While club football was drawing into focus, Dick remained a key player in the Scotland under-age teams. In 1982 he would play a lead role in Scotland winning the European Under-18 Championships, starring opposite future Chelsea and Everton wide man Pat Nevin as the Scots topped a group that included a Holland side spearheaded by Marco van Basten – later a team-mate of Dick's at club level – before seeing off Czechoslovakia in the final.

'I'd never come across Ally before,' Nevin told *Nutmeg* magazine, 'but his name had been bandied around a fair bit in the press. Expectations were high.

'He was a year younger than me, but even so he was considered an older hand. We were chosen for a Scotland under-18s friendly at Fir Park; we played on opposite wings and both of us scored. In one of the newspapers the next day, the headline was brilliant. It read "Nevin and Dick shine."'

Dick would compete in an even more talented Scotland side at the FIFA World Youth Championships the following year, held in Mexico. Their progress this time was halted at the quarter-final stage.

Despite a glowing youth career on the international scene, and despite spells at Tottenham and Ajax, Dick never earned a senior cap for Scotland, his prospects hampered by serious knee and ankle injuries.

Before spending seven years in charge of the Scotland national team, Andy Roxburgh oversaw the Scottish youth sides, and it was he who managed the under-18s to European Championship glory in '82.

'He was one we identified quite early as someone of potential,' Roxburgh says of Dick. 'Very few make the first team of their clubs when they are teenagers; Paul McStay was one and so was Ally.

'He was very much the flying winger. But when we played those [European Championship] finals, our striker, Eric Black, was withdrawn. He was Aberdeen's striker and they had a cup final, so Alex Ferguson had to keep him back. Ally Dick and Pat Nevin were our two wingers, but because our strikers had been withdrawn, I decided to play them as strikers. When you think about false nines, that's very much how they played.

'He was clearly a player of potential. He was doing well at Tottenham and then he went over to Ajax. In his case, it seemed to just fade away because he had injuries. He was a shining light as a teenager and never quite realised his potential.'

* * *

Dick had the football world at his feet in 1981. Wanted by every major club in the land, the 16-year-old surveyed his options carefully, but it didn't take long for the ambitious youngster to settle upon a destination.

'I used to go every weekend and summer holidays to a lot of clubs to train,' Dick recalls. 'I went to Aston Villa a lot, I went to Man City, QPR, Crystal Palace. I realised I liked London, so in my head I knew [that was where I wanted to play]. But I never told anybody.

'After being at a few London clubs when I was 15, I'd been to Tottenham three or four times and always had a laugh. I felt part of it. I thought, "Right, that's the club for me." I felt at home there.

'I told my parents that was where I wanted to go. They said, "Keep your eye on it. You might change your mind." I still continued to go to other clubs, but in the back of my mind – Tottenham. Then when I was 16 and I was able to sign legally it was still Tottenham.

'I remember the day it was in the papers I'd decided to sign for Tottenham, and Crystal Palace turned up at my door. The guy says, "Whatever they've offered you, we'll give you double." It was nothing to do with money. I just enjoyed it [at Tottenham]. It was a great laugh. There was a nice family atmosphere. I was a quiet guy – I was confident but quiet – and I fitted in there.'

In addition to Spurs making Dick feel at home, the fact they had just won the FA Cup certainly didn't hurt their hopes of winning the teenager's affections. Moreover, Spurs were the most stylish side in the land, boasting such exotic talents as Glenn Hoddle and Argentinian duo Ossie Ardiles and Ricky Villa. Tottenham sealed their FA Cup triumph the same week Dick signed, beating Manchester City 3-2 in a dramatic Wembley replay. The famous, slaloming winner scored by Villa, swerving his way through what felt like the entire City team before slotting past goalkeeper Joe Corrigan, would surely have captured Dick's imagination, appealing to his inner entertainer.

'They flew me, my brother and my dad to the Saturday game, which was a draw, then they played the replay on the Wednesday. They said, "We'll fly you down again." But my dad was working, so we said, "Leave it." And that was the game Ricky Villa scored the goal. That was the week I committed to Tottenham.'

Once he'd finished his schooling at 16, Dick left home for London, more than 400 miles south of Stirling, a seven-hour journey by car. He did so alone, leaving behind his family and moving in with a host family arranged by Tottenham. Although club trials and Scotland youth-team excursions meant Dick was as well travelled as a 16-year-old could hope to be in 1981, he could have been forgiven for feeling daunted by such a drastic move. But the Scot had no reservations about moving south of the border. He had long been sure of a professional future in the game, and he knew England was the place to be if he was to become a top player.

'I knew when I was 13 years old I'd be a football player,' Dick matter-of-factly states. 'When I was 13, I was playing in the under-15s. I was always playing two years above and I was still the best player. Celtic were asking me to sign at that age. I knew I was good. I knew I was better than most.

'When I was 14, it was guaranteed – as much as you can guarantee it – that I was going to be a professional football player. I knew that there would have been a lot of clubs offering me a contract, and I knew I would have a choice of all the top clubs, so I didn't have to wait around and play for Stirling Albion for a couple of years, or even Celtic.

'A lot of people said, "Start off here [in Scotland] and build up." But Scottish football was kind of dodgy in the early 80s. I always wanted to play in England, so I thought, "Why put it off when I can do it now?" I don't regret a thing. I think I did the right thing. I did what I wanted to do and I've loved every second of it.

'I was very mature for my age. I handled all that pretty well,' Dick says of moving to London. His landlady, whom he describes as 'very mumsy', was a mother of ten, with three of her children still living at home. Taking the teenager in as one of their own, the host family 'really looked after me,' he says. 'I was only there for a year and a bit before I bought a fancy house in a nice part of London, but I still used to go back, it was perfect for me. I'd been there before and stayed with that family when I was there training for a week, so I knew them, I liked them.'

On 20 February 1982 Dick became the youngest player ever to play for the Tottenham first team. Aged 16 years and 301 days, he started a First Division match against Manchester City at White Hart Lane. Although, 26 years later, John Bostock (Chapter 14) would break Dick's record as the youngest-ever Spurs player, to this day Dick remains the youngest both to start and feature in a league game, with Bostock coming off the bench in a 2008 UEFA Cup tie against Dinamo Zagreb.

Not only was Dick unaware of his little piece of history at the time, but his ascension to the first team took him wholly by surprise.

The summer he'd signed for Spurs, he'd been involved with the senior side during pre-season, making the odd ten-minute cameo in friendly matches. But when the 1981/82 campaign began in earnest, he spent his time with either the youth team or the reserves, which was exactly as he'd envisioned his early Spurs years, having joined the club so young.

Dick described his call-up to the first team as 'a total shocker. I woke up one morning in my digs, was getting my breakfast and the landlady put the newspaper in front of me. It said, "Ally Dick prepares to make senior debut." That was the first I'd heard of it. But I went to training on Friday and my name was in the 11. The manager told me I was going to be starting the next day.'

Even for the perma-laidback winger, the thought of starting a First Division game at White Hart Lane, aged just 16, caused sweaty palms. 'That was nerve-wracking,' he admits. 'I'm usually quite calm about things, but I think this was the first time I was nervous before a game. My legs felt numb.'

Ultimately, Dick found himself more comfortable at first-team level than he had been in the reserves, where the roughhousing and lax approach to properly applying the laws of the game was a shock to the system. 'When I turned up for the first reserve game, the guy I was playing against had a big beard and he kicked the shit out of me,' Dick recalls, wincing at the memory. 'And he was talking to me: "I'm going to break your legs." That was me learning football. I found the pace and physicality of it tough going. I was quick so I could get away, but that first year was tough, that initiation to reserve-team football. First-team football I always found easier – you played with better players, much more technical. But the reserves: with a handful of people watching, you get away with murder.'

Dick's seamless assimilation to senior football saw him become understudy to Tony Galvin, Tottenham's first-choice left-winger. Galvin, a Republic of Ireland international, was nine years the Scot's senior, robust and rarely injured. In an era long before squads 25-men strong, and with only two substitutes permitted, Dick's first-team exposure was limited. He did, however, turn out in the second leg of the 1984 UEFA Cup Final. Anderlecht were Tottenham's opponents, and Spurs had returned to White Hart Lane with a credible 1-1 draw from the first leg.

The Londoners found themselves trailing their Belgian visitors 1-0 by the time Dick came off the bench in the 77th minute, Alexandre Czerniatynski having put Anderlecht ahead on the hour. Ossie Ardiles had replaced Gary Mabbutt five minutes earlier and Dick came on for defender Paul Miller as manager Keith Burkinshaw threw caution to the wind in search of an equaliser.

Captain Graham Roberts eventually scored with eight minutes to play, taking the game to extra time. Spurs won a penalty shootout, thanks to goalkeeper Tony Parks saving Arnór Guðjohnsen's decisive kick, to claim a second UEFA Cup, following their 1972 triumph over Wolverhampton Wanderers in an all-English final.

For Dick, though, the victory was bittersweet. Not long after coming off the bench, he injured his ankle, he believes, by treading on a sprinkler that hadn't been fully depressed beneath the turf. Ligaments were ruptured. It was the first of a series of serious injuries that would eventually contribute to his departure from top-level football aged 23, and eventual retirement at 32.

'The groundsmen will fight to this day,' Dick says, 'to tell you it wasn't, but ... you know the sprinklers that come out of the turf? I think it was that bit of turf that I stood on that gave way under me. [That was] the first time that I tore my ligaments, by just sort of jarring my ankle slightly, hyperextending it, in the UEFA Cup Final.

'I'd only been on for 15 minutes. I got injured and I couldn't come off. I wouldn't have come off anyway. I kind of limped through the next 45 minutes with torn ligaments.

'At the end of the game, everyone was saying, "Come in tomorrow [to get the injury assessed]." We went to a nightclub that night and I was limping around, sweating. Then next day they sent me to the hospital and I ended up staying there for a few days, getting my leg in plaster. It wasn't an operation, it just had to be stabilised for six weeks. That was my first injury that needed hospitalisation.'

After six weeks in plaster, Dick's injured knee felt right as rain. The following season, however, he would suffer an ankle injury from which he never fully recovered. Eager to impress in a reserve fixture his parents were in town to attend, he found himself 'going in for tackles I wouldn't normally go in for'.

In one such challenge, his studs caught in the turf. 'My ankle went back on itself,' he says. 'The [physio] said, "A couple of weeks; ice it and you'll be fine." I started playing again in about eight weeks, but it was still sore.

'After about three months, they sent me to see a doctor – the same doctor who did Paul Gascoigne's knee operations. They sent me to [the doctor's] house, because he lived quite close to me. So I went to this big, beautiful house in the centre of London. I explained to him about my sore ankle and he got a big needle, cortisone, and gave me about eight injections, all around my ankle.

'I went home and my ankle was great – it's gone, totally gone.' Although the initial pain was treated, Dick was later told by a physio at Ajax that his ankle should have been destabilised after the cortisone injections, and that playing on it without allowing it the proper time to heal likely caused lasting damage. 'Ever since then,' he says, 'I've had to wear ankle strapping. That's what stopped me playing in the end – it wasn't my knee.'

With his progress at Spurs checked by injuries, the club's signing of Chris Waddle in 1985 effectively put paid to Dick's prospects at White Hart Lane. Waddle, a recent England international, joined from Newcastle United and scored twice on his debut. Waddle was also a left-winger and shared stylistic similarities with Dick – a gifted dribbler with a desire to get fans out of their seats. With Galvin still around, the Scot was nudged further down the pecking order.

'That's me fucked,' thought Dick after picking up the *News of the World* one morning to read the headline 'Spurs sign Waddle.' He stayed with Tottenham for another year and credits the England winger, star of two World Cups, as a 'good person to learn off'. But Waddle's arrival made Dick's eventual exit an inevitability.

Rangers were keen to take Dick back to Scotland, and manager Graeme Souness personally called the player to sell him on the move. Dick was happy to join, but he informed Souness of his religious background – although he was never especially religious, he had attended a Catholic school. Souness assured Dick this wouldn't be an issue. But this was a full three years prior to Mo Johnstone's taboo-busting move to Ibrox, becoming the first Roman Catholic to sign for Rangers since the First World War. The *Daily Record* got wind of Rangers' proposed move for Dick, running the presumptuous and inflammatory headline 'RC [Roman Catholic] signs with Rangers.' The deal was swiftly scrapped.

* * *

When one door closes, another opens. Dick's potential move to Rangers was beyond resurrection, but an unexpected option soon presented itself. 'Then, about a week later, Johan Cruyff phoned up,' Dick says, wearing an expression of incredulity. 'I thought it was my mate having a joke.'

Ajax had contacted Rangers over the possibility of signing Scotland international winger Davie Cooper. They were told in no uncertain terms that Cooper was not for sale, but Souness informed Johan Cruyff, his opposite number at Ajax, there was a young wide man of a similar profile to Cooper looking for a new club. He recommended Ajax take a look at Dick.

Dick picks up the story: 'That's when Ajax phoned me to come over. They'd just finished the season. They'd won the Dutch Cup. At the end of the season, they usually do a little tour to play the smaller clubs so the smaller clubs can make some money. It was five games in five days, and I played in all the games. They were like Sunday League teams, they were bad, so it was good for me – I looked fantastic. At the end of that, they called me and said they wanted me to sign.'

Dick found the intense focus of training tough – 'Those boys were fit … it was full on' – and far advanced of the rudimentary practices still common in England at the time. He was also struck both by Cruyff's methods and his forceful personality. The Ajax and Barcelona legend is revered as one of the greatest footballers of all time – perhaps the best ever from Europe. And as a coach, his ideology – an extension of the Dutch Total Football model he helped shape with Rinus Michels in the 1960s and 70s – laid the foundation for decades of success at Barcelona, whom he managed from 1988 to 1996. He was regarded as one of the game's great thinkers. And no one was more enamoured with Cruyff's genius than Cruyff himself.

'You definitely know when you're in his presence,' Dick remembers. 'He's got this aura, a glow effect around him. He was something special.

'He was very arrogant, had an arrogant air about him. It was tough to grasp his methods, because obviously they were talking in Dutch the whole time. But he'd turn to me and explain everything in English, then I'd pick it up.'

One of Cruyff's many maxims was that 'Playing football is very simple, but playing simple football is the hardest thing there is.' And mastery of the basics formed the core of his methodology.

'Everybody thinks it's this secret, unusual, fantastic way. It's nothing like that,' Dick explains. 'It's simple, very basic. They get the basics very spot-on. We'd do the same thing, day in, day out. But that's what you become good at. You do it without thinking – one touch.

'These guys had it down to a fine art when it came to possession – playing the ball, moving away – and closing down. One thing I noticed right away: the goalkeeper – even back then, in the mid-80s – was great with the ball. Stanley Menzo, you'd knock the ball back to him and he was the sweeper, basically.'

Dick had joined a talent-rich Ajax team who had been Eredivisie champions a year earlier. Among their number were several players who would go on to win the 1988 European Championships at international level, such as Frank Rijkaard, Marco van Basten and Arnold Mühren, while a teenage Dennis Bergkamp was making an impression as a pacey right-winger. Another star of Euro '88, Ronald Koeman, a 23-year-old midfielder at the time, would leave for PSV shortly after Dick's arrival. Dick admits he didn't know who Koeman was at the time, but he quickly discovered the magnitude of the departing Dutchman's talent. 'When I got to Ajax, Cruyff said, "You play on the left. When you get past [your maker], rather than cross all the balls, look to the edge of the box. Drive it to the edge of the D for him," – this wee blond guy. And every time I played the ball to him, he hit it sweet as a nut; he must have scored five goals, straight in the top corner.

'I always remember saying to the guys, "He's a good player, eh? He hits a nice ball." Little did I know, it was Ronald Koeman. He'd just signed an £8m deal to go to PSV.'

Even without Koeman, who bequeathed his No.8 jersey to Dick, Crùyff's Ajax side was resplendent with world-class stars. 'When I got changed at Ajax,' Dick remembers, 'it was Arnold Mühren, me and Marco van Basten.

'Mühren was about 38 at the time, but he was the perfect player to play with as a winger: he'd get it and give it to you, so you had plenty of chances to cross in to Van Basten, Johnny Bosman, and Frank Rijkaard would be steaming in – all great in the air. A lot of chances were converted.'

Rijkaard and Van Basten would join AC Milan at the end of the 1986/87 season, joining up with fellow Dutchman Ruud Gullit to win back-to-back European Cups in '89 and '90, but not before helping Ajax clinch the Cup Winners' Cup. Dick's season was ended in the second round of the competition, however, rupturing a cruciate knee ligament in a 4-0 defeat of Olympiacos in October.

'At Ajax, there was no reserve squad. If they had injuries, they'd draft someone in from the youth team. You had 18 professionals, that's it. So you're in the first team right away.

'The left-winger who'd have been my opposition, my challenger, was a Dutch international winger called Rob de Wit. At the time I'd signed, he'd had a stroke that summer, so the position was all mine. At the beginning of the season, I started all the games. And in the Cup Winners' Cup I started all the games.

'When the Olympiacos game came around … that's when I got injured. I toe-poked the ball to get away and the guy came in sideways and got me. I knew right away something wasn't right. I got up and tried to run it off, but I came off at half-time.'

The injury ruled Dick out for eight months, missing Ajax's 1-0 win over Lokomotive Leipzig in the Cup Winners' Cup Final. He had been hopeful of returning in time to take part in the final –

which, held in Athens' Olympic Stadium, would have made for a satisfying closing of a loop, having suffered his injury against Greek opposition – but he 'didn't want to push it' and risk further complications.

Although Dick recovered sufficiently to be available for selection by the start of the 1987/88 season, injury problems persisted. Ajax again reached the Cup Winners' Cup Final and this time Dick was in the squad, but he didn't make it off the bench as the Amsterdam side slipped to a 1-0 defeat against Mechelen. He made just six appearances that term.

By his own admission, Dick was never the most dedicated trainer. He loved nothing more than showing off in front of a full stadium, but the hard hours on the training field were a nuisance. His fitness level had dropped during his eight-month absence and it would never truly recover.

'I didn't play much that season,' he says. 'I got the odd game. A lot of injuries. I struggled a bit. I remember I went on holiday that year and came back very unfit, overweight. I was unfit, had a bad knee – I knew I wasn't going to be first choice. I tried to get back in but I was struggling.'

Cruyff left Ajax in the months before the Cup Winners' Cup Final defeat to Mechelen – who were managed by Aad de Mos, the former Ajax boss sacked two months prior to Cruyff's appointment in 1985. Before Cruyff left, though, Dick had managed to anger the headstrong Dutchman by confessing a desire to leave, further contributing to his lack of first-team opportunities.

'At the time, I was homesick,' Dick says. 'I heard Celtic were in for me and I was in the right place to come home. Near the end of the second year, I went in and asked Cruyff if it was true [that Celtic were interested]. I said, "If it's true, I'd like to go."

'I thought I was doing the right thing. I found out it was the wrong thing to do – never let them know you want to leave. I was a young guy; I didn't know that was a bad thing to do. I didn't tell them I wanted to leave; I just told them if Celtic came in, I'd definitely be interested.

'I was on the fringes then. You know you've gone back a bit then. If the left-sided player was injured, it wasn't automatically me who'd come in. I never threw my toys out of the pram or anything, but I gave up a little bit. I was fed up in Holland and I just wanted to go.'

Dick left Ajax in 1988. At 23, his résumé boasted a UEFA Cup victory and runners-up medals in the Cup Winners' Cup and UEFA Super Cup, in addition to his youth honours with Scotland. Yet, while records of his total appearances vary from source to source, he likely had fewer then 50 senior games under his belt.

The rumoured Celtic interest never did materialise. Upon leaving Ajax, Dick returned to England, training with Wimbledon and Southampton in an effort to regain fitness and earn a contract, before signing with Brighton & Hove Albion. He would last just eight months with the Seagulls, though, fighting a losing battle against mounting injuries.

'I was always injured,' Dick says of his ill-fated spell with Brighton. 'Right from the get-go, I had a bad back, probably from my knee. I battled for fitness the whole time. I could never get to that fitness level that everybody else had.

'I never made it easy for myself: I was lazy, I hated training. It was very difficult for me to get ultra-fit.'

Dick decided to take some time away from the game when he left Brighton in an effort to allow his body to heal. In the early 1990s, he was tempted back into football by an offer to play for South African side Hellenic. What was supposed to be a three-month deal was eventually extended to six. Although meeting his future wife while based in Cape Town retrospectively colours his time with Hellenic positively, he again found himself 'constantly injured', while registration issues meant he only played a handful of games.

Next came a spell in Australia, with Melbourne's Heidelberg United – 'I loved it. The pace was slower, perfect for me. If I wasn't feeling great I didn't have to train. It was very relaxed. I probably would have stayed there longer but the manager got sacked.'

A chance to return to South Africa presented itself and Dick signed with Seven Stars, the club who, coincidentally, would later become Ajax Cape Town, a sister club of the famous Amsterdam side.

During his time with Seven Stars, Dick took the opportunity to coach in nearby townships as part of an outreach project the club ran. A humbling experience, he encountered startling poverty, with many of the children shoeless for the sessions.

'The kids would get two slices of bread and a slop of strawberry jam. That was their lunch. It was the same everywhere we went. It broke your heart.

'We used to turn up for training sessions, there'd be 40 kids and 20 of them never had shoes, they'd just be barefoot. It was that poor. They were lovely wee kids, polite as you could get. But it broke your heart. Every day, you realise how lucky you are. We used to give out free crisps – we were sponsored by a chip company. I think they just turned up for the crisps, they were so poor.'

When his time in South Africa came to an end, the 32-year-old Dick joined Alloa Athletic, signing for a Scottish club for the first time in his professional career.

'The very first game, a bad tackle comes in and tears the ligaments in my ankle, the same one. That was it. I'd been on the park ten minutes. I still thought I'd play, but it just never started again.'

* * *

Dick has spent most of the two decades since his retirement working as a regional distribution manager for the *Daily Mail* and then chocolate manufacturer Mars. Football has flitted in and out of his life. He took part once in 'The Masters', a series of six-a-side tournaments for retired pros broadcast on Sky Sports during the 2000s, representing Ajax. In 2011 he tried his hand at coaching, leading sessions for young players at Stirling Albion, and he now oversees a local university team, but the effects of his old injuries still trouble him.

'I used to join in training,' Dick says. 'Now I've noticed I can't do that. I join in for ten minutes then I have to stop, my ankle gets stiff and sore the next day. It's rotten when your head wants to do something but your body won't allow you.'

The ankle issues, which date back to the 1984 UEFA Cup Final, when he was just 19, now prevent Dick from walking long distances, while his surgically repaired knee's lack of mobility means he has to kick a leg out straight when bending to tie his shoelaces.

'I remember the first couple of weeks at Tottenham, we'd do stretching and I could kneel down and lie flat on my back with my knees bent. I remember watching all the other guys and there were only two other guys who could do it. The older guys were bolt upright, and I was laughing at them. When you're 16, you think, "Never in a million years will that happen to me."

'You think you're invincible at that age but it catches up. I've had operations on both my knees, and they throb, ache, are sore. I can't bend my one knee completely. It was quite flexible before that, so that's kind of weird. And it interferes with your everyday life, playing with your kids and stuff.'

When the injury he sustained against Olympiacos in his first season with Ajax was assessed, the specialist told Dick he wouldn't play football again. The doctor was only half right. He was just 21 at the time and he would play on for 11 years, but never consistently at a high level. His Ajax career wound down quickly thereafter and his return to English football was as brief as it was uneventful.

'When I was at Ajax and I got injured, I accepted it pretty quick. I know a lot of guys strive and want to get back to the top, but I accepted the fact I would never be at the top. It probably helped because I'd done a lot, had a lot of medals,' Dick says, explaining how focusing on what football gave him, rather than what it took away, helped him achieve a healthy perspective.

'I never regretted anything. I always considered myself very lucky that I'd done all that before I got injured. I was happy with that and I accepted it. I think that was key to me being balanced and happy and well adjusted. I'd been involved in five European cup finals before I was 22 – I was very happy with that.'

Upon joining Tottenham as a 16-year-old, Dick was only given 25 per cent of his weekly wages, with the club funnelling the rest into a pension fund which, he says, is still fully intact. While this gave him a degree of financial peace of mind as his career in football wound down, he didn't reap the kind of rewards from the game that would have allowed for a life of leisure post-retirement.

Dick was 27 when the Premier League was formed in 1992. He should have been at his playing peak as satellite television was flooding football with money. With a little more luck, or were he to have benefitted from modern medical and sports science better treating and working to prevent the injuries that plagued him, Dick, Graham Hunter firmly believes, would have been a superstar.

'Today,' Hunter is adamant, 'make no fucking mistake about it, he'd be earning Ángel Di María money. He'd be better than [Raheem] Sterling has proven himself to be. I'm not being derogatory about Raheem Sterling, but, for my money, Ally was a better player.

'And when I talk about his technique and his left foot: it was from the fucking gods.'

A Different World

JINKING around his kitchen floor, dropping a shoulder as he saunters by the fridge, feet flashing, betraying the embers of a talent long dormant, he's right back there, at Manchester United's old training ground, the Cliff. I sit at the table, just a few feet away, but it's Bryan Robson and Norman Whiteside he sees. His stubble may be flecked with silver, his joints creaking almost audibly, but he still knows how to sell a dummy, spin on a sixpence and misdirect.

Now in his late 40s, Giuliano Maiorana's football career is almost three decades back in the rear-view mirror, but his power of recall is impressive. The memories of his playing days are still vivid, and how couldn't they be? Plucked as a teenager playing part-time football in the tenth tier of the English game and thrust into the limelight at Manchester United, he went from selling designer Italian clothes at a Cambridge high-street outlet to sharing a changing room with household names, players he'd watched star in an FA Cup Final just a few years previously. His life had suddenly begun to mirror countless fictitious stories of rags-to-riches sporting glory, from television, movies and literature. This was real life, yet it seemed scarcely believable.

'I remember the ball going out and over the line, I was there and I back-heeled it,' Maiorana says, recalling an early training session with United following his move from lowly, non-league Histon, re-enacting the scene as though to convince himself of its authenticity. 'Steve Bruce has run that way, and then I back-heeled it again,' he pivots once more, 'and he was like that [mimics a flummoxed look]. I'd only been there three weeks, from Histon.

Everyone was laughing and I felt embarrassed. I did it without thinking. In a way, I thought, "I shouldn't have done that.""

The drastic rise in ability levels of his new team-mates, compared to the part-timers he'd lined up alongside before, who would cram twice-weekly training sessions around day jobs and family lives, was a culture shock to Maiorana.

'I remember training with Bryan Robson. They'd be feeding him balls and he'd just be whacking it to the left, whacking it to the right. The level was ridiculous.' And the impressionable youngster couldn't help but feel a little star-struck. 'I've seen him in FA Cup finals and now I'm just walking past him,' he remembered of his first encounter with Norman Whiteside in a corridor at the training ground. 'Even in the canteen at the Cliff, you'd get a plate and it would have a little Man United logo on it. You didn't get that at Histon.' But the teenage winger, as Bruce would have attested to after being spun inside out, held his own.

Indeed, Maiorana impressed sufficiently during his maiden match in a United shirt, a friendly fixture against Birmingham City in November 1988 – a game organised to raise funds for Blues midfielder Ian Handysides, who had been diagnosed with a brain tumour earlier that year, from which he would tragically die in 1990 at the age of 27 – that he was brought off at half-time and immediately offered a four-year professional contract. The £30,000 United paid as a transfer fee for Maiorana reportedly saved Histon, who were £23,000 in the red, from extinction.

'I remember walking on to the pitch and there were thousands of people. I was used to playing in front of 50 people – Histon's a really small village. I remember seeing Trevor Francis running towards me. It was surreal. I didn't do too bad in the game; I won a penalty.

'I remember the ball going out for a goal kick for them, and I went to get the ball. Their ground had a race track around it and there was a medical bed on the track, and the ball got stuck underneath this bed. I was on my hands and knees trying to get this ball. I got it and threw in back to the keeper. The keeper looked at me really weird: "Cheers, mate." There were ball boys there!

'I was just a kid. It happened that fast for me. It was ridiculous. It was a rollercoaster.'

United manager Alex Ferguson wrote in a column for the *New Straits Times* the following month: 'That was one of the best displays I have ever seen from a trialist. The player marking him, Ray Ranson, is an exceptionally experienced full-back – but Maiorana gave him all kinds of problems.'

Culture shock notwithstanding, Maiorana's week-long trial with United couldn't have gone any better. However, this was not a gifted prodigy reared in the academy of an elite club, accustomed to the accepted behaviours and inherent subjugation that are part and parcel of life as an emerging player at a big club.

This was a young man whose extraordinary talent had long gone unnoticed; who, at 19, no longer harboured ambitions of a top-level professional football career.

In the late 80s, the scouting process and recruitment of young players was not quite the arms race it is today, when a player rarely gets beyond the age of ten without having been scrutinised and either inculcated in an academy or deemed surplus. But still, few saw their first shot at joining a professional club arrive beyond their 18th birthday.

Maiorana feels that the same rough edges and idiosyncrasies that compelled him to drop to his belly to try and fish the ball from underneath a stretcher against Birmingham, and that rendered him awestruck and unsure of whether he had contravened an unwritten rule when skilfully outwitting a veteran defender in training, sat uneasily with Ferguson.

The relationship a young player enjoys with his manager can be crucial to his development; earning the trust and confidence of the boss will lead inevitably to opportunities, opening doors that for others may remain closed. Maiorana made a rip-roaring start to life at Old Trafford, making a handful of senior appearances in the First Division after penning his four-year deal with the club – including a virtuoso display on the left wing against Arsenal, in which he twisted the blood of England full-back Lee Dixon. But he soon found himself on the margins, banished to the reserves without a route back.

'Most of the players, if not all of them, at that club had gone to the Lilleshall School of Excellence at 14 and been moulded into being a player,' Maiorana explained to me when I first interviewed him for *FourFourTwo* in 2016. 'I hadn't been moulded into a footballer – I was different. It's not as if I was rude or disrespectful – I never have been – but it gets to a stage when somebody's always having a go at you, and you think, "Is it worth it?"'

He expanded on his issues with Ferguson when I met him at his Cambridge home to interview him for this book: 'From day one it was okay. It's just that [Ferguson] wanted to mould me into something that I wasn't. He wanted me to shave. My beard wasn't even that long; I'm Italian for god's sake, it was just a five o'clock shadow. And "Cut your hair," when it wasn't even that long.

'When I went there I had been working in an Italian boutique shop. I was wearing Timberland while they were all wearing Adidas and tracksuits. I never used to wear tracksuits. I used to wear jeans, turned up, with Timberlands and no socks – that was the fashion back then. He walked past and said, "Get some fucking socks on your feet! And have a fucking shave!" Just grinding at me all the time. And then I wasn't in the first team and he'd walk past me, blanking me. When I injured my knee, I used to be in the gym on my own. He used to walk in, and as I was about to say hello he'd walk off.

'I wasn't a "yes man". I look back and think I'm glad I didn't sell my soul, because a lot of people do.'

* * *

'I remember him coming, remember seeing him, then he just disappeared off the radar,' says Jim White of *The Telegraph*, echoing many fans' memories of Maiorana at the time, this player who burst on to the scene before inexplicably vanishing from the first-team picture. Some are aware of the cruciate knee ligament injury that he picked up in a reserve match in 1991, and point to that as the likely reason for his demise, yet that doesn't account for the fact his last first-team appearance came in 1989.

Debuting two years earlier than the Welshman, Maiorana, wearing the No.11 shirt, with his floppy dark hair rippling in the breeze and a dazzling ability to swerve between and beyond multiple defenders at once, was in many ways Ryan Giggs before Ryan Giggs.

'Other people have said that: "You look like Giggs." And sometimes they didn't even know I used to play for United,' Maiorana says. 'I couldn't get away from it. It was body feints. I used to try these flicks. I used to have a defender on my back and I'd get the ball, dink it and then go like that,' he demonstrates flicking the ball up and back-heeling it over his head, 'and the defender wouldn't know where it was. That's how I used to like to play football: being three, four, five steps in front of the defender. Like with Lee Dixon, if someone's up your arse and you do a back-heel, before they even know where it's gone you've turned.'

Such skills inevitably fostered a degree of hype around Maiorana, who quickly endeared himself to a support base with a long-held appreciation of fine wing play, dating back to the days of George Best and, earlier still, Billy Meredith and Johnny Berry.

White continues: 'I remember being very excited by him and there was this kind of promise that United were going to rebuild with young players. There was a whole flurry of guys who were called the "Fergie Fledglings"; he was on the back of that. There was a kind of buzz around him. There always is with junior wingers coming through the ranks. I don't think anyone ever bestowed on him the "new George Best" line that most of them have to suffer, but there definitely was a bit of buzz about him.'

Alan Tonge was an apprentice at United when Maiorana arrived, and he would later appear regularly with him in the second string. I asked Tonge, discounting the factors largely beyond the winger's control that ultimately saw him ostracised, whether Maiorana was talented enough to make a lasting impact for United at first-team level. 'Oh, definitely, yeah,' began Tonge's unequivocal reply. 'I think it was quite a quick transition for Jules. It wasn't one of those scenarios where they thought, "We'll get Giuliano when he's 18 or 19 and we'll have to wait until he's 23 to get a first-team appearance out of him." I think he played in the reserves, then got his opportunity quite early.

'The club at the time was still in a bit of a transition, because Fergie came in in '86 and he was still finding his way a little bit.

He didn't win a trophy until 1990, which was the FA Cup win. In that four years, I don't think we were performing very well. It was a funny time. I think Fergie was still laying his foundations in a way. There was quite a bit of pressure on the players back then because we weren't in the momentum of winning trophies. It was a strange one. There was certainly pressure on Sir Alex, but there was a bit of pressure on the players to perform as well.

'[Maiorana] played in Ian Handysides's testimonial. He must have had a really good game because they offered him a deal after that. It was a poor pitch – Old Trafford was a bit of a mess back then – and I think there had been a lot of rain in the Arsenal fixture; it was a bit muddy, a bit sloppy on there, but he did well. He gave Dixon a little bit of trouble, something to think about.'

Such promise, yet Maiorana only ever made eight first-team appearances for United, the final two coming from the bench in October 1989, less than a year after the excited half-time offer of a four-year contract that followed his fearless 45 minutes on trial against Birmingham.

* * *

As we sit in the kitchen of his Cambridge home, just before breaking for a tour of the upholstery business started by his father that he now runs alongside his brother Sal, stationed just behind the semi-detached house, Maiorana tells me how, as a youngster, his skills were no secret locally, yet went largely unappreciated by talent spotters.

Aside from a couple of unsuccessful trials with Cambridge United, Maiorana's wasn't the typical tale of a supremely talented pre-teen; he wasn't ferried around the country to attend trials with various clubs; there was no queue of sides falling over themselves to woo him into joining their academy.

'I never played for one of the best teams. I'd play with my friends. One year, one of the best teams asked me to join them. I went along, played for them for three months but never liked it. All I wanted to do was enjoy playing football.'

His father, who emigrated to England from Italy with Maiorana's mother before starting their family, was fanatical about football, an avid Juventus supporter, and would later make weekly 360-mile round trips to Manchester to watch his son turn out for United. Maiorana Sr ran a local amateur football team, Italcam – Italians from Cambridge – and playing for his dad's side was the height of the young winger's ambition until he was spotted and snapped up by Histon of the Eastern Counties League, England's tenth tier.

'It was during a five-a-side game that I got spotted,' Maiorana says. 'It was on the AstroTurf at Histon, pre-season. The manager of Histon, Alan Doyle, he knew somebody on our side. He said, "Who are those two lads there?" And pointed to me and my brother. They asked us to go to pre-season and that's how we ended up going to Histon. I thought I played about 30 games for the first team, but Alan Doyle, the manager, he thinks I played about 16 to 20 games before United came along – it was ridiculous.'

The young winger who'd grown up on a diet of Italian football and idolised Napoli's Diego Maradona made a fast and lasting impression at Histon. Doyle was convinced the teenager's talent ought to be displayed in loftier surroundings than Histon's modest Bridge Road stadium, with its capacity of 3,800 but where home crowds rarely threatened four figures. Doyle tipped off a scout with connections to United about this uniquely talented gem he'd unearthed, thus setting in motion a giddily rapid ascent up the Football League ladder for Maiorana.

'I got told on the Wednesday night United were watching me,' Maiorana remembers. 'I thought it was rubbish. I didn't believe it. Then on the Saturday, I got told they wanted me to go up [to Manchester for a trial]. I was hoping it was going to be in the next few weeks – I was shitting myself, basically. Then on the Sunday: "Jules, we've got to leave at five o'clock [in the morning], they want you there tomorrow." I remember going up there on the M6. Alan Doyle came with me. We got stuck in traffic and I was thinking, "Thank God for this." We got to Old Trafford half an hour late. I was so glad we were late. I didn't fancy training. But as soon as we got there they said, "Hello, Jules. We haven't started training yet because we've been waiting for you." I thought somebody was taking the piss. Brian Kidd [one of Ferguson's trusted coaches who later became assistant manager at United] said, "What's your name?" "Giuliano." "Alright, what do they call you for short?" "Giu." "Alright, Jules ..." And I'm thinking, "Jules?! Well, I'm only going to be here for a week, they can call me what they like." And it stuck.'

The gravity of the situation Maiorana found himself in was not lost on Alan Tonge. The former United apprentice is cognisant of how, despite appearing to be the chance of a lifetime, suddenly finding himself in the most professional of environments, in the pressure-cooker surrounds of one of the world's biggest clubs, would not have been easy for Maiorana to adjust to.

'It's like the equivalent now of someone coming from Salford City or Chorley,' Tonge suggests, 'from a lower league, and to an opportunity [to play for United]. It was very, very rare. I was an apprentice when Giuliano arrived. It was a bit of a baptism of fire for him. He arrived on a morning and got into his training stuff and was straight into training.

'It was quite a bizarre scenario because one week you are playing in the Southern League, or whatever it was he was in, and the next you are training with Bryan Robson and some of the players who were [at United] at the time. That must have been a difficult thing to contend with from Jules's perspective.'

Maiorana recalls his initial struggle to adapt: 'I come from a close-knit Italian family. Leaving my family to go up there, to be in digs with 12 other people, all younger than me ... They used to sleep with footballs. I played football because I loved it, but they were from a different world to me; they'd been at the Lilleshall School of Excellence when they were 14. I was used to my mum's lovely Italian cooking. All of a sudden, I was eating fish and chips and shepherd's pie.

'I was in these two houses that were knocked into one. I didn't have my own bedroom, sleeping with people I didn't know and eating English food – it was all weird. I'd never been north of Peterborough before.

'Going from a university city like Cambridge and going up there [to] an industrial, massive, massive city – the "capital of the north" they say it is. It was a big shock for me.

'When I got my car, I used to jump in my car and I didn't have a clue where I was going. I used to get lost just for the purpose of getting lost. Just to get out of the house.

'I think most of these kids had had a lot of trials, so they knew how to mingle better than I did. I used to just drive around.

'I was used to working nine until eight. We used to get in at half nine, ten o'clock and finish at midday. I couldn't go anywhere, couldn't knock on anybody's door, couldn't go to meet anybody. It was a lonely place at first. But the players in there were lovely people. I adapted and got used to it – I'm not going to war, am I? The digs were alright, to be fair, but at first it was strange.'

Being a couple of years older than most of the boys he shared a living space with, Maiorana excused himself from the hazing and hijinks that the youngsters would get up to. 'They used to do things to each other, but when they tried to do them to me I'd give them a dead arm: "If you want to do that to each other, fine, but leave me out of it."'

He remembers befriending Adrian Docherty, the supremely gifted Northern Irish winger and subject of Oliver Kay's magnificent biography *Forever Young*, whose own prospects were ruined by a knee injury similar to that which Maiorana later suffered, before tragically dying aged 26 having fallen out of the game altogether. 'I used to play guitar with him a lot. I remember him saying to me, "I like getting up and seeing the sunrise and playing the guitar and having a couple of beers. People think I'm weird." I would say, "There's nothing weird about that, mate."'

Although the transition to digs was difficult for Maiorana, he credits the camaraderie that developed between the boys with easing his assimilation. 'Anyone who got in the first team,' he says, 'we'd pat them on the back.

'There was a game against Nottingham Forest, I was in the squad but didn't get in the team. Tony Gill did and he came up to me straight away and said, "Sorry, Jules; I thought you were going to get picked in front of me." That's a great thing to say.'

* * *

Two months on from his deal-clinching display in the testimonial against Birmingham, a string of impressive performances with the reserves earned Maiorana his competitive first-team debut. Millwall were the visitors to Old Trafford and the young winger was brought on as a second-half substitute.

'When [Ferguson] asked me to come on, I said, "Can I go to the toilet?" Maiorana says, recalling the bowel-loosening effects of the butterflies in his stomach.

'Ferguson's last words before I went on were: "Get out there, son, and run your fucking bollocks off." I looked at him, looked away and thought, "Alan Doyle would have given me better words of wisdom for Histon."

'I ran on, went down the wing. I could hear the crowd – "United! United!" – fading in and out of my ears as I breathed in and out. I did a 360 to see all the people at the game. If anything, I was used to being outside watching in; this time it was the other way around. It was ridiculous.'

Maiorana again belied his youth and inexperience with an exciting, confident, dribble-happy cameo. He would have to bide his time for his next taste of first-team action, though, another substitute outing against Luton Town at Old Trafford in late March.

On 6 April 1989, Maiorana's patience and progress were rewarded. Arsenal, soon to be crowned First Division champions, came to Old Trafford, and Maiorana was starting.

'It's like rock stars say: no matter how many times you get on stage, you still get nervous. But it's how you react on the pitch. I remember being in the changing room, my head was still in the clouds. Ferguson said, "Norman Whiteside has said he isn't going to play unless Jules plays." Everyone was laughing. He went through the team: "... and number 11: Maiorana". I thought, "Fucking hell."

'I remember not knowing who to warm up with, so I just joined some group. And then the whistle blows and you just get on with it. Luckily for me, as soon as I went over that white line, it didn't matter whether I was playing at Old Trafford or for Histon, it was just me expressing myself as a footballer.'

And express himself he did. In direct opposition with right-back Lee Dixon, who'd be an England international within a year, Maiorana ducked and weaved, flicked and feinted – those fluid motions recounted in the kitchen. Time after time, he would take the ball in stride and run, run, run at the Gunners' vaunted back four. Time after time, his more experienced colleagues sought him out whenever they had the ball. It was a performance that cemented his first-team status, helping mid-table United to a 1-1 draw with high-flying Arsenal and earning him three more senior outings before season's end.

However, a stark downturn in fortune wasn't far away.

* * *

'I was on the floor, screaming. It was like an electric shock in your knee.'

The game in which Maiorana suffered the injury that would effectively end his chances of a career in top-level football had started brightly. It was a reserve fixture against Aston Villa, in April of 1991.

'In that game, I took the ball from outside our own area – I can still see me doing it now – running the whole length of the pitch with these Villa players on my heels,' Maiorana remembers. 'And all you've got to do is [demonstrates body feint]. You see all these players today, showboating to get past people. When I did something, I did it to get past a player, never to take the piss.

'And I would see their legs, little gaps, and I'm still running, dropping my shoulder.' He becomes animated once more, shoulders bobbing and weaving like a boxer. 'I got outside the area and I smacked the ball. It was going in one corner but it took a deflection and went in the other. Most of the players were coming up to me: "Fucking hell, what a brilliant goal!" I said, "It's not my goal, though." It was a deflection. It wasn't a clean goal so I didn't want it.'

The same, inimitable, maverick style of play that saw him stand out at Histon and allowed him to rise rapidly to the summit of the footballing world proved irksome to Ferguson. 'I used to do overhead kicks from throw-ins on the halfway line, and back-heels and flicks. Once,' Maiorana confided during our first interview, 'Ferguson had me in his office and said "You've got to stop doing those tricks." I just replied, "To be honest, boss, that's how I like playing football." I like to get fans off their feet. I used to like trying to do things that people would leave the game remembering.'

In a cruel twist of fate, it was this same will to entertain that led to Maiorana's cruciate knee ligament rupture against Villa. Rather than the result of a bad tackle or an awkward twist, it was a collision with Villa striker Dwight Yorke – who would star for United later in the decade – as Maiorana attempted to acrobatically scissor-kick a dropping ball to safety from deep inside his own half that did the damage. 'I should've headed it,' he admits, 'but that's the way I played football. I'd never had a bad injury before. I was thinking, "I hope it's not a broken leg," – that's how stupid I was. I didn't know much about being injured.'

The narrative runs that Maiorana was never able to recover full form and fitness after his knee was surgically repaired, hence his release from United in 1994. However, he refutes this version of events, feeling his reserve-team performances post-injury were as good as ever, and that it was ultimately his relationship with Ferguson that put paid to his United career.

'When they released me in '94, and Ferguson said my knee wasn't up to it, I said, "Wait a minute." I said, "I know I've got a dodgy knee but don't you say to me that I will never be able to play at the top level again."

'In my last season, we played at Tranmere [reserves]. When I walked off after the game, people were saying, "Fuck me, you're a hell of a player." Then all of a sudden, three months later, they are trying to tell me I'm not good enough because of my knee.

'I was still playing well. Tony Gill, bless him, when he broke his leg badly, we used to be at the Cliff and you could see he was kind of limping as he would run. He would ask us whether he was limping or not and we were heartbroken for him; we couldn't tell him that he was. It wasn't like that with me: I was still fast, I could still shoot, I could still play football.

'Brian Carey [a young central defender in United's second string] said to me, "Since you've done your knee you look stronger and faster than before." But Ferguson: "No, no, son." I think I must have seen red because somebody said to me that I walked out kicking bins and everything.

'What I do remember is walking out of Old Trafford saying, "If this is what football is about then football can go fuck itself. I'll miss football and football will miss me."'

* * *

The injury was, of course, a major setback for Maiorana, requiring surgery and months of gruelling recuperation. Advances in sports and medical science mean players nowadays can expect to make a full recovery from an anterior cruciate ligament (ACL) reconstruction. But the process was less sophisticated in the early 1990s and this particular type of injury threatened careers.

But there was a gap of almost two years between Maiorana's injury in April '91 and his last first-team appearance in October '89. Prior to the advent of the Bosman rule in 1995, allowing freedom of movement for out-of-contract players, footballers were bound to their clubs regardless of their contractual situation. Maiorana felt trapped at United and held back by Ferguson.

'I went to see him before I did my knee,' he explains. 'I said, "I want to leave. You're not playing me." He said, "I'll never let you leave this club. We had David Platt and Peter Beardsley here and we ended up with egg on our faces." He didn't want me to play for United and he didn't want me to play for anyone else, and that's a disgrace.

'I was a fading memory. And when I left, people just forgot about me. Some people, who didn't know I got injured, thought, "He looked promising but he never weighed up to what people thought he would be."'

Maiorana believes the genesis of his strained relationship with Ferguson dated back to his first outing for United, against Birmingham.

'After the Birmingham City game, we were on the bus coming back, Clayton Blackmore was sat at the back, I was sat in the middle because I didn't know anyone, and Clayton said, "Jules, do you want a beer?" I didn't drink but I'd just signed for Man United, so I thought, "Yeah, I'll have a beer." David Wilson came up to me and said, "The boss has said you better put that beer down now," which I can understand. "If not, he's going to come here and go fucking mad at you."

'So I did, I put the beer down, didn't give any attitude and walked to the front of the bus like he'd told me to. And I noticed the difference between the first-team players, who seemed all relaxed, having a drink at the back and having a laugh, but at the front of the bus [where the younger players were sat] the atmosphere changed, because Ferguson was there and they were all shit scared of him. I could sense it. And because I wasn't ...' He trails off, leaving hanging the insinuation that Ferguson resented his lack of deference.

Alan Tonge suggests, 'He wasn't institutionalised like a lot of the apprentices were. He was his own man, Giuliano; he had quite a strong sense of self. That's the kind of lad he was. I think that was a problem for Jules, because he had quite a strength of character about him. He wasn't being rude to Ferguson, because Jules is a top man, he's not rude to anyone. But I think he found the culture of the club quite strange around that time.

'He wasn't misbehaving, but he got spoken to like he was. Sometimes, in the football environment, if you're not careful you get spoken to like a little child, and I don't think that sat too well with Jules. It didn't sit too well with a lot of young professionals. But that's how it was back then: "You do as I say or you won't be around here much longer." I think he struggled with that a little bit.

'He was someone a little bit different in that environment, that's what I remember about him, because he had the courage of self to stand alone and be comfortable with himself instead of kowtowing to somebody else. That's what I respected about him. A lot of players go the other way and go into this kind of robotic, rigid personality. You almost have to act to get on sometimes.'

Maiorana felt singled out, treated unfairly by Ferguson. And he believes this mistreatment was overt, obvious to other coaches and players at the club, including Darren Ferguson, the manager's son.

'I wasn't in a good place when I was playing for Ferguson. When I wasn't in the first team and I wasn't in the reserves, I wasn't in a good place. But all I wanted to do was go on a football pitch and show people what I could do with a football.

'Once, when we beat Leicester [reserves] 4-1 – I'd scored one, set one up and hit the post – [Leicester manager] David Pleat gave me a pat on the back after the game: "Fucking superb tonight, son. Brilliant." I walked into the changing room and everyone was saying the same. Ferguson walked in: "Well done, boys.

Everyone can have the day off tomorrow, except you, Maiorana. You're going to come in and run your fucking bollocks off." [Reserve-team manager] Brian Whitehouse looked at Ferguson and just turned around; he was gutted. Darren Ferguson had his head in his hands.

'And other things happened, at dos and events. I was wearing an £800 suit, which I'd got cheap from the shop I used to work at, and a pair of £140 shoes, which I'd got cheap as well. I had a waistcoat on, a shirt. I was stood talking to somebody when Ferguson walked past and said, "Look at the state of you. You've always got to be fucking different." I said to Darren, "What the fuck is up with your dad?" And there was a YTS player sat there with a blazer on, with a polo shirt and no tie, but he didn't say anything to him.

'How can they treat youngsters like that? If you don't like somebody, be a gentleman about it: shake his hand and say, "Sorry, we don't want you here." Don't do what they did to me. It's morally wrong. If you don't want me at United, let me go and play somewhere else. That's what I in part blame [Ferguson] for: he didn't allow that.'

At least, that is, until it was too late for Maiorana to resurrect his career. He was eventually released in 1994, aged 24, almost five years after his final first-team game for the club. Any memories of his early promise were now distant, any interest from other top clubs had evaporated.

Maiorana remembers vividly how he was informed of United's intention to let him go. He'd been home to visit his parents in Cambridge when Ferguson had called and spoke to his father.

'"Ferguson phoned up. He said he's not going to give you another contract." He'd just said it over the phone to my dad. I got hold of him: "Alright, come and see me next Friday at Old Trafford." In the meantime, I got a letter: "You're free to approach any other club ..." So I went in there, chucked the letter on the table. I said, "There you go, boss. You know what's in there because you sent it to me." I undid my jeans [to show the scar on his knee from the operation] and said, "Would you give me a job, looking like this?" He just looked at me. "Would you give me a fucking job?" "Sit down, son, sit down."

'I ended up getting another year because he knew I would have gone to the papers. As I'm walking out, he's tapped me on the back and said, "You know what, Jules? I really like you." So condescending. I patted him on the back and said, "Do you know what, boss? I really like you too."

After leaving United, Maiorana was training with Cambridge City when he was contacted by former Old Trafford team-mate David Wilson, urging him to join him at Ljungskile SK in Sweden. Wilson spent a decade in Scandinavian football after joining Finnish side RoPS from Bristol Rovers in 1993, and he played more than 130 games across two spells with Ljungskile. Maiorana, though, lasted just five games in Sweden.

'I just wasn't meant to be a footballer,' he admits with a regretful sigh. 'That was the hardest decision of my career at that time: I knew I was coming back home and finishing football. Back to reality. I was back here, driving the van, doing a delivery one day and Soul II Soul, 'Back to Life', came on [the radio] – I was that close to driving the van into a wall.'

* * *

Maiorana's time at United straddled the years before and after the formation of the Premier League. The rebranded top flight would change English football in ways previously unimagined, attracting a global audience and pouring billions of pounds into the game through lucrative sponsorship deals and television rights contracts. It was an era in which players' wages began to multiply stratospherically. Maiorana's years in Old Trafford purgatory meant he never reaped such rewards, though, his weekly earning peaking at £400.

But it was not so much the denial of earning potential that troubled Maiorana after his retirement. Instead, it was how early retirement and unfulfilled potential robbed him of a platform to showcase his abilities that darkened his days, leading him to seek help from a psychiatrist in the years after he gave up on football.

The unique trajectory of his career was akin to finding a winning lottery ticket, only to have it torn up before his eyes. He was a creative soul robbed of an outlet.

'When I was playing, I used to go to bed thinking, "What can I do with that ball?" Thinking of ways to get past players and things like that, then trying it in training. Because I was so used to thinking that way, when I had to give up it was still going through my head. It was driving me insane.

'I was fighting my demons. It was a fucking nightmare. I used to go to bed thinking, "Football ... No, you can't think of football, think of something else." Then, as I was drifting off: football. It was fucking horrible. I wouldn't wish it on anyone.'

Maiorana's experience at United left him, by his own admission, incredibly bitter for many years. Unable to glean any positivity from his journey in the game, he tried his utmost to avoid football altogether, but found the national game to be ubiquitous, offering constant reminders of the past he was trying to escape.

'When I gave up football, I didn't want to talk about football,' he says with a slow shake of his head. 'I had a mate who used to run a team around here and I'd go and coach. He used to say to the kids, "Whatever you do, don't mention United to him." I used to go mental.

'I went over to Sweden to get away from it. One day, in '95, I opened my curtains to see a little Swedish kid in a United top with a number 11 on the back. I used to say that if I went to the moon I'd find a United top.

'When you retire from football, no matter which way you look, there are reminders of football; if it's not in the park, it's in the papers; if it's not in the papers, it's people with football tops on – it's everywhere, in your face. You can't get away from it, and that makes the process of getting better even longer.

'You've got to understand, when I gave up football, I put football at the back of my mind; I hated the fact that I played for United because it didn't turn out well for me. People used to say to me, "Yeah, but you played for United ..." But I didn't give a shit, that didn't mean anything to me.

'When United used to play in the Champions League, I used to get out the house; I couldn't watch them; I was dying for them to lose – I hated them. When they beat Bayern in the [1999 Champions League] final, I phoned my brother up. He said, "Giuliano, it's the 88th minute, they're still 1-0 down." Then, two minutes later: "You're not going to believe this: it's 1-1." I was down the pub, having a pint by myself. "You are not going to believe this: 2-1." I said, "You are taking the piss.'"

Time has given Maiorana perspective, though. He is now able to reflect on his difficult years at United without slipping back into that dark place, revelling in sharing the story of his remarkable journey. He recognises that if his chance to play for United had never come, he wouldn't have met his wife, Val, a Salford native. Through their son, Sal, born in 1997, he has even rediscovered his passion for football, following United's fortunes, free of resentment.

'My thinking wasn't like that for years,' he admits. 'I've had to teach myself to think positive. For the first seven, eight, nine years, the thoughts I was having weren't right. I used to laugh, and then I'd think, "What are you laughing for? You're not a footballer any more." Silly, stupid things come into your head, all kinds of shit.

'I always say you've got to see the positives. My dad died when he was 59. I was with him near enough every day of his last ten years, in the workshop, talking, having a laugh, working. What's more important: those last ten years of your dad's life, or playing in Serie A in Italy and earning millions?

'Since I've given up football, I've worked with my family every day. We always get on. It took years for me to think the way I do, but I got there in the end. I'm all good now, thankfully. If you'd have knocked on my door 15 years ago, I probably would have told you to piss off.'

Shattered

6 APRIL 1994. A date forever etched on Ben Thornley's conscience. The day a budding football career, almost certainly set for England caps and multiple major honours at club level, was altered by a bad tackle from a frustrated veteran in a reserve match.

Thornley was one of the stars (arguably *the* star) of Manchester United's FA Youth Cup-winning side of 1992. Among the likes of David Beckham, the Neville brothers and Nicky Butt, he was the one earmarked for the brightest future in the Old Trafford first team. A right-footed left-winger – a stylistic trait now common, but one that made Thornley a rare breed in the early 1990s – with pace, skill, creativity with either foot and a scoring touch. A lifelong United fan raised in Salford, he was a young man living his dream. Having progressed through the Red Devils' youth ranks to make his senior debut against West Ham United in February 1994, an injury to Ryan Giggs meant he was set to play a part in an FA Cup semi-final encounter with Oldham at Wembley Stadium, just a week before his 19th birthday.

I met Thornley in Essex, where he now lives with his partner, dividing his time between there and trips to Manchester for his work as an analyst on United's in-house TV channel MUTV, as well as occasional appearances as a matchday hospitality guest at Old Trafford. He is a warm and engaging character, affable and open, making it easy to picture him as the kind of player who could bring levity and bonding to a tense dressing room, as he was later described by a former team-mate. But when the subject of his career-threatening injury is broached, he recalls the day the trajectory of his life was changed with almost harrowing vividness, his eyes narrowing as he prefaces his account of that unfortunate spring evening by stating its date, as if to press home its trauma: '6 April 1994'.

'Giggsy was struggling with an injury and the manager [Alex Ferguson] wanted to make sure, because of the type of pitch that Wembley was – it was a killer of a pitch that sapped your legs – that I had some sort of match practice under my belt. So he sent me out on the Wednesday night against Blackburn [reserves] and he just said, "See how you feel."'

In this book, many of the players featured speak of moments in which their fate hung in the balance after a decision that at the time seemed of little consequence. Indeed, it is a fact as true in everyday life as it is in the unique milieu of football stardom that experiences are often shaped by chance, for better and worse, leading to thoughts of what might have been, the bedrock of regret. Thornley's story is not without its own *Sliding Doors* moment, where, but for youthful exuberance and being caught up in simply enjoying what he was doing, things could have turned out differently, cruelly punished by fortune for not taking the chance to be substituted when it was offered to him.

'We were 3-0 up, I'd scored two and made the other one. Jimmy Ryan, who was the coach at the time, said to me, "What do you want to do?" It just never dawned on me. It was like, "I'm here, I'm having a great time." It turned out to be one of the worst decisions I've ever made.

'You just don't think about it at the time. I could've scored my hat-trick so why would I want to come off? I was enjoying myself too much.'

Late in the second half, disaster struck. Thornley's enjoyment of the game had come largely at the expense of Blackburn Rovers full-back Nicky Marker, a comparative veteran. As Thornley sees it, Marker had grown frustrated at chasing the teenage winger's shadow all game. His frustration manifested itself in an aggressive, high and late challenge on the United youngster, obliterating his knee and hamstring.

'I was 18 and he was 29 at the time,' Thornley explains. 'He had just had enough. You could see from where the tackle happened – which was virtually in the middle of the pitch, and he's a right-back – he had come for me. When you see the tackle, it was that high off the floor, straight into my knee as I passed the ball to Clayton Blackmore, who'd gone up the outside. And as I planted my foot after passing it he'd just come straight in, and that was it.

'I felt it straight away. Gary Walsh was in our goal, and this was a third of the way into their half, but Walshy heard the snap. The manager was there. He grabbed my dad and they came flying down at Gigg Lane to the pitchside. He knew straight away, and the medical team knew straight away, that I had to get myself to hospital, because they'd heard it and they'd seen it. They knew that it was bad.

'It wasn't just my cruciate. It was MCL [medial collateral ligament], hamstring, everything. Everything needed stitching up and repairing as well. Jonathan Noble, a guy I'm obviously very grateful to, who repaired my knee, said that when he opened my knee up it was like putting a book on its spine: everything just fell apart. He said that, along with Jules [Maiorana, the subject of Chapter 2], it was one of the worst ones he'd ever seen.'

The dream was put on hold. By the mid-90s, cruciate injuries were not necessarily the career-enders they had previously been, but full recoveries were rare, especially in cases as severe as Thornley's. The FA Cup semi-final was now no longer a consideration; his only ever Wembley appearance would remain an England Schoolboys outing in 1990. An arduous, year-long rehabilitation lay ahead, watching on as United secured their first-ever double, and as a procession of former youth-team colleagues got their first-team breaks.

* * *

These days, Manchester United boast a worldwide scouting network, with a net cast over all corners of the globe and the latest analytics and video compilation packages poured over in an effort to unearth the next superstar; whether it's a kid from Urmston or Iceland, Longsight or Lebanon, no stone is left unturned for fear of being beaten to a top prospect by a rival. But before the riches of the Premier League (founded in 1992) came streaming in, and before United became a global marketing juggernaut, the talent-identification process was simpler and, largely, conducted closer to home.

Through a fortunate geographical quirk, the Red Devils' old training ground, the Cliff, was a stone's throw from where Salford Boys, a team comprised of the finest local talent, played their home games. As such, it became regular practice for either Alex Ferguson himself or one of his trusted sidekicks to make the 50-yard stroll across to Lower Broughton Fields to watch the teenage hopefuls in action, keeping an eye out for any particularly gifted lads who might be worth offering a trial to. And that's exactly how Thornley was spotted. He was 13 at the time and on Manchester City's books, despite being a United supporter. But, on the advice of his father, he had decided against signing schoolboy forms with City, leaving him free to explore interest from Nottingham Forest and Ipswich Town when contacted. And eventually United, too.

Brian Kidd, a former United player who would go on to serve as Ferguson's assistant manager from 1991 to '98, was overseeing the club's youth system and already aware of Thornley as being one of the area's standout talents. The glowing report that came back from the scout sent to watch him in action for Salford Boys only cemented in the minds of Kidd and Ferguson that this was a young player they needed to sign, and they approached Thornley's father to enquire about the youngster's availability. Rather than break the good news to the teenager there and then, Thornley's dad thought surprising his son would be the most appropriate way to let him know of United's interest.

'I came home from school on a Friday night,' Thornley remembers, his eyes growing wide as he is transported back in time. 'My little mate from school, who we used to take turns sleeping at each other's houses, came back with me. I said, "It's my turn to stay at Geoff's house tonight so I'm going down there." My dad said, "You can't. Geoff's welcome to stay here, but for the time being I need you to not go anywhere." I was naïve; I didn't think anything of it. I kicked up a bit of a stink. Seven o'clock comes and my dad says, "Can you go and answer the door." If there was a camera on my front porch to see my face when Alex Ferguson and Brian Kidd were standing there …

'They said, "We'd like you to come and join us." They had contracts drawn up – not just for now, but for when I was 16 or 17. It was unbelievable. I said to him, "Yeah, I'll leave Man City." I still didn't sign any schoolboy forms, which is what they were called back then, with Man United. I honoured evening training, I honoured school holidays when they had get-togethers with people like Keith [Gillespie] coming across, Sav [Robbie Savage] coming up from Wales and Becks [David Beckham] coming up from London, and we played matches against different clubs, against each other and training sessions. That was not an issue at all. But one thing I said I wouldn't do was sign anything. I said, "If you still want me when I'm 16, then I'm doing you a favour, because you might not. I'm not going to sign anything with you until I'm 16 and we agree amicably that, yes, I still want to sign for Man United and, yes, you still want me to sign for Man United." And they did.'

As is the case with many talented young players who get picked up by big clubs, Thornley's extraordinary ability was evidenced by the fact that he had always played in older age groups before joining United. He played his first organised, competitive match for his school as a seven-year-old in a team of players as old as 11, and scored, too. He was also deployed in central midfield, a common tactic of coaches at that level, in order to get their best player into the position from which they can exert the greatest influence. But when he arrived at United, he was among a glut of gifted central midfield players. Recognising his pace and unique two-footedness, it was suggested that he moved out wide. With Gillespie occupying the right flank, the left wing became Thornley's new home.

'The one thing I will always be grateful to my dad for, in terms of me being a professional footballer, is that, from a very early age, he got me to kick the ball with both feet,' Thornley says. 'There was nobody else who was an instigator in that. It was him, straight away.

'We used to live in a semi-detached house, and on one side was where my mum and dad and the neighbours would park their cars. Any time they were all out, I used to stand in the far side and whack the ball against the wall of my mum and dad's house. Any other time it's bloody annoying if there's a constant bang, bang, bang when you're sitting in the front room. But whenever they were out I used to try – because I favoured my right foot at the time – to force myself to use my other foot. And I became a very accomplished player with two feet.'

Thus, a style began to be forged. Nowadays, old-fashioned wingers are seldom seen at the highest level, with wide players whose first thought is to cut inside on to their stronger foot de rigueur. The opposite was true in the early 90s, though: a winger was tasked predominantly with attacking his marker around the outside and whipping crosses into the box; right-footed players on the right and lefties on the left. But Thornley set about carving out a niche for himself as an early approximation of the inverted wingers that have since proliferated, confusing his opposing full-backs by being equally as able to take them on in the customary fashion as he was drifting inside on to his right foot, aiming shots at goal and sending dangerous, in-swinging crosses toward the far post.

'Eric Harrison [United's youth-team coach] loved that,' Thornley says of his unique playing style. 'I remember going on loan to Huddersfield in 1996, before I actually signed permanently with them, and that was what got me my England call-up in the summer for the under-21s.

'It was something that came to the fore in the year we won the Youth Cup, because I didn't just put crosses in and beat full-backs, but I actually finished as the top scorer in the Youth Cup that year for the team, just from cutting in. I had a decent shot on me. I definitely remember scoring one like that against Manchester City in one of the rounds – I scored twice, actually. So, yeah, it came to the fore, and I wanted to continue it into my overall play. And, obviously, if the injury hadn't have occurred, it would have been a really useful weapon for me I suppose.'

David Preece, a retired goalkeeper and now a prominent member of the football media, played with Thornley at Aberdeen and had earlier watched on from the bench for Sunderland as the United winger starred in a Youth Cup victory at Roker Park. When I asked the former keeper for his impression of Thornley upon seeing him first-hand, he was effusive in his admiration of the winger's ability.

'He stood out massively,' Preece says. 'He was so quick. He had the ability where the full-back could close him down correctly and think he was doing his job well, but Ben would still manage to get the ball in. He had this amazing ability to get the ball in.

'Even when he came up to Aberdeen it was exactly the same. A lot of the balls he used to put in, he'd put them into great areas for the striker. He had this great knack of putting it between defender and goalkeeper, so strikers could get on the end of them and have an easy job.

'He had that ability to go down the line on his strong left foot – he had a great ability to cross the ball. But if that was shut down he'd just shift it on to his right foot. I remember at Aberdeen he scored a couple of crackers from distance. He just dropped his shoulder to come inside on to his right foot and let go.'

Taken on as a first-year apprentice at 16, Thornley wasn't moved into digs like some of the youngsters who'd come from further afield, and thus was not subjected to some of the antics that a group of young men living together, away from home for the first time, inevitably got up to. That didn't prevent him landing the unfortunate nickname 'Squeaky', though, due to his high-pitched, Salford accent. But he does remember some of the unsavoury behaviour that has become infamous from the old days at the Cliff.

With testosterone levels high and a dressing room hierarchy of first- and second-year apprentices established, the teenagers were at times willing participants, at other times goaded into acts of hijinks and misbehaviour. Mostly mindless fun, but occasionally bordering on bullying.

'Robbie Savage was an absolute belter at chatting a mop up, for example,' Thornley recalls. The second years would often abuse their seniority by instigating the kind of hazing rituals synonymous with American college fraternities. Remembering one of the more humorous examples, Thornley says, 'One of them was Deiniol Graham, who I'm actually really close to now, but at the time he was a bugger. He came in and we had to lie on the physiotherapist's table and pretend that there was a woman underneath you – shagging the bed.

'So he comes in, Deiniol, and he went, "Oh, who's this then?" And it was Mark Rawlinson that was on there. Deiniol had a look at what was going on and he went out into the kit room then came back again with a calendar. He started turning the pages until he got to Clayton Blackmore, when he had all those highlights in his hair. He said, "I want you to kiss Clayton Blackmore." And he did as well. I bet he's glad social media didn't exist then as it does now.'

It wasn't always so light-hearted, though, and there were times when the fallout caused more than simply cheeks reddened with embarrassment.

'There was one lad who was a right bugger. He was a couple of years older. He was really, really bad. It's funny to laugh about it now but as 16-, 17-year-olds you're thinking, "No." He came in and he got his cock out. He started dangling it in front of people. The dressing rooms were in a horseshoe shape, with benches along the side and then one at the top. And Butty [Nicky Butt] was sitting right in the middle. He said, "I don't care what happens to me but if you put that anywhere near me I'm going to fucking punch you." He's done it a couple of times. He bust Keith Gillespie's nose once. He's a lot better now obviously because he's a lot older, but at the time he was a proper snapper. He could handle himself, I'm pretty sure about that. Even from being a kid and playing against him, when he was with Greater Manchester Boys and I was with Salford Boys, I always remember his upper-body strength: for somebody who didn't look it, he was really, really strong. And he did, he whacked him.

'That then kicked off a chain of events whereby it happened again and one of the lads was whacked with a ball in a towel. He had a cup of hot tea that he picked up off the bench – it always used to happen at lunchtimes – and he threw it. It didn't scald anybody, but something ensued. The next day, he didn't come in. His dad had phoned up that night to say that his son's head had swollen up and this is what had happened. The foreman at the time, a lad who was a year older than us called Andy Noone, he came down to tell us that Eric Harrison wanted to see all the first-year apprentices straight away.

'I know that if it happened to my lad I'd be straight on the phone saying, "What the fuck's going on here?" Eric Harrison told a few of the lads, "If I ever hear any more of this you'll not be playing in my youth team. There'll be other lads who'll take your place." He'd sent out the message to stop all this bullying and that was the end of it. It never happened again from then on.'

* * *

Thornley's move to the wing was an unqualified success. He was quickly establishing himself as one of English football's brightest prospects amid a generation of players at United who were turning heads every time they played. This stable of prospects, including eventual United regulars Beckham, Butt, Giggs, Scholes and the Neville brothers, and others like Savage, Simon Davies and Gillespie who enjoyed success elsewhere, have since been immortalised as the 'Class of '92', owing to their FA Youth Cup triumph of that year. But the umbrella term for this group of players is somewhat of a misnomer. Giggs was a year older than the rest and already a first-team star who was borrowed by the Youth Cup side at the semi-final stage for an extra competitive edge. And Scholes and Phil Neville belonged to the year below and didn't kick a ball on the cup run of 1992, although they did feature when United reached the final of the same competition a year later.

Of the regulars in the '92 cup-winning youth side, Thornley was the standout star, finishing as top scorer in the competition that year. Gary Neville was the leader of the team, captain and central-defensive rock, despite later developing into one of the English game's finest right-backs. In an interview for Sky Sports, he spoke glowingly of Thornley, recognising the winger as a vital component of United's Youth Cup success.

'For anyone who has got to the end of their career, there will always be a player that you've played with and you'll think if that boy hadn't have got injured or if something different had happened then he would have been a top player,' Neville said. 'For me, that was Ben Thornley.

'In fact, he was probably our best player. If you think about David Beckham at that age, Paul Scholes at that age, Ben

Thornley was above them in terms of the level he was playing at between the ages of 16 and 18. He was prominent in the FA Youth Cup Final victory in 1992, played in every single round and was brilliant in every single round. But then he got that terrible injury. It was a real shame. It's something I think about even when I see him now.'

When I put Neville's praise to him, Thornley pinpoints his ability to perform when the chips were down, raising his game under pressure, as perhaps being what set him apart from the other youngsters at that time. 'I think it was because there were times when we were under pressure a little bit – in the first year and the second year – and it always seemed to be me who got us out of the shit,' he says. 'Against Spurs, we were 3-0 up but there was still that bit of nerves. And within ten minutes I'd scored and it killed it. The second leg of the final against Palace, we were 3-1 up from the first leg, but within a few minutes of kick-off they'd brought it back to 3-2. But a couple of minutes before half-time, I scored to get the two-goal lead back, and it calmed everybody down a little bit. It always seemed to be me, not Giggsy, who brought us back to a position where we could relax, where they could breathe. I was a kid. I didn't really know what pressure was.'

Despite being the side's standout performer, when it was proposed that Giggs would be joining the team for the semi-final against Tottenham Hotspur, Thornley feared for his place. He needn't have.

'I was nervous about the fact that Giggsy came into the team. Eric [Harrison] noticed in a couple of training sessions leading up to it that I wasn't myself. Even though the team was laid out, and I could see that I was in it and that it was Sav that was missing out. I didn't know whether things would change. So he pulled me in and said, "What's the matter with you?" I told him I was a bit concerned with the fact Giggsy's going to play and he plays in my position. He said, "Don't worry about it. Yes, he's going to play, but if you're fit and playing at your best, which you have been, you will be in my team. If you continue like this, you'll be leaving me, you'll be skipping the reserves and going straight into the first team."

'I didn't need to worry about what Giggsy or anyone else was doing. And I played every single game for two years.'

As it turned out, Giggs was fielded as a striker in place of Savage, and Thornley kept his place on the left wing. The coaches insisted Giggs play out of position in an effort to ensure Thornley's rhythm was not upset, evidence of his standing within the team.

By this point, the word was already out: this was a special generation of players United had on their hands. Before advancing deep into the latter stages of the Youth Cup in 1992, they had tasted success in prestigious tournaments against high-calibre opposition, and all without the added help of Giggs.

Thornley said, 'We'd played in the Milk Cup in Northern Ireland and we won that. And we beat some really decent teams. It showed that this group of lads were winners.'

The moment that crystallised this gifted group of boys' status as genuinely impressive young players came on a frosty November evening in the north-east of England in the Youth Cup. Sunderland were the opponents at the Black Cats' old Roker Park stadium.

Trailing at half-time, the United hopefuls (not that they knew it at the time) had reached a crossroads on their journey to stardom. Had they lost, the very best of the bunch would still have been given their first-team chance at some point, but the legend of the Class of '92 would have been much different. And to add to their adversity, the young Manchester side walked out for the second period to be greeted by a blanket of snow, spread crisp and even over the turf, having fallen heavily between the referee's half-time whistle and the changing-room bell ringing to signal the end of the 15-minute interval. If their cup run was to continue, United would have to show some mettle.

'We came back out and it was like, "What's going on here?"' Thornley explains. 'We had to use an orange ball in the second half – it was just a blanket of white. Unbelievable. We won 4-2. This was without Giggsy as well. They knew from what they'd seen up to that point that we had a talented side, but I think, with the position we were in in that game – difficult conditions, already 2-0 down and having never really played in a national competition before – it showed that we had a bit of character as well. We ended up scoring four unanswered goals in the second half.

'From then on, I'm not saying it was easy, but we had the belief. Even when we played Spurs in the semi-final, after 20 minutes the tie, not just the game but the whole tie, was dead and buried: we were 3-0 up and they'd had Nicky Barmby sent off. That was it. We went down there, we didn't even take Giggsy to the second leg. Within three minutes I'd scored and it totally killed it. And they were real favourites to win it. They had Sol Campbell, Nicky Barmby, Darren Caskey, Paul Mahorn, Danny Hill, Andy Turner – all lads that, if they hadn't already played in the first team, certainly went on and did so. They were paying them big money as well, maybe £700-800 a week. We hadn't even signed pro. We were still getting £29.50 in a little brown envelope. Their lads were earning big, big money, so it was a real coup.'

Crystal Palace were United's opponents in the final, played across two legs in May of 1992. The first leg was at Selhurst Park, with the return being under the bright lights of Old Trafford in front of a 14,000-strong crowd.

The away tie was negotiated with relative ease, securing a 3-1 lead to take back to Manchester, thanks to a Butt brace, with Beckham adding the third. Given an early scare in the return leg as Andy McPherson headed beyond Kevin Pilkington in the United goal to put Palace in front early in the first half, it was Thornley, with a wonderful solo run and low finish, who settled the Red Devils' nerves by equalising before half-time. United ran out 3-2 winners on the night, lifting the prestigious cup by virtue of a comfortable 6-3 aggregate scoreline.

Beckham, who only became a starter at the semi-final stage thanks to an injury to Keith Gillespie, noted in a 2015 interview that the Youth Cup Final remains his fondest Old Trafford memory, above anything he achieved at the Theatre of Dreams at first-team level, and ranking higher, even, than his free kick against Greece that sealed a place at the 2002 World Cup finals for England. Thornley remembers riding such a wave of confidence at the time that the final was 'a breeze', with the young side feeling virtually unstoppable.

* * *

The following season, Thornley split his time between United's youth side, 'A' team and reserves. Another FA Youth Cup Final was reached, with Phil Neville and Paul Scholes now regulars, but Leeds United proved stronger over two legs. Revenge, however, was exacted in the 1993/94 campaign, when many of the same players faced off again at reserve level.

'They had pretty much seven or eight of the youth team that played against us in May, and we had the same,' Thornley recalls. 'We beat them 7-1. It was virtually the same team, so you can imageine how sick we were that we'd given such a poor showing in the youth team months earlier. We'd played them again and demolished them.'

By now, Thornley was 18, a regular at reserve level and knocking on the door of the senior side. Having been invited to travel with the first team on a handful of occasions to ease him into the fold without actually being named in the matchday squad, a debut was beckoning. A senior bow came in February of 1994 against West Ham United at Upton Park. Named as a substitute for the game, Thornley replaced Republic of Ireland international full-back Denis Irwin in the second half, with United chasing the game. They eventually scraped a 2-2 draw thanks to a goal from former West Ham midfielder Paul Ince, who had become a figure of hatred at his old stamping ground due to his acrimonious £1m switch to Old Trafford in 1989.

Ince's mere presence in the United line-up meant an already lively home support offered a particularly hostile welcome to their visitors from Manchester. Ordinarily, the 18-year-old Thornley might have been beset with nerves ahead of his maiden first-team outing. But forced to warm up in the infamous Chicken Run, the gulley that ran parallel to the touchline, right in front of the boisterous home support, the teenager craved the sanctuary of the pitch.

'Horrendous, absolutely horrendous,' Thornley says of his Chicken Run warm-up. 'I remember warming up with [United back-up goalkeeper] Les Sealy, bless his soul. He played at West

Ham afterwards. Somebody was having a go at him and he turned around and mentioned something about money – he was a proper cockney gobshite, Les, and he didn't care who he upset, either. I could see the looks of these guys' faces when I was warming up. And of course I got the abuse as well: "Who the fuck's this?" That sort of thing. It was quite an intimidating place to be warming up.'

He'd travelled with the squad to games before, but he'd never made it to the bench. He knew the trip to West Ham was different when, after training on the Thursday, two days before the match, Brian Kidd informed him that they were only taking 16 players to east London – the 11 starters plus five substitutes – and that he was not to forget his club blazer and tie.

'It was a tight game. Incey equalised in the last minute to make it 2-2,' Thornley remembers of the match. 'It wasn't as if the manager had decided that it was 3 or 4-0, we can put him on for a few minutes. He actually had the belief in me that I could go on there and make a difference.

'I came on for Denis and, although I did nothing to be directly involved in the goal, I certainly remember doing one or two things. One of the last things I did was skip past somebody on the far side and he hacked me down. The ref didn't blow for a free kick because it was the end of the game, and he didn't book him either. But there were two or three of my team-mates who surrounded the referee and said, "What was that?" He knew what he was doing. He wasn't having it [being beaten by a youngster] at all. Which was incidentally how my injury came about. Nothing more than that.'

At this point, United were motoring towards a first-ever double, aiming to retain the league title they'd won the season before and add to it the FA Cup. After a tumultuous two decades for the club, they were finally heading in the right direction, seeds sown and beginning to germinate into a period of unprecedented domestic dominance and progress in Europe. But just six weeks removed from his debut, Thornley's future career prospects were thrown into doubt.

* * *

There was a distinctive, horrifying snapping sound heard around Bury's Gigg Lane. Blackburn defender Nicky Marker's challenge contorted Ben Thornley's leg and left him writhing in pain on the turf. But the true severity of the damage done was only fully understood once surgeon Dr Jonathan Noble operated on the injured knee. As soon as Noble glimpsed inside Thornley's shattered knee, the extent of the devastation was apparent: his anterior cruciate ligament (ACL) and medial collateral ligament (MCL) were both shredded, and his hamstring was also torn.

The decision was made to repair the MCL at the expense of the ACL. The former, which runs down the inside of the leg, gives the knee joint stability, while the latter provides mobility. It is possible, through strengthening of the surrounding muscles, to get by without an ACL, and to this day Thornley does not have a functioning cruciate ligament in his affected knee. The hamstring had to be fixed, and would require immobilisation of the leg to properly heal – the opposite of what is needed after ACL surgery, when movement is encouraged at an early stage of recovery. It was decided that the MCL would take priority and the leg would be put in plaster for six to eight weeks.

Thornley's experience in the immediate aftermath of sustaining his knee injury was the polar opposite of what Adrian Doherty had gone through. In *Forever Young*, Oliver Kay's book about the young Ulsterman's life, Doherty's initial treatment after sustaining his injury is painted as bumbling and insufficient, without proper, timely diagnosis and having to wait almost a year before receiving the necessary surgery. Perhaps owing to the sheer impact of the challenge that caused his own ligament ruptures, there was no underestimating the scale of the damage Thornley had suffered. He instantly received expert help from United's medical staff, for which he remains grateful.

'I was in the right place, no question about it,' he says. 'I was in the wrong place to get the injury but I was in the right place to have it rehabilitated. Fortunately for me, David Fevre, who is still the physio at Blackburn Rovers where Kiddo [Brian Kidd] had taken him when he left United, had just come across from Wigan in rugby league. He had quite an extensive knowledge of rehabilitating and treating serious knee injuries because they were a lot more common in rugby league than they were in football. He was brilliant with me through the whole summer.'

The gym at the Cliff was downstairs. It was an impersonal, basement-like room filled with fitness equipment, into which the only natural light creeps through narrow windows high up near the ceiling. Like the training field, it is a place of work. But unlike the training field, it can be a lonely place, bereft of the camaraderie, the japes and banter that make training sessions with the team something to look forward to, and something invariably missed by footballers upon retirement.

There's none of that in the gym for a player recovering from a serious injury. It's just you, your physio and weeks upon weeks of hard, painful rehabilitation exercises. It was doubly tough for Thornley. He was part of a special generation of young players at United, many of whom were either making their first-team breakthrough or on the cusp of doing so.

'When all the lads are coming back for pre-season training and it's nice outside, you're stuck in this gym,' he says, remembering those initial dark days. 'It gets to you mentally, it's not just physically. Because you'll have weeks where you think, "Brilliant, I'm not that far away." Then you'll come in the following Monday and just feel like shit: you can't do anything, you can't lift anything and you can't move. It aches and you feel like you're three stone overweight.

'You're there first thing in the morning, doing double sessions because you've got a terrible injury and there's loads and loads of different stuff you could be doing. Boring exercises. I have to show that I'm being professional about it. I can't be disappearing with a cruciate knee ligament injury, having not played for a few months and not due to play for a few more. I can't be coming in at ten o'clock and leaving at half past 12 when I've had my dinner. I need to be coming in at half eight in the morning, when the physio is arriving, getting on with my stuff.'

Was it hard to stay positive? 'It was, but the people that I was friends with at the time and the club that I was at, I couldn't have been in a better place. I had mates there: I had Gaz [Gary Neville], I had Becks [David Beckham], I had Keith Gillespie and Sav [Robbie Savage]. They were all close friends. Even though I obviously wasn't training, they never excluded me from anything that was going on outside of training. If they went for a game of snooker, I'd always get asked. If they went for a few drinks, I'd always get asked. If they went for something to eat or to the cinema or to watch a game, I would always get asked. It wasn't the case that I was out of sight, out of mind. And that helped.

'When you're in that gym, that's how it feels at times, because there's literally no one else there and the sun's shining outside. It was the one time you wanted it to piss down in pre-season so you weren't that hot. You were stuck in a gym indoors, but you knew that you had to be.'

After an aborted attempt at a comeback in November 1994, it was a year before Thornley's knee was back in a condition that would allow him to play. Any player who has experienced and recovered from a career-threatening injury will attest that you have to learn to trust your body again. Memories of the physical pain and emotional strain of the initial breakdown and the lengthy, arduous rehabilitation all lurk in the recesses of your mind, creeping to the fore any time you enter a challenge or accelerate towards full running speed.

'I was nervous when I was going to be tackled – that's a definite,' Thornley admits. In many cases, there also must come an acceptance that, even if able to play to a high level again, you are no longer the player you were before. Whether the injury robs a yard of pace, precludes quick changes of direction or forces a re-evaluation of certain techniques, there is an inherent adaptation period and a certain honesty required in assessing what this new reality holds.

'I noticed that, because of the amount of time I'd been injured, my body shape had changed. I wasn't as light as I used to be. And, therefore, the speed I had before the injury, I'd probably lost half a yard or a yard. In the position I was playing, that was crucial. That was a real contributing factor. Fortunately, I was fairly quick anyway, but without the injury there's no question about it, I would have been quicker.

'Some people have an injury whereby they can get back to the position they were in before; mine was so bad that, no matter what I did, there was no way [my knee] was ever going to be fully

100 per cent. And it was never going to be because I still don't have a cruciate.'

Then comes a delicate balancing act: brutal honesty and self-doubt at one end of the scale, the optimism and positivity required to get through the ordeal and salvage a career at the other. Unsurprisingly, mental loop-the-loops take hold.

'It didn't change the way I played the game, but it did change my outlook,' Thornley says. 'There were certain times I'd think, "Do you know what, this isn't working." And the moment I felt that, I'd go and have a really good game – I'd create a goal or score a good goal. Then I'd be thinking, "I can do this."'

To his credit, Thornley remained a United player for more than four years after his injury was sustained. And he was the most eager participant in pre-season training ahead of the 1995/96 campaign. Most players dread pre-season, when intense cardio work is prioritised in order to rediscover peak fitness following the summer holidays and ahead of the new term. But Thornley had been injured for the entirety of the last summer and a bout of appendicitis scuppered his 1993 pre-season, so he couldn't wait to put in the long miles by July of '95. He was never able to crack Ferguson's first team on a consistent basis, making just eight more senior appearances for the Red Devils, clocking a miserly total of 264 Premier League minutes. But he was on the fringes of a squad that won the 1996/97 Premier League title, and featured five times as Arsenal dethroned United the following campaign. He even played in the pivotal game at Old Trafford in March 1998, when a Marc Overmars goal tipped the balance of the title race in the Gunners' favour. Recalling Ferguson dishing out his famous 'hairdryer' treatment after the loss, Thornley says, 'I don't remember him having a go at me – and, trust me, if the manager has a go at you, you remember it. But there were three or four players he really laid into.'

Post-injury, Thornley got a taste of regular first-team football thanks to loan spells with Stockport County and Huddersfield Town. The latter, in 1996, was a particularly enjoyable period, buoyed by the confidence shown in him by manager Brian Horton and feeling a developmental growth as a result of further honing his craft in the more physically demanding First Division.

Thornley's form at the McAlpine Stadium led to an England under-21s call-up for the prestigious Toulan Tournamant in France that summer, and the United youngster was minded to stay at Huddersfield and start afresh a level down from the Premier League. However, Ferguson, at the time, was only willing to part ways with the then-21-year-old if a particularly attractive offer was presented, the kind of which Huddersfield didn't have the means to put forward.

By the end of the 1997/98 season, though, Thornley had reconciled with the idea that the dream of playing consistently for the club he grew up supporting was effectively over. He decided to take hold of his future by approaching Ferguson and asking that he be allowed to leave.

'I went and saw the manager and said, "Listen, I came for two years, I've never been any trouble for you. I am eternally grateful for everything that you've ever done for me, in terms of my rehabilitation and my football education, the way you've looked after me. I would love to try and repay you by showing that I can be a professional footballer in a squad somewhere, which, let's have it right, isn't going to happen here on a regular basis." He stood up and shook my hand. He said, "You're right, son." And that was it.'

That wasn't quite it. United and Huddersfield still couldn't agree a fee, so a tribunal intervened to decide the figure the West Yorkshire outfit would have to hand over for Thornley, by now 23. There were no hard feelings at Old Trafford, though, and Ferguson sent Thornley a letter expressing regret at how things never quite worked out as planned for the Youth Cup star of '92, wishing him well in future endeavours, insisting that the player could always knock on his door. A nice touch from the often-intimidating manager, and Thornley feels his strong relationship with 'the Gaffer' has played a part in his being invited to work for MUTV in recent years – 'because he's still massively influential'.

* * *

On the face of things, Huddersfield Town represented a sound choice of club for Thornley at this stage of his career. With their new, state-of-the-art stadium and ambitions of breaking into the

Premier League, the Yorkshire side could offer him a platform to rebuild his career away from the limelight. During Thornley's first season with the Terriers, local businessman Barry Rubery completed a protracted takeover of the club, promising the requisite finances to make a promotion push reality.

* * *

If regular football was the main driving force behind the switch then Thornley's 42 appearances and five goals in the 1998/99 campaign would have pleased the 23-year-old, who was finally now starting to learn how much of his pre-injury abilities remained when tested competitively. But Huddersfield finished tenth in Division One and manager Pete Jackson was dispensed with, as Rubery sought a higher-profile figurehead for the club's new era. In an apparent attempt to add a little pizzazz to the previously unfancied second-tier club, the new manager's identity was teased on a billboard in town, depicting a blanketed figure above the line 'Who will it be?'

It was former Manchester United captain Steve Bruce, his appointment at Huddersfield confirmed in May 1999. By this time, Thornley's former team-mates had just secured another league and FA Cup double, and were gearing up for a Champions League final against Bayern Munich in Barcelona. Several of his former youth-team colleagues were now regulars at Old Trafford, with David Beckham, Paul Scholes, Ryan Giggs, Gary and Phil Neville and Nicky Butt all key figures in the club's most glorious season. Thornley, who had just finished mid-table in the second tier, harboured no feelings of resentment, however, and flew to Barcelona to cheer on his close friends, just as he had when watching Scholes, Neville and Beckham play for England at the 1998 World Cup in France. He celebrated with the players after their dramatic 2-1 win, too. There was one former team-mate he wasn't banking on bumping into, though: 'I went out there [to the Camp Nou] and, when I looked up, Brucie was sat above me. I had a plastic pint glass of beer in my hand. He pointed at it and shook his head.'

Huddersfield finished eighth in Bruce's first season, just two points outside the play-off places, with Thornley again a key player. But fortunes quickly reversed the following term. Bruce was sacked early on, replaced by another former United star, Lou Macari (who Thornley now works alongside for MUTV). And, as it became apparent the funds promised by Rubery were not going to be forthcoming, Town limped towards relegation. The drop to Division Two brought cost-cutting measures. Thornley was out of contract and was unlikely to have been offered new terms even if he had wanted to stay.

* * *

Reading were also in the Second Division, but, unlike Huddersfield, they appeared to be on a positive trajectory under Alan Pardew. They'd finished third in 2000/01, narrowly missing promotion, but boasted the newly built, 24,000-capacity Madejski Stadium and were being backed by the millions of their owner whose name the stadium bore. They would finish second in 2001/02, earning promotion to Division One.

Pardew offered Thornley a two-week trial in the summer of 2001 and was impressed with what he saw. However, the former Manchester United starlet ranked only second in Pardew's list of desired targets for the wing. The manager informed Thornley that he couldn't offer him a deal right away as he was still waiting to hear back from his number-one choice for the role.

'I'm thinking, "Right, ok, what the bloody hell has he got me down here for?" Thornley remembers. 'This guy was coming from Rotherham, and he was stalling, he wasn't sure. So I think [Pardew] had got me there in case the other guy wasn't coming, then I was there and a ready-made replacement for him. But he hadn't heard from him. My two weeks was up and I was waiting for an answer, and he had to say no, just in case this kid who said he was going to sign signed.'

Pardew would contact Thornley again weeks later after being let down by his first-choice winger. By that point, Aberdeen had offered a two-year deal which he had accepted on the basis that it offered security and at least two more years of doing what he wanted to do: play football professionally.

It was a big step for Thornley: moving to the north-east of Scotland to play for an unfamiliar side in a new league meant leaving Salford for the first time; even when playing for Huddersfield he'd commuted. But he also speaks of enjoying the freedom, the chance to start anew, that comes with such a drastic change of scenery.

'When I lived up there I loved it. I didn't have anybody looking over my shoulder. I was in the team and things were going well.'

Things certainly were going well. 'Thornley has made an immediate impact, scoring three goals and providing some much-needed ammunition to a hitherto shot-shy attack,' *The Herald* reported in September 2003, just a few weeks into the Englishman's stay north of the border.

The Dons finished fourth in the Scottish Premiership in 2001/02, Thornley's first season with the club, and his three league goals meant only four team-mates outscored him. David Preece was Aberdeen's back-up goalkeeper at the time, and he remembers the impact Thornley's arrival had at Pittodrie: 'When he got there he'd already had the injury, so he was carrying a bit more weight than before when I'd seen him. Some days he maybe couldn't train as much because of his knee. But that season he was still a big influence on the pitch. He scored a couple of great goals and he was a great asset going forward.

'Bringing someone like that into the dressing room could have easily upset the apple cart,' Preece continues, discussing Thornley's effect on team morale. 'I don't know if overawed is the right word, but he could have been a bit different. But that couldn't be any further from the truth: he is one of the few players I've known who could really gel a dressing room together with his personality. From the minute he came in the dressing room it was almost like he'd been there two years. Just a hell of a lad; everyone got on with him. We had some success after he had left, but he was a big part of why we had a strong group together and a strong team spirit. Just because of the way he was. He gelled everybody off the pitch. Everybody gravitated around him.'

Thornley's Aberdeen experience took a sharp turn for the worse during his second season with the club, starting only twice. Ebbe Skovdahl, the Dons' veteran Danish manager, offered no explanation as to why the winger was no longer relied upon.

'All of a sudden it changed and I wasn't in the team,' Thornley remembers, 'and nobody could really understand why. The manager was a bit of an oddball. And I couldn't really see anything changing. Then Steve McMahon got in contact with me. He said, "Do you want to come and sign for me at Blackpool in January? I see you're not playing and we need somebody who can put a decent ball in."'

Resigned to the fact that he was no longer a starter for Aberdeen, Thornley admits that drinking and womanising became his primary pursuits at this stage, in lieu of getting his kicks on the football pitch. Where once his affable, party-loving personality made him a popular figure, 'one of the lads', his nightlife revelry took on an altogether darker complexion, framed now in a context of unhealthy escapism.

'I didn't ever really go off the rails as such, but [Skovdahl] was never going to include me to play, and I never travelled anywhere. I was always one of the first-team squad that was left behind. So from Friday to Monday I just went out and got pissed. I went out drinking and womanising and whatever else.

'I trained Monday to Friday as hard as I could, and then as soon as Friday afternoon came, when all the lads were leaving to go back to their families or leaving to go to an away game in Edinburgh or Glasgow or wherever it was, I'd be out. I'd be out with the physio, I'd be out with the lads who were injured, or with mates who had come up to visit.

'I was 26 or 27 years old and I wasn't involved in playing. I'd trained hard all week and this was sort of my reward, if you like. I could go out, have a few beers, then come back in on the Monday morning. That was how it worked for a couple of months.'

Having resolved to call time on his Aberdeen career and push for a mid-season move to Blackpool, who were a thoroughly average team in the English third tier, Thornley went to see Skovdahl in his office, expecting some pushback from the manager who'd want any parting of the ways to be on his terms. But Skovdahl acquiesced without hesitation or debate. It was almost as though the manager couldn't have cared less about the decision. That's because he didn't care: he'd just tendered his resignation.

'I'm thinking, "This is weird. He just let me go." And it was because he'd left himself. The very day I left, he left as well,' Thornley says. 'It would have been nice for me to have stayed until the end of the season without Skovdahl being there. The fact that he never even told me that he wasn't going to be there, that would have influenced my decision, because I had a couple of training sessions when Steve Paterson came in, between 20 December and when I was leaving in the new year to go back to Blackpool.'

Paterson wanted Thornley to stay and couldn't understand why his predecessor had allowed the winger to leave. But Thornley had already penned his contract with Blackpool and was just waiting for the January transfer window to arrive for the move to be rubber-stamped.

* * *

Arriving at Blackpool, Thornley found 'a poorly run club' in utter disarray. He'd only signed a six-month contract, but his half-year at the seaside was no holiday. Training was disorganised and unproductive, scarcely more than a kick-about; there was chronic disinterest among the squad; and manager Steve McMahon was barely clocking part-time hours, splitting his time between Blackpool and his home in Spain. 'We trained and played not far from the airport, and back then he had a place in Spain,' Thornley explains. 'Blackpool airport did a flight on a Saturday evening from there to Spain, which he took on a regular basis. So he'd fly out on a Saturday after a game if we were at home, and we wouldn't see him again until the following Thursday or Friday.

'I just didn't enjoy it. I was so glad that I only signed there until the end of the season, because I would never have wanted to stay, even if they'd have offered me another five years.'

At 28 years old, most footballers are reaching the peak of their powers, likely on the most lucrative contract of their career and performing to their highest standard. Thornley had left Blackpool to join Bury, where former United team-mate Chris Casper had become the Football League's youngest manager, on a game-to-game deal. The same summer, David Beckham left United to join Real Madrid; Thornley was now in Division Three, turning out for a mid-table side, on a non-permanent contract.

When he gave Bury an ultimatum, insisting they increase his pay by half once he had played a certain amount of games for them, it was 'see you later', as he puts it.

A month shy of his 29th birthday, in March 2004, Thornley was out of the Football League, signing for Halifax Town on a non-contract basis. He played three games for Halifax in what remained of the 2003/04 campaign, but again felt as though the club wanted more from him than they were willing to pay for. 'I just couldn't be doing with thinking, "I'd rather just go out and get a job and know that I'd get paid at semi-pro level,"' Thornley says of his mindset at the time, having now fallen fully out of love with the game.

Yet he speaks of rediscovering his enjoyment of football after becoming semi-professional, and the relief of stepping away from the professional game. The stakes are lower and the hours are shorter; what you give up in money you get back in time. Time to be spent with family, with the son he had with his Aberdonian ex-wife. His spells with Bacup Borough, Salford City, Wilmslow Albion and Witton Albion – the club he eventually retired with in 2010, and where he played with his brother Rodney, who is now a masseur at Manchester United – allowed him to once again be valued as a player. Regardless of how his powers had diminished, at this level he could do things those around him daren't dream of.

'I was enjoying playing,' he says. 'From the previous year or so, from the Blackpool thing, the Halifax thing, the Bury thing, I actually enjoyed it more, because I hadn't been enjoying playing.

'I trained twice a week, knowing that I was going to play on Saturday. And it was still a decent standard.

'I actually started to look forward to it again. I started to enjoy playing football again. I think it's because these clubs are striving to be professional that they take it really seriously. It makes you feel almost at home that that's the way they run it.'

A circular progression, from amateur to professional to amateur again, is nothing rare in many footballers' careers. Even those who play at the highest level often see out their final seasons at a lower competitive standard – some drop down the domestic football pyramid, others move to lucrative, emerging leagues like Major League Soccer or the Chinese Super League. This allows them to take a backward step or two, savour every moment and enjoy playing for playing's sake, just like a kid discovering the game on a playground.

But Thornley's career never reached the highs his talent merited: his arc ought to have peaked much higher. He is completely at peace with his life in football, though. He refused to let the injury that so brutally disrupted his progress hold him back any more than was unavoidable. He still plays, joining up with former team-mates for 'legends' games for United and for fun in an amateur league in Essex.

To some, having your dreams shattered while your peers, your close friends, all go on to achieve theirs, would be a source of intense bitterness. But there's not a hint of envy in Thornley. Indeed, his perspective on his unfulfilled promise is that it was taken out of his hands: some squander theirs, but his was stripped from him. A lack of ability was certainly never in question.

'At Man United, my career was cut short, and that was the bottom line,' he reflects. 'It wasn't because I wasn't good enough or I was a pain in the arse, or I got hooked on birds or drugs or booze. It was because of the injury.

'Those lads were always going to be top, top players. And there's no jealousy, no envy. If anything, it's made me very proud that I was part of a team that produced such great players, and I was their level. That's the way I'll always think about it. Don't get me wrong, I wished it to have been different; who wouldn't, given the opportunity to have five, seven, maybe eight years in United first team? But it didn't happen.'

Any regrets? 'Obviously I'd love to have played more games for United. And wherever I have been, because of the type of player I was, the one thing I should have done more of was score goals.

'But I have absolutely no regrets. I've done something that millions and millions of people around the world want to do, and that's pull on a red shirt and play for Man United. No matter how long I got, no matter how long I did it, it is something that nobody can ever take away from me.

'It could have been better, but it could have been a hell of a lot worse.'

Such Great Heights

MERSEYSIDE hums on derby day. Any time red meets blue in Liverpool, there is a vibration throughout the city, its frequency building in the days and hours before kick-off, a portent of promised drama, of energies clashing at high speed.

Liverpool bleeds football. Its two major footballing forces, Liverpool and Everton, are clubs rich in history. While no football league has courted globalisation quite like the Premier League, shifting focus beyond the confines of locality in search of profit, the Reds and the Toffees retain a unique connection with their support bases. As the game becomes increasingly gentrified, with complaints of many fans being priced out, Liverpool and Everton remain proud of their working-class roots. With their stadiums just a mile apart, separated by Stanley Park, this rivalry sees families, friends and work colleagues mixing red and blue. The notion of bragging rights is one often sneered at, but here they matter.

Danny Cadamarteri found out just how much victory in the Merseyside derby means to Everton fans on 18 October 1997. As he was leaving Goodison Park after the Toffees' 2-0 win, a rabble of Everton fans, proclaiming him their new hero, raised the young man above their heads and carried him off down the street, leaving his mum, who'd been by his side, bemused and more than a little concerned.

Everton led in the game thanks to a Neil 'Razor' Ruddock own goal. Then, with 14 minutes to play, perhaps taking advantage of tired legs, Cadamarteri robbed Liverpool defender Bjorn Tore Kvarme on the halfway line, made a beeline for the Reds' goal, sidestepping Ruddock along the way, and fired unerringly into the bottom corner. It was Cadamarteri's fifth goal in just his sixth start for the Everton first team, and having turned 18 only six days earlier it made him the youngest goalscorer in the history of the Merseyside derby. Ruddock, one of English football's pre-eminent 'hard men' in the 90s, was so impressed by Cadamarteri's daring and pluck that he sought out the Everton youngster to offer a respectful handshake before the teenager was substituted to a raucous ovation three minutes from time.

'Was it a foul?' Cadamarteri ponders of his, shall we say, enthusiastic challenge on Kvarme. 'In this day and age, Liverpool might have got a free kick – it was probably a foul. Razor's come charging in from the side,' the now-38-year-old continues in his raspy Yorkshire tones, remembering the goal still talked about reverently inside Goodison Park, 'and I've nipped it past him to score. I spent the whole of the game trying to stay away from him in case he tried to kick lumps out of me.

'The build-up for the game was immense. We had a lot of Scousers in the team among the young lads who were coming through: Michael Branch, Michael Ball, Gavin McCann was in the squad, who was a born-again Scouser, a Lancashire lad who'd been at Everton from a young age, and we had Dave Unsworth. Then we had the old guard: Dave Watson, Graham Stuart; "Big Dunc" [Duncan Ferguson] was obviously in the squad. It was all everybody spoke about all week. Then we were there: it was Merseyside derby day.

'You go to Goodison and all the way there every street is rammed. When you get to the stadium, it's jam-packed. And it's deafening. I'd played in the Premier League a few times, at St James' Park, which has a great atmosphere, but Goodison on Merseyside derby day is something else. We had a good day that day. And, of course, the infamous goal at the end of the game, where I allegedly fouled Kvarme and ran off and scored. It was a great day.'

A great day that was supposed to have heralded the arrival of a gifted young striker of Everton's own, a talent capable of rivalling Michael Owen, who was emerging simultaneously on the other side of Stanley Park. Cadamarteri was hailed as the brightest of a crop of youngsters ready to return the good times to Goodison, his combination of pace, youthful gusto and bouncing dreadlocks bewitching fans.

'I remember him bursting through on the scene because it was so dramatic and so exciting,' says David Prentice, the *Liverpool Echo* journalist who has covered Everton for more than 30 years. 'It was the same season Michael Ball had come through. With the pair of them, it was like there was going to be a new dawn for Everton led by these two youngsters.'

However, it would be almost a year before Cadamarteri next scored a first-team goal, and he would leave Everton a forgotten squad player in 2002, with just 15 goals from 110 appearances, never to play in the Premier League again.

* * *

Cadamarteri made his first-team debut in the final game of the 1996/97 season. Joe Royle had been sacked as Everton manager at the end of March after a run of just two wins from 13 league games. Club captain and veteran centre-back Dave Watson took caretaker charge of the side for the remainder of the campaign, picking up enough points to ensure safety from relegation and a 15th-place finish.

With Chelsea visiting Goodison to bring the curtain down on a forgettable season for the Toffees, Watson unexpectedly selected Cadamarteri as a substitute, alongside fellow youth-team star Michael Ball, whom Watson had given a debut weeks earlier.

The first-team call-up was a great surprise to Cadamarteri, who had played a Lancashire League game for Everton's 'A' team the morning of the Chelsea fixture, only to then be told to report to Goodison. 'I never felt there was an indication that I was seen as a hot prospect,' he admits, feeling Ball, Michael Branch and Richard Dunne all enjoyed higher billing than him among the generation of academy hopefuls. 'They were the ones we thought were really fancied by the club. It was probably more of a surprise that I broke in, got an opportunity and did really well.

'It was a no-time-to-think kind of situation. I think it was Anders Limpar or somebody had pulled out with injury. I didn't have a suit, so I went back to my digs and borrowed one of my landlord's suits and went down to Goodison.

'I went down there and didn't know where to go. I got sent down to the changing rooms that we used to clean. Dave Watson said, "You're in the squad, lad. Jimmy's gone down to the club shop to print you a shirt." It was the last game of the season so they'd run out of some of the numbers for the shirts. So I had number 28, and what they'd done is, they'd done the shirt then marker-penned the nine to look like an eight. I've got the shirt framed at home.

'I'm on the bench and it gets to half-time. He said, "You're coming on at half-time." "I'm coming on?!" This was as the whistle for half-time went. He brought me on at half-time against Chelsea at Goodison Park – no time to prepare.'

In addition to the suit, Cadamarteri's landlord had sent him off to Goodison with one specific instruction: to 'smash' Dennis Wise, the combative Chelsea captain roundly unpopular with opposing fans. Do that, ran landlord John's thinking, and you'll get the fans onside; do it at the Park End and they'll 'love you forever'.

'So, I've come on and it's just in my head: I've got to smash Dennis Wise and I've got to smash somebody down by the Park End.

'One ball goes in behind and I'm chasing it, running towards the Gwladys Street Stand and not thinking about anything else. I'm running up against Marcel Desailly, who I used to watch on Channel 4's *Football Italia* [when he played for AC Milan] – I've been sat at home watching *Football Italia*, seeing Marcel Desailly, but now I'm running down the pitch and it's him, going shoulder to shoulder. I've gone shoulder to shoulder and I've knocked him over – the fans went, "Wheeey!" I'm buzzing.

'About 20 minutes later, the ball's gone into the channel down by the Park End, and Dennis Wise is running on to it – this is the moment.' Cadamarteri leans forward in his chair, his eyes glistening as he recounts the moment in a rhythm evidently perfected over years of retelling. 'I've run in and gone bosh! Dennis Wise goes up in the air. As soon as I've hit him, the whole of the Park End has erupted: "Wheeey!" I had goosebumps. But then I thought, "Oh my god, I've just smashed Dennis Wise ..." I turned around and he's jumped up. He grabbed me by the hand and said, "I love that, son." I was buzzing.'

In the context of where we are sat, a meeting room in the heart of Burnley's state-of-the-art training complex, where Cadamarteri now coaches the Clarets' under-18 team, it seems especially incredulous that a 17-year-old should be asked to play twice in a single day, much less that the second game should be his senior debut. 'We talk about physical loading,' Cadamarteri says, 'not wanting young players to do too much ...' Not that it held him back: despite Everton's 2-1 defeat, he was named man of the match for his exhilarating cameo against the Blues.

The following season, Howard Kendall returned for a second spell as Everton manager. Cadamarteri admits he had 'half expected' to be among the first-team squad for the campaign, having starred in the final match of the previous term. Instead, though, the teenager was returned to the youth team. His pre-season focus was affected by his father falling ill, with Cadamarteri travelling back and forth to his dad's hospital bedside in Sheffield around his training schedule.

Football was a welcome distraction during a difficult time, and a first-team opportunity soon arrived. Selected among the substitutes for the fifth game of the 1997/98 season, away to Derby County, he came on as an early replacement for the injured Michael Branch. Everton lost 3-1, but Cadamarteri impressed sufficiently to be awarded a starting berth for the next game, at home to Barnsley, scoring his first senior goal in a 4-2 win. Tragic circumstances prevented the 18-year-old from truly enjoying his coming-of-age moment, though.

'My dad was still really ill and he passed away. So, I played in the game, did well and scored. I got man of the match in the game. But my dad had never got the chance to see me play in the first team, so I had mixed emotions: the highlight of your life, a debut at Goodison Park, scoring, man of the match, but I'd just lost my dad ... mixed emotions. But I think the thing that kept me on the straight and narrow was that I was in the first team now.'

Not only was he in the team, he quickly became one of Everton's most important players. 'Daniel, as a young kid, had no fear – he just did his natural thing,' Michael Ball says of his former roommate when I ask why he thinks Cadamarteri was able to make such a sudden impact at first-team level. 'Daniel was all about reactions and his strength. Technically, he probably wasn't the best, but his reactions to situations is what surprised and shocked the opposition. He was so unorthodox no one could handle him. He was sort of a secret weapon at the club.'

The goals kept coming for Cadamarteri, netting five in a run of six consecutive starts, culminating in his solo effort against Liverpool, a game in which he was preferred to record signing and England international Nick Barmby in the Everton line-up.

Amid this run of attention-grabbing form, one game, and one goal, carried particular emotional significance for the young man who'd recently lost his father.

'My dad was an Arsenal fan,' Cadamarteri says. 'I was desperate to play in this game [against Arsenal on 27 September 1997]. So I played in the game. We were 2-0 down, come back, Bally scores, I score the equaliser. It's 2-2, I'm buzzing. But then I've got mixed emotions because I'm an Arsenal fan and I'm thinking, "My dad will be turning in his grave if Arsenal don't win the league this year and it comes down to a point or two."'

Arsenal, in what was Arsène Wenger's first full season in charge, went on to win a league and cup double that season. This side containing Tony Adams, Patrick Vieira and Dennis Bergkamp, though, had been run ragged by Cadamarteri's instinctive and unpredictable forward play.

Cadamarteri's rise to becoming an Everton regular as a teenager came as a surprise to many. Unlike Michael Owen at Liverpool, or Wayne Rooney at Goodison in the early 2000s, who were both known to fans as prospects of elite potential long before their debuts, silence preceded Cadamarteri's emergence.

The young attacker grew up in Cleckheaton in West Yorkshire and was scouted by Everton while playing for his local side as a central defender. Perhaps the fact that Branch and Ball, viewed as the most gifted Everton players of the same generation, were local Liverpool lads meant they garnered more attention than Cadamarteri, with the out-of-towner slipping under the radar.

Even the reporters covering the Everton beat were unaware of the rapid, dreadlocked forward's imminent arrival on the senior scene. 'You'd imagine a guy with a name like that would have stood out,' says the *Liverpool Echo*'s David Prentice. '[But] I don't remember him coming through.

'That was the era when you had Francis Jeffers and Wayne Rooney a couple of years later, and we did hear of these names two or three years before they came into the first team. That wasn't the case with Danny; he did just literally explode on to the scene.

'I think he was helped in that season by Howard Kendall, the manager. Howard was always happy to blood a youngster, to give him a chance and see how he did. Danny, initially, grabbed his chance with both hands very quickly. But I can't say there was any fanfare or build-up to it; he did literally just appear on the scene one autumn, and he sadly faded just as quickly.'

Michael Ball remembers this period similarly: 'Liverpool had Michael Owen [who was preceded by] big talk. Everton had Michael Branch, but when he got his opportunity, it didn't really work for him. Danny then started to become, "Can he be the next one to make it through the ranks?"

'When Danny came to the club, at the time the talk was all about Michael Branch. He was making noise and they believed that he was going to go on to the next level very quickly. Me and Michael were at Lilleshall [the National School of Excellence]. Daniel, as a young kid, wasn't involved in the England set-up, so he wasn't in a high regard in that sense. But I remember when Daniel came to Everton, he had the physical presence – he was naturally powerful, naturally super-fast.

'I wouldn't say it was a surprise,' Ball continues, reflecting on Cadamarteri's first-team breakthrough. 'Daniel, in his age group and the year above, could out-muscle and out-sprint everybody. The club, at the time, were struggling with injuries and suspensions. They put belief in Daniel. It probably surprised a few people inside the club that he was the choice, but he grabbed it with both hands. He got his opportunity and, within five games, he smashed it. It was great to see, because he'd had a few personal problems.'

By the time the dust had settled on his Merseyside derby masterclass in October 1997, the 18-year-old Cadamarteri was one of the hottest properties in the Premier League. Several national federations began investigating his diverse heritage in the hope of discovering his eligibility, with five different national teams all courting his allegiance. He was chosen to represent England at under-18 and then under-21 level, while the dynamic nature of his play and carefree demeanour leapt from the screen as his first strides in senior football were broadcast on *Match of the Day*.

But Cadamarteri's sudden rise proved mercilessly temporary, followed quickly by an equally stark fading from view. The goal against Liverpool was his last for 350 days, with his next strike not arriving until October of the following season. Although he remained a regular feature of Everton's first team throughout 1998/99, playing at least some part in 30 of the club's 38 league fixtures, he scored just four goals that term.

The signing of striker Ibrahima Bakayoko in October 1998, along with experienced marksman Kevin Campbell's arrival on loan from Trabzonspor later in the season, limited Cadamarteri's opportunities in the centre-forward position, with the teenager increasingly forced out on to the wings, inevitably hindering his goals return.

His superlative early form saw him rewarded with a lucrative contract by the club, and many fans came to accuse the youngster of losing focus at this point. But Michael Ball believes Premier League defenders had learned quickly how best to combat the Everton striker, and that this was the main factor behind his plummeting productivity.

'I wouldn't say Daniel got his big contract and fell away,' Ball says. 'I just feel that clubs understood how to play against him, and Daniel then struggled to get consistency. He relied on his power and pace to get him into goalscoring situations; his natural ability was maybe not as good as his strength. So when clubs got wise to him, that's when Daniel started to struggle a little bit.

'He was very raw. I think because he was so raw, coaches struggled to find his best position. And because he was so fast, they tried to use his pace to hurt the opposition. That probably didn't help him.

'Daniel was an impact player and an instinct player: you give him a chance, he doesn't have to think about it, he puts it away. As soon as you put him in a one-v-one situation and he had to think and calm himself down a little bit, he struggled.'

By the end of the 1998/99 season, it had become clear Cadamarteri's ability to impact games the way he had in those early appearances had waned. A peripheral figure come the start of the following campaign and without a goal in almost a year, he joined First Division Fulham on loan in November of '99. 'I just needed to get away from Liverpool and just have a bit of a change,' he says of the temporary switch to Craven Cottage. But indiscipline and immaturity led to Fulham cancelling the loan deal early, after he was sent off in a game against Blackburn Rovers for stamping on former Liverpool player Jason McAteer 'because he was a Red'.

The 2000/01 season brought a slight return to form for Cadamarteri at its midway point. He appeared to develop an on-field understanding with Kevin Campbell, scoring in back-to-back wins over Arsenal and Chelsea. This renaissance proved to be short-lived, however. In September 2001, the Everton forward appeared in court, facing charges of assault relating to an incident in which a 25-year-old woman claimed to have been punched in the face by Cadamarteri in a late-night fracas. Judge David Lynch insisted he was in 'no doubt' that Cadamarteri had indeed punched the woman, but decided against levying a custodial sentence as 'it was not an unprovoked attack'. The Everton player was fined £2,000 for his indiscretion. A club spokesperson commented on the conviction, saying, 'The matter will be discussed by the club, manager Walter Smith and the board of directors in the very near future.' It was decided that his contract, which was due to expire at the end of the season, would not be renewed. Although he did play again for the Toffees – his final first-team appearance coming against Aston Villa in January 2002 – Cadamarteri, now 21, was let go in February.

* * *

'I surprisingly had quite a few options,' Cadamarteri says of the interest in him when it had become apparent his time at Everton was expiring. Among those courting his signature were top-flight opportunities in the form of La Liga's Málaga and Hibernian of the Scottish Premiership. A move closer to home most appealed, though, even if it meant a step down to Division One.

'Bradford had come in for me, which was on my doorstep. I just wasn't ready to move away,' he explains. 'I was engaged at the time, I had five sisters and had not long lost my dad. I wasn't mature enough to move away. I was 21 or 22. It just didn't appeal to me.

'Bradford has just come out of the Premier League and still had a lot of big-name players. I could go back home, be around my schoolmates, friends and family and just restart again. I made that decision and went to Bradford. I loved being back home. I just needed to get my football back on track. I went there as quite a big signing, a big name, and I was a local lad as well. I enjoyed how it relaunched my profile.'

But Bradford City's relegation from the Premier League had sent them into dire financial straits, with debts of £13m and administration looming. As one of the club's highest earners with staggered pay increases written into his contract, the Bantams couldn't afford Cadamarteri, and his release was negotiated after two and a half seasons.

After turning down an offer from Stoke City, next came a spell with Leeds United, whose own hard times had forced them into the second tier. Elland Road proved an even shorter residence for Cadamarteri, who, in a heated exchange, told manager Kevin Blackwell he was 'not a proper manager'. He left for Sheffield United without ever making a competitive appearance for Leeds.

'I didn't have a great relationship with Kevin Blackwell,' Cadamarteri concedes, 'so he didn't stand in my way. Sheffield United just bought me from Leeds. It was better to move on.'

Minor injuries and stiff competition for places up front – 'He horded strikers,' Cadamarteri says of Neil Warnock, his manager at Sheffield United – meant he was on the move again after just one season at Bramall Lane, staying in Yorkshire and returning to Bradford, now in the third tier.

Cadamarteri was making headlines again in May 2006. A routine post-match drugs test after a League One match against

Oldham came back positive for traces of the stimulant ephedrine. The Bradford forward was charged and hit with a six-month suspension. Cadamarteri has always maintained his innocence, however, attributing his positive test to having taken Day Nurse, an over-the-counter medication, to combat the effects of flu.

'I'd been off all week with flu,' he begins the retelling of the incident that threatened to leave his career and reputation in tatters. 'The physio had told me to stay away from the training ground while I was struggling with it.

'I was off over the back end of the week before and the weekend. They said not to come in Monday but to come in Tuesday afternoon. I came in and I was still struggling a bit. They said, "Go back home for a few hours, then we'll see how you are and maybe stick you on the bench."

'I had this Day Nurse and I felt great. I went back to my house and got my head down for a few hours. I phoned the physio to say I was feeling a bit better. They put me on the bench and I was feeling alright.

'I came on and ran around like a mad man and did well in the game. At the end of the game, it was the usual thing: the doping control had selected me and I went off and did my pee, and I thought no more of it. Then a week later, the physio phoned me up and said, "You know that pee test you did? It's come back as positive." I said, "Positive? What do you mean?" "You've failed that drugs test."

'I'd had the normal training supplements, the only other thing I'd had was Day Nurse. I didn't think it was an issue. We went through the whole process of having B samples tested. But there's a stimulant in Day Nurse called pseudoephedrine, which is a mild form of ephedrine.'

Cadamarteri arranged for his B sample to be tested by an independent lab in Derbyshire, in order to ascertain an exact volume of the offending substance. The sample, he says, was found to contain 50 milligrams of pseudoephedrine, twice the body's natural amount, but some way short of the typical levels expected of deliberate, performance-enhancing foul play.

As a result, a potential two-year ban was avoided, with the matter instead becoming one of negligence. Cadamarteri thought he might get away with just a fine, losing no playing time. On the advice of the PFA [Professional Footballers' Association], he pleaded guilty to the charge, with the hope of avoiding a drawn-out case while not affecting the outcome. No such leniency was afforded, and a subsequent appeal also fell on deaf ears. He was banned from football until January 2007, by which point he'd be 27.

He never returned to Bradford, though. The club dismissed Cadamarteri from his contract after he was charged. He feels this was a cost-saving move on the club's part, who insisted he'd be offered a new deal when he was eligible to play again. 'They were hoping I'd take reduced terms as an avenue straight back in,' he says. But, after proving his test failure was a mishap rather than misconduct, Cadamarteri insisted Bradford had no grounds for terminating his contract, forcing the club to come to a settlement on his release.

* * *

Cleared to return to football in January 2007, Cadamarteri signed for Leicester City, playing a couple of games for non-league Grays Athletic in order to regain fitness before joining up with his new club.

He never did stay anywhere for long after leaving Everton at 22. A year at Leicester was followed by two spells with Huddersfield Town, either side of a season and a half with Dundee United in Scotland, which brought his first and only major trophy, the Scottish FA Cup, and allowed him to fulfil a dream of playing in Europe. A knee injury, suffered while playing for Carlisle United in League One, forced Cadamarteri to retire in 2014, aged 34.

Cadamarteri's studiousness is perhaps an aspect of his personality many would be surprised by. As a young player, his game was built around instinct and natural athleticism, yet he kept a diary of training sessions, noting down the methods and practices of the coaches he worked under. He was also able to see beyond the circus that surrounded Paul Gascoigne, whom he played with at Everton, and insists 'Gazza' was a great role model for him as a young player – 'He ran his socks off in training and he was fantastic on the pitch. He was a great example to watch ... He'd go and have a run in the morning before he trained. If you talk about the old mentality of being first out and last in, that was him.'

After retirement, he segued quickly into coaching, first with regional side Howden Clough and then with Leeds United Ladies. He would consult the handwritten book of session plans, borrowing those he remembered enjoying and discarding those he didn't respond to.

Cadamarteri moved into youth coaching at Sheffield Wednesday's academy, where his eight-year-old son Caelan-Kole is currently earning rave reviews, before turning down an offer from Huddersfield to assume his current post with Burnley's under-18s.

Cadamarteri's playing career has equipped him with a deeper understanding of the young players now under his tutelage. He's been the new kid on the block, the great hope of a desperate fan base, but he has also learned the hard way lessons of conduct, misadventure and how quickly a budding career can unravel. When it comes to the accusation that he was never able to fulfil his potential as a young player at Everton, though, Cadamarteri feels history has perhaps judged him unfairly.

'A lot of people say, "You had an unbelievable start but then you had a goal drought." But I didn't really have a goal drought. It kind of came with circumstances: we had a number of young players playing in a squad that was struggling, battling relegation. I played a number of positions as well. I'd had that run of games and scored a lot of goals, but I started to find myself playing wide right, wide left, and even in the full-back positions a couple of times. People didn't realise because the games weren't aired as much.'

David Prentice believes the petering out of Cadamarteri's Everton career became a matter of mindset, and that his rapid ascent ultimately contributed to his precipitous fall. 'I think it's difficult to understand why it went wrong so quickly,' Prentice begins. 'People made obvious jokes about how he got his dreadlocks cut off and, a bit like Samson, he seemed to lose his talent at that time.

'I genuinely think he began to believe his own publicity a bit too soon. I wouldn't say he became "big time", but maybe he started to think he had already made it, that he was already a player. And through overconfidence maybe he didn't show quite as much commitment as he should have done and started to fall away as quickly as he'd appeared on the scene.'

Finally, I asked Michael Ball for his theory as to why his former Everton colleague and roommate was never quite able to reach the heights anticipated of him. Ball's forthright assessment is one that will apply to many faded prodigies, suggesting Cadamarteri's lightning-bolt arrival set expectations at a level he could never realistically reach.

'Daniel's enthusiasm – his pace, his bounciness, his dreadlocks – brought that glimmer of hope to the club. I know a lot of fans think he should have made it, and his big contract [was his downfall], that he never fulfilled his potential. My thinking was, was the potential really there, or did he play five unbelievable games?

'His reactions were so good that he was so hard to defend against. But then you get a little bit wise over the years, you don't get as tight any more. Daniel couldn't find another way, because he only knew one way: his instincts, his power and pace. Players and teams got quite cute against him and Daniel couldn't find that other avenue.

'I still feel he had a good career for the talent he had.'

Fixed

LONG drives through the north-east United States, taking in the orange and brown abundance of New England's forestry in autumn, or the luscious green landscapes of Maine, New Jersey and Vermont in spring, offer hours of meditative contemplation. As the road's white lines twist and turn endlessly ahead, the setting lends itself to reverie.

In these moments, as he travels between his base in Connecticut across the broad web his current remit captures, John Curtis could be forgiven for allowing his mind to wander back to the late 1990s. Back to when he was breaking into the Manchester United first team as a teenager, tipped to be a defensive stalwart at Old Trafford, as well as for England, for years to come. He might, understandably, relive his career as a footballer, only affixing an imagined trajectory more befitting of what was promised at the outset. Then, though, would come the stinging realisation that, despite a 14-year playing career that included several Premier League seasons, Wembley appearances and a League Cup winners' medal, it could have been more; it was supposed to be more.

But there are no such reminiscences and daydreams for Curtis. His second life, as a coaching instructor for the United States Soccer Federation (USSF), has given him a frank perspective of his playing days. Mistakes made and lessons learned from his own experiences are now stored, analysed and filed, forming the tools of his trade.

'It's the penny-drop moment,' he says. 'I can remember the moment the penny dropped for me: I was at Northampton Town and I can remember playing against Chesterfield away. I was in my 30s and I finally realised what it was all about and what you needed to do as a professional.

'The penny drops for the top players when they are 16 or 17 years old, but it didn't really drop for me until late in my career. What does that mean? I think it basically means suddenly realising what is required: doing whatever is necessary to win. And that is what a coach's angle is all about. Not at the youth level; we try to disguise that fact. But, ultimately, that is what it's about: it's about winning. Certainly at the professional level.'

In footballing terms, Northampton Town is a long way from Manchester United. In Curtis's case, there were 12 years and spells at ten other clubs between his United debut and signing for fourth-tier Northampton in 2009.

Perhaps second only to budding Argentinian playmakers being dubbed 'the next Maradona', the 'future England captain' moniker seldom proves prophetic for the young players labelled with it, as proved to be the case with Curtis; the closest he ever got to the senior international stage was an infamous England B outing versus Russia, staged at Queens Park Rangers' 19,000-capacity Loftus Road in the build-up to the 1998 World Cup. Although a regular at under-21 level, the United youngster was part of a cast of junior players making up the numbers so Three Lions boss Glenn Hoddle could run the rule over fringe players such as Les Ferdinand, Jamie Redknapp and hat-trick scorer Matt Le Tissier – 'It was a true mix of the haves and the have-nots in terms of who was going to get selected for the World Cup squad,' Curtis remembers.

At club level, it was a similar tale of inertia on the precipice. Promising beginnings at United, where he was the recipient of the club's prestigious Young Player of the Year award in 1997 before impressing with his poise and maturity in early first-team outings, ultimately levelled off to a standard not quite befitting of a team obsessed with achieving top honours at home and in Europe. Instead, Curtis's longest tenure at any one club, in terms of total appearances, was a two-and-a-half-year, 87-game spell with Nottingham Forest during a particularly grim period for the two-time European champions as they languished in the third tier.

Curtis's was still a playing career that would be the envy of most who have ever harboured dreams of becoming a professional footballer, and former team-mate Ben Thornley is quick to point out that Curtis was a 'good player. John was athletic, quick, and committed,' and he 'still had a good career'. And Thornley is of the belief that, were it not for the fact that as a right-back Curtis faced the ultimately insurmountable challenge of unseating Gary Neville, by then well established as the undisputed first choice for club and country in the position, he could have enjoyed a long and successful career at Old Trafford. Not doing so, Thornley adds, 'was no slur on John whatsoever, with either his ability or attitude'.

However, Curtis sees things slightly differently. As a young player he was the subject of hype and hysteria, destined, it seemed, for the very top, but he believes he developed a 'fixed mindset'. He was, he says, eager to protect the status he had earned as one of England's brightest young hopes, rather than opening himself to the trial-and-error process that breeds improvement, fearing mistakes rather than valuing the important lessons they bring. And while he acknowledges being recognised with individual accolades, such as being named Manchester United's Young Player of the Year, is flattering, he questions whether such commendations were healthy for his psychological development as a young man.

'It is an amazing achievement, really, when you look at who has won that award in the past,' Curtis offers. 'But that's another thing: are these awards good? Do these awards cement that fixed mindset?'

* * *

By the age of 14, Curtis was perhaps the most sought-after young player in the country. A regular England youth representative, word of his talent travelled fast as he impressed during his stay at the FA's National School of Excellence at Lilleshall in Shropshire. Having been spotted playing regionally, the Nuneaton-born youngster progressed up the England schoolboy ranks before being recommended for a placement at Lilleshall, the country house and estate which acted as a central coaching base for the country's most gifted young footballers, churning out England internationals such as Sol Campbell, Jamie Carragher and Michael Owen while in operation from 1984 to 1999.

Growing up in a part of the Midlands where most pledged allegiance to either Coventry City or Leicester City, Curtis admits he 'was never a mad football fan', preferring cricket and proudly claiming to have opened the bowling for Warwickshire under-13s. As such, when a swathe of clubs began to covet his signature, he was able to select a destination on merit, rather than being swayed by any pre-existing biases.

The clubs competing for his registration would invite him to train with them, and he did so regularly, joining up with Aston Villa and Stoke City, among others, during school holidays. Indeed, it was while playing in a tournament in Scotland with Stoke that Curtis was first moved from his original midfield station to centre-back. Named Player of the Tournament, the move stuck, and he starred in the role for England before later switching to right-back as the United first team drew closer.

He never committed to signing forms with Stoke, or anyone else, however, leaving his options open until he joined Manchester United at the age of 15. Back then, the Red Devils were not yet the dominant force of English football they were soon to become under Sir Alex Ferguson, so what drove the decision to make a home of Old Trafford?

'I signed for United towards the end of my first year at Lilleshall. We were invited up to watch Man United play Blackburn in their final game of the 1992/93 season – it was the first time they'd won the league for a long time. The atmosphere at Old Trafford that day was unbelievable, and I said to myself, "That's where you want to play." And I signed for United shortly afterward. Then, upon leaving Lilleshall, I joined United as an apprentice initially, and then I signed as a professional at 17.'

Curtis moved into digs on Hugh Oldham Drive, overlooking the car park of United's old training ground, the Cliff, where Ferguson's car could be seen parked up by 6am every morning, without fail. 'It was just me and a landlady,' he remembers, 'in a little terraced house in Salford. It was a little bit strange because I was on my own. The reason I was on my own is because I was doing my A levels. So, rather than being in digs with a load of lads around and getting easily distracted, they arranged for me to be on my own, which was good. But in hindsight it might have been nicer to go in digs with the boys.'

Many young footballers in this situation struggle with the move from their homestead, leaving parents, friends and family behind, but this was nothing new to Curtis, who'd boarded at Lilleshall for two years previously. He adapted quickly and approached his new life in typically workmanlike fashion. His assimilation was also aided by the fact he'd already played for the United youth team while still at Lilleshall and was part of the 1995 FA Youth Cup-winning side, captained by Phil Neville – 'I played in the semi-finals and the final. It was a very good team.

'I remember my youth-team debut down at the Valley. We played Charlton. Lee Bowyer megged me and ran past me, but luckily I got back and tackled him. It was sort of a welcome to under-18s football when you're a 15-year-old. It was a big jump.'

The natural progression once a player outgrows youth-level football is to start turning out for the club's reserve team. However, Curtis initially found his path to regular reserve minutes blocked by 'Class of '92' alumni such as the Neville brothers, Paul Scholes and Nicky Butt, who were themselves straddling the second string and the first team.

'The reserve team was full of those guys,' Curtis recalls, 'and the senior players who weren't playing. From playing with Ashley Westwood, David Johnson and people like that [in the youth team], to suddenly playing with the likes of Scholes and Choccy [Brian McClair] was a big jump up.'

As with any step-up in competition he'd faced up to this point, though, Curtis met the challenge head on and soon established himself at reserve level, sufficiently impressing to claim the club's Young Player of the Year award at the end of the 1996/97 season. It was a moment worth savouring for Curtis: 'You have to think who is involved in selecting the Young Player of the Year: it was [youth-team manager] Eric Harrison, the gaffer [Ferguson], Jim Ryan, the reserve-team manager – those kind of people would have been putting my name forward for that particular award.'

Reserve football conquered, a first-team bow wasn't far away. Curtis's debut came in a League Cup tie against Ipswich Town in October 1997, just a few weeks after his 19th birthday. Inauspiciously, United lost the game 2-0. His Premier League beginnings offered much more positive signs, though, with his first senior appearance at Old Trafford coming in a 7-0 thrashing of Barnsley just two weeks later.

'It was fantastic. A fantastic game to play in. There were a few injuries. I'd played in the League Cup a few weeks before and it was fantastic to play in that game and do so well. As a young kid, it was an amazing experience. Playing at Old Trafford, it was always full. Capacity crowd, great atmosphere because the team was doing well – to be involved with that, with the great players that were on the pitch at the time, was an amazing experience for me. Looking back, I can remember smashing someone in centre-midfield in a tackle and thinking, "This is what it's all about." I enjoyed it.'

By the end of his third league game for United, a 2-0 win at home to Everton on Boxing Day, Curtis had a 100 per cent win record, with United scoring 15 times and conceding only once. He would taste defeat in his next three outings, however, first in a shock reverse at the hands of Coventry in United's last game of 1997, then away to Sheffield Wednesday before the Red Devils famously slipped up at home to Arsenal in March.

Having at one point opened up an 11-point lead at the top of the table, defeat to the Gunners at Old Trafford, thanks to a single Marc Overmars strike, tipped the momentum in Arsenal's favour, with Arsène Wenger going on to claim his first Premier League title.

Ferguson's post-match bollocking method, known euphemistically as 'the hairdryer' for the proximity and ferocity of its delivery, is notorious, and he is said to have unleashed a particularly thunderous outburst after this game. Curtis had been a second-half substitute, and some suggest his struggle to contain Overmars, the lightning-quick left-winger whom he came in direct contact with as United's right-back, crystallised in Ferguson's mind the idea that the young Englishman was not of the requisite calibre for a long-term future at Old Trafford. But

Curtis disagrees, feeling history has remembered his display harshly.

'The hairdryer was very often out, so we as young kids were kind of well-versed in it. That was what Eric Harrison did so well as youth-team manager: he prepared you for that first-team environment. It was ... interesting.

'I always get a lot of stick for that game, but people often forget that Marc Overmars scored when I wasn't even on the pitch – he didn't score when I was there. This was an Arsenal team that was full of world-class players. Those two clubs going head-to-head for the Premier League every season, a bit like United and City are now, it was two big-hitters with world-class players in every position.' Whether related to the Arsenal defeat or not, Curtis would only make six more Premier League appearances for United before joining Blackburn Rovers in a £1.5m deal in June 2000.

Curtis admits that, with hindsight, he has pondered whether he should have left United sooner. With his first-team prospects fading, he joined Championship Barnsley on loan in November of 1999, relishing the chance to play regularly and compete at a high level. He then made a permanent switch to Blackburn the following summer. But he resolves sticking around that extra year was beneficial, being part of United's famous treble triumph of 1998/99.

Although he was not selected for the Champions League Final that year, a dramatic, come-from-behind win in stoppage time against Bayern Munich in Barcelona's Camp Nou stadium, and despite not accruing enough appearances to end his United career with more than a Charity Shield winners' medal, Curtis has gleaned valuable lessons from being in the winning environment Ferguson had fostered – even if he didn't actually witness the spectacular late turnaround against Bayern first-hand.

'Me and Jordi Cruyff were in the squad but not on the bench. We were sat up watching the games with the fans. Bayern Munich were winning and we made our way down through the stands to say commiserations to everybody. Then we heard a massive cheer. We were like, "Wow, brilliant. Let's get down there for extra time to see if we can get on the bench or watch it from the tunnel."

'Jordi [a former Barcelona player] obviously knew his way around the Nou Camp, so he was leading. He said, "Come on, if we go down this way we can get down to the tunnel and watch it." And as we go down the winner goes in and the whole place erupts. So we actually missed both of the goals, but it was an amazing experience to get on the pitch afterwards, and amazing to experience the celebrations.

'That whole season, to have a front-row seat and be a fly on the wall for everything – the FA Cup Final, all the league games – it was truly amazing.

'I look back as a coach now and think how lucky I've been to be able to work with some of the greatest players of that particular generation, in a club that, certainly at that point, had the best youth-development program, the best first team, the best manager. Looking back at that, you just think, "What an experience." It was an honour, and it has set me up now as a coach.'

Jim White of *The Telegraph* has decades of experience covering United, and his summation of Curtis's time at Old Trafford chimes with the player's own. 'I've got the feeling with him that he was one of those guys who was old before his time and then got overtaken by others,' White suggests. 'Both the Nevilles, really, were able to develop more as players. If we're going to make a really harsh parallel it would be with him and Luke Shaw [who was enduring a difficult spell at the time we spoke], because I would have said Luke Shaw, at 18, was the future of the England defence. When he was at Southampton, everyone wanted him; he looked so accomplished, and then, both physically and in terms of game management, he has not been able to make the next step.

'I remember Fergie once saying, "What we do at United is ensure players have a good career as a footballer when they come through our academy. It may not be at United, but we equip them to have a good career in football." And I always had the feeling [Curtis] was one of those: looked fantastic when he was 15; less so when he was 25, but was equipped with the self-confidence that comes with being at United to have a career in the Championship. And there's a lot of these guys around who have had fantastic careers, just not with United.'

For Curtis, the decision to leave United, 'was very, very easy, because I'd got to the stage that I was 20 and I wasn't playing regularly. I was completely demoralised, to be honest.

'I was in an environment that wasn't good for my development any more. I had seen everything that it had to offer, and it got to the stage that it was detrimental for me to stay, so it was a no-brainer.

'I went to the gaffer and said, "Gaffer, I need to play." And two weeks later I was playing against Man City at Maine Road in the Championship. So that was credit to him. He recognised that and he helped me straight away. By the October of that season [1999/2000] I was playing in the Championship for Barnsley. It was like it was a breath of fresh air for my career; it invigorated me.'

The move away from United, getting out of the 'pressure-cooker environment', as he puts it, lifted a weight off the young man's shoulders. The quotidian pressure to deliver, to win and keep winning, rarely pausing to take stock of any achievement before marching on in relentless pursuit of the next, can be draining mentally. More so, perhaps, as someone on the fringes, fighting for relevance at the same time.

'You feel 10ft tall, because everything was lifted. It's like having the weight of the world on your shoulders playing for Manchester United, and at Barnsley that wasn't there any more. So I arguably played some of my best football during that loan spell with Barnsley. I really, really enjoyed it.'

Then came an offer from Blackburn Rovers. Down in the Championship despite having been champions of England only five years earlier, the Lancashire club were intent on bouncing straight back up to the top flight. Their bid of £1.5m was accepted and Curtis became a Blackburn player in the summer of 2000, closing the book on his United career, which comprised 14 league appearances, just a couple of months short of his 22nd birthday.

An ever-present in Rovers' triumphant return to the Premier League, an injury early in the 2001/02 season ruled Curtis out for three weeks. The form of his replacement, Australian international Lucas Neill, meant he never reclaimed his first-term berth on a regular basis and was an unused substitute in

Blackburn's League Cup Final victory over Tottenham Hotspur that season.

'Had things worked out differently there,' Curtis wonders, 'had I remained in the team then, maybe it would have unfixed that mindset a bit more. Maybe I could have built on the confidence of that season in the Premier League – who knows?'

Instead, he began a search for regular first-team football which would last the best part of two years, encompassing fleeting spells with Sheffield United (loan), Leicester City, Portsmouth and Preston North End (loan), before settling at Nottingham Forest in 2005.

Preston had wanted to sign Curtis permanently, offering a contract. In Billy Davies, Curtis feels he 'had a manager there who liked me and really supported me', and not signing on at Deepdale is a regret he carries with him.

'It was a poor decision based on money. I was on Premier League money at Portsmouth, thinking I could keep Premier League money. It wasn't a decision about football. It was a decision about money, more than anything else, and I live to regret that.'

He joined Forest mid-season, and the East Midlands club were relegated from the Championship to League One at the end of the campaign, becoming the first former European champions, having won the European Cup in 1979 and '80, to be demoted to the third domestic tier.

Daniel Storey, the former deputy editor of Football365 and a lifelong Forest fan, remembers this period of his club's history well, if not fondly.

'Forest were a bit of a disaster club at the time,' he says, 'and we were picking up former Premier League players, or players on their way down rather than on their way up. We were effectively only buying free transfers at that stage.

'So I suppose [Curtis] kind of got lumped in with a group of players we didn't really think were good enough for Forest, but they clearly were because we were a League One club at that time, we just didn't want to believe we were a League One club.

'It's probably unfair on the individual, but that was a rotten time to be a Forest fan. We got relegated in 2005 and that's when he came in, effectively as a League One defender at that point. I think he played around half the games in his first season then nearly all of them in his second, sometimes at centre-back, but more often than not at right-back.

'He was kind of jobbing at that point. It was probably fair to say the hopes of him becoming a future England captain were gone by then, but there were a lot of players at Forest at that time who looked like they were fighting a battle; it probably wasn't a very nice place to be playing football, and they probably had to self-motivate to enjoy themselves, because we were wretched.

'He was a committed professional. There were a few players at Forest then who you doubted whether they wanted it; I'm sure he really wanted it.'

For Curtis's part, he enjoyed his two and a half years with Forest, a club he describes as 'in the Manchester United ilk, with the history and heritage it's got'. Indeed, it was only the last embers of ambition that caused his exit. Although all pretentions of international pedigree had long extinguished, he still believed he belonged at least at Championship level. At the end of his second full season at the City ground, he rejected an offer of fresh terms and instead signed for second-tier Queens Park Rangers.

However, if Forest were a club in disarray, QPR were utterly calamitous. Recently taken over by Flavio Briatore, the Italian businessman and owner of the Renault Formula 1 team, their ambitions outweighed their means, and the subsequent injection of finances was not matched by sense employed by the club. 'I will never invest in a football club again,' Briatore, who stepped down from his post at QPR in February 2010 following a Football League 'fit-and-proper-person' investigation, would later say on an Italian chat show. 'It's only ever a good idea if you're very rich and looking for ways to waste your money. In two years, you'll be very poor and won't have that problem any more.'

Within a week of Curtis's arrival at Loftus Road, John Gregory, the manager who'd signed him, was sacked. The defender's first-team chances evaporated and he was released in December 2007, having made only five appearances for the club, the last of which came in September.

* * *

The end of his time at QPR also marked the end of Curtis's career in high-level football. Released without a club to go to, a year-long injury kept him from actively pursuing other opportunities. After calling in favours to work with Notts County to rehabilitate, and turning out for non-league Worcester City to gain match sharpness, he joined Conference side Wrexham on a short-term basis before signing for Northampton in League Two, but he was released at the end of his first season at Sixfields.

Ever since leaving Manchester United, he struggled to regain an upward trajectory for more than a fleeting moment, with setbacks and back-steps occurring with the kind of regularity that would test anyone's resilience. Curtis says he managed to maintain context and perspective throughout, though.

'When you leave a club like Man United to go to Barnsley, or to a Championship club, from a psychological standpoint, it is a really massive step backwards. So to go from not playing at a Championship club to playing for Worcester City in the Conference North, that sounds like it's a massive step backwards, but in my mind it wasn't, because I was already used to those kind of steps. So psychologically you become very pragmatic, kind of immune to it.'

Recognising his time in the game was winding down, Curtis elected to move to sunnier climes to see out the remaining years of his playing career, joining Gold Coast United in Australia's A League in 2010.

'I actually wanted to go to MLS,' he says of his move Down Under. 'I wanted to come to America, but the seasons don't line up. After that season at Northampton, when Northampton didn't offer me another contract, I didn't want to search around League Two or the Conference for a club to take me; who would you rather play for: a lower-league club – Woking or someone like that – or go and play on the Gold Coast in Australia? It was a no-brainer for me to go over there.

'I had to go on trial. I went over there, did one training session and the manager signed me. It's quite a funny story, actually. I got food poisoning in the flight over; I got zero sleep. I spent the night that I got there throwing up and then went to training the next day – almost 40 hours with no sleep. And then I did well enough in training for the manager to sign me. It was certainly a fun experience.'

With one eye on his post-playing career since his early 20s, Curtis had always envisioned segueing into coaching. He studied for his first coaching badges while at Nottingham Forest, and curses not having done so earlier – while still a youngster at Manchester United, even – feeling the new perspective it gave him was hugely beneficial.

'Coaching while you're playing is a fantastic thing – I'd recommend that to any player. The FA do coaching courses as part of their youth-development systems now, but they only touch on it. I would advise any player to dive into it and get involved with the club they are playing for, get involved in the academy. Even if it's just the under-9s, under-10s, it would be an eye-opener.

'If I could go back in time, I would have coached at Man United. I would have gone down to the academy every night and watched the training sessions, watched the coaches and gotten involved. It would have made me a better player, I believe. I think it would make any player a better player if they could develop as a coach. They'd understand the coach's angle a lot more, and what the coach is actually after. It will make you a better player.'

Now, the lessons Curtis learned the hard way as a player are not only being passed on to the players he works with in his role with the USSF, but are also being applied to mould and improve other coaches, passing on a greater sensitivity to the issues that held him back.

'A lot of the coaching I do focusses on the psychological aspect. It's nice that I can look back now as coach, because I've lived those experiences, so I can pass those experiences on.

'My son is on the verge of the England under-18 squad for rugby. I know nothing about rugby; all I can do is advise him with a football perspective, and advise him on mindset, thinking that the mentality in professional, high-level sport is the same, or at least very similar. I do my best to try and protect him and not [let him] make the mistakes I did, not let him get fixed early.

'Fix your mindset when you're 85, not when you're 19.'

From Club to Club

'**H**E should be a multi-millionaire. He was brilliant.' Even at the elite, professional level, there are a handful of players to whom football comes comparatively easily. They glide effortlessly along the turf, they see things quicker, in sharper focus than their peers, and barely break a sweat in executing techniques that demand full focus and meticulous measurement from others.

Making his way through the youth ranks at Wolverhampton Wanderers during the late 1990s, Ryan Green was one such player. He would later settle into a right-back remit, but at academy level he was a virtuoso. Played in defence, as either full-back or sweeper, enabling him a full view of the pitch, he would stride forward with the ball at his feet, breaking beyond opponents at speed and spraying passes left and right.

'He was so athletic,' former team-mate Matt Murray enthuses. 'I remember him getting the ball in the youth team, picking the ball up at sweeper and running through everyone to score. He was so quick and he could kick with both feet. He was strong, he was athletic, he read the game. It was all so natural to him.

'Ability-wise he was better than [England international and £24m Manchester City purchase] Joleon [Lescott]. Greeny would beat most people for range of passing. He would beat most people in a sprint. Greeny was brilliant. Of course, Joleon had ability, but Ryan Green could do everything: ping it with his left foot, ping it with his right.'

But Murray also offers the same caveat that has followed Green his whole career, from his eventual Wolves departure and through spells with Millwall, Sheffield Wednesday,

Bristol Rovers, Port Talbot Town, Merthyr Town and Hereford United. With a winding career path that initially looked set to trace a steep upward trajectory, the defender, 37 at the time we met in the lounge of a gym in Cardiff, never parlayed his unquestionable potential into anything close to what was predicted of him.

'Joleon was the best he could be,' Murray continues. 'Joleon and people like Jody Craddock will look back on their career and say, "I was the best I could be." Not many people can say that,' – the inference, of course, being that Green is not one such player.

He knows it, too, frankly admitting, 'Instead of being a top player, I'm probably a medium player. I probably would have been a Premier League player if I had a good attitude. If I had the attitude I have now, at my age, I'm sure I would have been a Premier League player.'

Green was a senior international at 17, becoming the youngest player to represent Wales, a record he took from Ryan Giggs, and he made an impression in the Wolves first team while still in his teens. He had the world at his feet. Yet, at 33, as he slipped into part-time football with Welsh side Merthyr, who play in the lower reaches of the English football pyramid, he found himself working on the railways to make ends meet.

'It was difficult,' Green confides. 'You're used to only doing a couple of hours and earning good money. Then you are doing all the hours under the sun for £20,000 a year. It was a wake-up call. I was thinking, "Bloody hell, I do all these hours for £20,000 a year when I could earn that easily playing part-time football."'

Adored by Hereford fans for his three stints with the club, supporters of the Edgar Street club banded together to crowdfund the cost of cortisone injections for the Welsh defender in 2016, when the club were unable to cover the costs of treating his Achilles problem. It was a heart-warming gesture, but also served to remind of how far from his Premier League-level potential Green's meandering career had taken him.

'Chris Evans, who was the academy director, and I used to discuss Ryan as being like a Rolls Royce,' former Wolves youth coach Chris Turner, who also went on to sign Green at senior level when he became manager of Sheffield Wednesday, explained to me. 'His pace, whether you played him in midfield, whether you played him at centre-back or full-back – he just oozed class. He was like a Rolls Royce of a footballer. He could change pace, he was physically strong in the tackle. A great talent that. As he says himself, I don't think he realised how good he was.'

* * *

From football-obsessed kid to fully fledged professional, Green has been playing the game as long as he can remember. Although he still doesn't cut an imposing figure, standing 5ft 8ins, he has always had a natural strength and was physically mature compared to many of his opponents at school and junior level. This, married with his technical gifts, meant he was easily identifiable as a young footballer of real promise.

'I was six years old, playing at under-10s,' he says. 'I scored on my debut, which was unbelievable. I was a midfielder. You used to just run around anywhere then. When I was a baby, my parents said I would take a ball to bed, wear my football boots to bed. I just loved football. I was always practising on the street. Nowadays, the kids are on the computer, but I was out on the streets, practising non-stop.'

Playing for Cardiff Schools, a select team of the area's brightest talents, Green stood out still, and soon garnered interest from professional clubs, with trials at Crystal Palace, Norwich City and Cardiff City. Then, as he describes it, 'Wolves came and sold the dream to me straight away.'

'I knew it was a big club. They were in the Championship then. I went up there and they sold me the dream, to be honest – a brilliantly run club. If you look at the players from our youth team who made it – Robbie Keane, Matt Murray, Joleon Lescott, Jermaine Easter – I think there's more than ten who made it professionally. Lee Naylor, Keith Andrews as well. It was Matt Murray in goals, myself. Adam Proudlock made it for a little bit as well.'

Green made the move to Wolverhampton, a distance of around 120 miles, at the age of 15, leaving his home town of Cardiff earlier than planned, having gotten into trouble at school and invited not to return.

Going straight into digs and focussing his efforts into football every day in a new city, adapting wasn't easy – he felt homesick and alone. But the arrival of Jermaine Easter, a school friend from Cardiff who would go on to become a Welsh international forward, later the same year helped Green settle, and his football benefitted.

'It was fairly obvious to me as I was head and shoulders above a lot of people back then,' he says matter-of-factly, with no sense of arrogance or conceit. 'They signed me on a professional contract as well, so you know you've got half a chance when they sign you on a professional contract.

'I was 16 when I started playing for the reserves. Men's football straight away. I thought I was [physically ready for it]. In the youth team, I was a lot stronger than most, but men's football was a bit of a shock to the system. You try to bully them in the youth team and they fly to the floor, but the men are not going anywhere.'

Sky Sports journalist Adam Bate, a lifelong Wolves fan, recalls the anticipation that surrounded the Welsh youngster's first-team breakthrough at Molineux. 'I still remember Ryan Green's debut against Sheffield United,' Bate begins. 'It was a night game at Molineux and there had been so much talk of this young lad because Bobby Gould had already given him his Wales debut. He played at right-back that evening and showed genuine quality going forward.'

It was a bittersweet first-team introduction for Green, however. Just three weeks after his 18th birthday, in November 1998, he replaced regular right-back Kevin Muscat and impressed sufficiently to earn a standing ovation as he left the field. It would have been a perfect start to life at senior level were it not for the fact he was being carried off on a stretcher at the time.

'I made my debut, hell of a game, but did my medial ligament. I tried to play on but you know when it's gone, so I had to come off. I think I was out for two months. Then I came back too early and did it again, but not so severely – I was probably out another month. It went away after that. I never had no problems with my medial ligament again.

'I was probably man of the match in the game. Kevin Muscat was one of the top players there anyway, he must have gotten injured or suspended – probably suspended knowing him.'

Green's injury and subsequent layoff prevented him from building on the momentum of his shining debut and allowed Australian international Muscat, seven years his senior, to resume right-back duties without contest.

A full international debut, remarkably, had come four months earlier, at the age of 17 years and 226 days, meaning Green had played for Wales before experiencing first-team football at club level. He had already been a regular for the Wales under-21s, having progressed through the under-18s and -19s ranks by the time he was 16. And a strong showing against a talent-packed Italy under-21 side, featuring the likes of Andrea Pirlo and Nicola Ventola, had convinced manager Bobby Gould to include the teenager, along with fellow prospects Craig Bellamy (a common direct opponent of Green's as a speedy winger at youth level in Wales) and Simon Howarth in his squad, which travelled to Malta and Tunisia for back-to-back friendlies in June 1998.

'My debut was against Malta. We won 3-0 [with Bellamy among the scorers], then we played against Tunisia. I started both games. And before those two games, we played Wrexham in a testimonial. That gave me a taster.

'I took Giggs's record [as Wales's youngest ever senior international], and then Lewin Nyatanga took it off me a few years later.

'At 15 I was getting in trouble, fighting and stuff, then two years later I was playing for my country. It was mental. But I always knew I could be a footballer, I always practised after school. My mates were drinking but I was always practising. I was always pretty confident. From the age of about 11, I knew I could be a footballer. I'm not being big-headed; I was just miles ahead of everyone.'

* * *

'It all seemed set up for Green to go on to become a Premier League regular at Wolves or elsewhere,' Adam Bate posits.

'Instead, he was hardly seen again. It was almost two years until his next Wolves appearance and after a brief run in the team – one that included a red card in the Black Country derby at West Brom – he was gone.

'Even though Green was less impressive during that second coming, many Wolves fans would have bet on his sale coming back to haunt the club. Although there were signs of that happening when he got a move back up the leagues to Sheffield Wednesday, that never really proved to be the case.

'Perhaps it was injuries. Maybe it was a poor attitude. It is difficult to say from the outside looking in. But what's certain is that Green did not come close to fulfilling his potential.'

Taking ownership of the faults that led to the promise of his early career remaining unfulfilled, when I first contacted Green to discuss the prospect of his involvement in this book, he freely admitted, 'Going out and drinking was my problem.'

There's a delicate balance to be struck as a high-level professional in an industry as physically and emotionally challenging as football. It's essential for mental wellbeing to be able to unwind, decompress and relax from time to time, inching open the release valve ever so slightly in order to prevent the pressure forming cracks. For some, this takes the form of enjoying a few drinks with friends every once in a while.

But players must also treat their bodies with extreme care; nurturing and nourishing their physical self is both a professional requirement and a venture beneficial to the individual's longevity and prospects of higher achievement. Balancing the competing desires of wanting to let loose and needing to retain physical shape is a delicate exercise. Green did not manage to do so.

'It's addictive,' Green says of his partying lifestyle. 'You have the pick of the women, you've got a decent amount of money. I had friends in Wolverhampton who I had met locally, and I'm still friends with them. They were good times, but I wish I'd maybe just gone out once or twice a week.

'Since I made it [into the first team], my attitude went downhill for ten to 12 years. I was going out clubbing – I was going out six days a week sometimes. I didn't have a drinking problem, never had a drinking problem, I just liked going out, as most young lads do. Mine was a bit more than the usual young lad; I was more like a student, going out every night.'

Chris Turner suggests, 'He got side-tracked, which prevented his further development. He was a Welsh international – he played a number of times for the first team of Wales. The boy had great talent but I don't think he actually realised how good he was.

'These are the sort of issues that people don't realise with young players: they do have the same cravings that outside of football people have.

'You have to be disciplined, and Ryan found that hard. You try and point him in the right direction, especially when he was in the youth team. Or you point him in the direction of players he needs to look up to and follow.

'Ryan's one of them who is a follower, but unfortunately he followed the wrong sorts at times, getting himself caught up where he shouldn't be. But these are the many drawbacks that a young footballer has that are out there, out to catch them and prevent them from being one of the top five per cent in the country and playing internationally for their country. Ryan had that ability, he just lacked that dedication at the right time to follow it through.'

Green was still able to play to a good level through his partying, and nights out on the town didn't affect his performance in training the following day as much as might be expected – 'Your body gets used to it,' he suggests, 'and when you're young you can get through it.' His lifestyle, though, wasn't going unnoticed by the managers he worked under. He admits that every coach he had during his late teens and 20s had words with him about curbing his off-field habits, eventually earning him a reputation that spread quickly, closing doors that his talent would have otherwise opened.

'You start to get a name for yourself. I went out on a Friday before a match and got fined by [Wolves manager] Colin Lee, two weeks' wages. You probably go down the pecking order then. And he'll talk to another manager, who will talk to another manager. You get a reputation. That's 100 per cent why I didn't make it as at least a Championship player.'

* * *

After making his debut in November 1998, and subsequently leaving the field injured, Green didn't reappear in the Wolves first team until September 2000. In the meantime, after constantly being overlooked by manager Colin Lee, the Welshman handed in a transfer request.

'I was just getting frustrated with not playing. And I knew I was good enough to play at that level,' he says. 'Colin Lee was in charge. He wouldn't let me go out on loan but I wasn't in the first team, I was just in the reserves, and you're not going to progress much at reserve level. I just got frustrated and put a transfer request in. But I withdrew the transfer request after he said I could go out on loan.'

Before any loan switch materialised, however, at the beginning of the 2000/01 season, a switch to left-back for hitherto first-choice right-back Kevin Muscat opened up a slot for Green to fill. He featured regularly in the opening months of the campaign, but Lee was sacked in December, replaced by Dave Jones in early January. When the new manager omitted him from the side to face Sheffield Wednesday in the FA Cup, Green again asked for a transfer and was loaned to Torquay United in March – where Lee had just become caretaker manager – and joined Millwall that summer, signed on a free transfer by former Wolves boss Mark McGhee.

After a strong start to life at the Den, including a debut in a thrilling 3-3 draw with Nottingham Forest, the first setback sent Green spiralling back into old habits.

'It was a bit unlucky for me: every team I went to, the Player of the Year and fans' favourite was a full-back. Matt Lawrence was right-back [at Millwall], he was Player of the Season the year before. He was out injured so that's why they signed me. I did really well. We were in the play-offs that year. Then he came back and he was back in the team. So I was a squad player and I started going out drinking then. The London life, as a 23-year-old boy, was massive. I was living the dream.'

Let go by Millwall at the end of the 2001/02 season, Green was again on the hunt for a club. A move to Bradford City in the First Division had been agreed, only for the collapse of ITV Digital to scupper the move. The broadcaster's multimillion-pound Football League television-rights deal had emboldened clubs below the Premier League, arriving as a saviour of the lower-level sides, only for the agreement to prove unsustainable. ITV Digital was left crippled by their ambitious Football League deal, and several clubs who'd banked on the revenue from the television contract plummeted into dire straits.

With the Bradford deal off the table, Green joined home-town club Cardiff City on a month-to-month contract. The Bluebirds were an upwardly mobile Division Two side at the time, who would eventually earn promotion to the second tier via a play-off victory over Queens Park Rangers at the end of the 2002/03 campaign. There proved to be no room for Green, though, whose only outing for the club after joining in November 2002 was in an LDV Vans Trophy fixture. He joined Sheffield Wednesday just two weeks later.

At Wednesday, for the third time in his fledgling career, Green was handed a chance at redemption by a former Wolves employee, this time ex-youth coach Chris Turner, who was managing the Owls.

Those who had been in the inner sanctum of the Black Country club around the time Green was progressing rapidly through the ranks clearly knew what talent the young full-back possessed and seemed prepared to overlook past indiscretions.

'He knew what ability I had,' Green says of Turner signing him for Wednesday. 'I played four or five games on the bounce then got injured. It was my knee, meniscus, so I was out for a month or so. The team were near the bottom and that was it, I was let go. They got relegated and I think they were trying to save money.'

Released by Wednesday, the summer of 2003 marked a low point for Green. He was still only 23, but for the first time in his career offers of employment were not forthcoming.

'That was the first time I struggled for a club,' he remembers. 'I had left Sheffield Wednesday struggling for a club, and my agent didn't sort anything out. I was looking on the internet myself, looking for clubs fairly close to Cardiff, and I saw Hereford's right-back had just gone to Telford – Matt Clarke. I thought I'd get my agent to ring Hereford. They were interested, they wanted to sign me. I played my first game in a friendly against Birmingham, did really well and signed.'

It was also the first time he'd dropped out of the Football League, with Hereford in the Conference, the fifth tier of the English football pyramid. Where once word of his natural ability had elicited excited whispers among coaches, the managerial rumour mill was now working against Green. Talk of his less-than-professional off-field behaviour was beginning to count against him. Managers talk to one another, especially when weighing up recruitment decisions. Before deciding on whether to take a chance on a player who had evidently not developed as expected, prospective suitors will have reached out to managers who'd worked with Green previously, and, it seems, few glowing recommendations returned.

'Reputation, yeah,' Green sighs when asked what he believes was the reason for the lack of interest at this juncture. 'When I was out of the team at Sheffield Wednesday, I did exactly the same thing: instead of getting my head down and trying hard to get back in the team, or getting fit, I was out drinking.

'They all had a word with me, every single manager, about my drinking. I just wasn't ready. To be honest, I didn't grow up until I was 30. I was a good player, but I'm drinking four to six days a week.'

* * *

A five-yard scurry, a crunching tackle and a calmly sprayed 20-yard pass gets Hereford back on the front foot. Green's breath is visible on this cold early November afternoon and steam rises from his glistening forehead. The 37-year-old centre-back understands the significance of the fixture – arguably Hereford's biggest since reforming in 2014 after the original Hereford United lost its battle with financial struggles – but he displays no signs of nerves or hesitation. He is the experienced head of the team, the veteran centre-back, with Dara O'Shea, an enthusiastic 19-year-old on loan from West Bromwich Albion, in his former role of marauding right-back.

Telford United, the side Green scored his first-ever professional goal against some 14 years earlier, are the visitors at Edgar Street to contest a place in the second round of the 2017/18 FA Cup. It would later be confirmed that the sell-out 4,700 crowd is the club's highest since its reformation, with a second-half goal scored by striker John Mills sending the home side through against the ten-man Bucks.

Green, marshalling the backline, calls on the experience and wiliness of two decades in the game to thwart speedy 20-year-old striker Marcus Dinanga, who only once escapes his attentions to meaningfully test the goalkeeper. Over ten yards, Green is still a match for most; longer distances yield diminishing returns, but there is unquestionably a quickness of thought, his brain processing scenarios more rapidly than those around him.

From my observation point in the press box, it's evident that Green, while no longer in possession of the athletic gifts that helped him stand out as a youngster, still enjoys his football. The competitive fire has not yet extinguished.

At 37 and now in his third spell with Hereford, he is adored by the Edgar Street faithful, not least thanks to his winning goal in extra time of the 2005/06 Conference play-off final – 'It came to my left foot and I just swung at it,' he recalls. 'If I had tried to control it, it probably would have ended up in the stands.'

That goal and, of course, his return to regular game time in what was his third season with Hereford, earned Green a move to Bristol Rovers, a League Two side with ambitions of progressing up the Football League.

And there were highs on the pitch once more, when he helped the Memorial Stadium side earn promotion to the third tier via the play-offs, which meant a Wembley appearance in front of 63,000. But a persistent Achilles problem and his penchant for the nightlife again proved to be his downfall.

Green recounts one nightclub tale of suffering a broken jaw after being punched from behind outside one club in Bristol, following some 'trouble' earlier in the night. He also shows me a faint scar on his face, the result of a drunken, glass-wielding ex-girlfriend of a friend taking her frustrations out on him on yet another wayward night out.

When his two-year Bristol contract was up, he was not considered for renewal. 'That's why I left Bristol Rovers: it was all over me going out drinking, really.'

Next came a return to Hereford to battle relegation from League Two for three seasons.

Succumbing to the drop in 2012, Green was released, leading to moves to Welsh Premier League side Port Talbot and Merthyr Town in England's eighth tier. Although he captained Merthyr to promotion, having to supplement his part-time football income by working a railway maintenance job, 4.30am starts for gruelling shifts of manual labour has coloured this period of his career darkly.

'It was probably the worst mistake of my career, signing at that level. I was just sulking, really. Sulking that I didn't have that much money offered from League clubs. Then, Port Talbot, local, offering me good money, a good signing-on fee – it was nice. But then you've got to play in front of 100 people, instead of 3,000 people every week. It's only part-time, and you start thinking, "What am I going to do after my career?" So yeah, that was probably the lowest point of my career.'

After helping Merthyr earn promotion, voted Player of the Year for his individual efforts, the club were fiscally unable to make good on their promise of a higher wage, so Green departed on amicable terms. He went 'home' to Hereford, who 'welcomed me back with open arms'.

Two promotions and a Wembley appearance in the FA Vase Final later, Green is still enjoying playing, hoping to play on as long as his body will allow. A property development venture, buying and renovating run-down houses in and around Cardiff, has given him financial security. He no longer has to play football, but the game remains his passion.

'I love my football. I don't want to give up. Football is my life and the thought of giving up is quite sad. I'm just trying to enjoy it as long as I can.

'If I can play until I'm 40, that'll be brilliant. But as soon as people start running past me week in and week out, I'll hang my boots up. I'll know when to hang my boots up. I've definitely got another year after this, which will take me to 38, 39. I'll just take each year as it comes then. I'm living the dream still, doing what I love.'

Green's penchant for partying earlier in his career doesn't appear to have impacted his longevity, but no one could contest its detrimental effect on his development and progression. Few would have anticipated the rickety trajectory his career was to take when he made his senior Wales debut at 17, or when he was applauded off the field after a valiant first outing for Wolves.

As one former team-mate confided, 'He wanted to be a footballer, but he didn't want to be a *professional* footballer.' Unfortunately for Green, that was true for longer than it needed to be, as he's all too aware.

'When did it click? Probably when it was too late.'

Chaos Theory

'PEOPLE think I took cocaine when I was a player: I swear on my kids, I never took cocaine while I was playing. But then I did it. I'd stay up two days. After a few months, I thought, "Hey, what are you doing? You're going to die if you carry on like this."'

Andy van der Meyde's post-football life has turned out to be almost as fascinating as his truncated time in the game. He was a Dutch international winger of Europe-wide renown at Ajax, having risen through the club's famously prolific academy. Spells at Internazionale and Everton proved less fruitful, as a series of off-field issues robbed any hope of continuity and stability. His last meaningful employment as a footballer was with Everton – he briefly resurrected his playing career back in the Netherlands after his initial retirement, before injury halted his comeback – deciding to hang up his boots when his contract at Goodison Park expired in 2009. He was 29 years old.

In the years that followed, Van der Meyde would capitalise on his fame in his home nation by, alongside his wife, starring in a reality TV series. The show proved so popular it was later adapted into a live theatre production that toured the country. Indeed, he is recognised in the street as we walk towards the coffee shop setting of our interview, past designer store after designer store in an upmarket district around the corner from Amsterdam's Museumplein, regularly frequented by Ajax players, stopping to exchange a friendly hug with an internationally known DJ.

Before the TV success, though, and before he began to tread a straighter path, Van der Meyde's life after football had taken on an altogether darker complexion.

Shortly after moving to Liverpool to join the Toffees, Van der Meyde's marriage broke down, the result of an affair with a dancer he met at a strip club in the city. He and his new partner had a baby daughter together, meaning Van der Meyde had reason to stay in Merseyside after his time at Everton ended, even if that relationship, too, had deteriorated. Known as a lover of nightlife, the Dutchman rented a city-centre apartment and indulged in days-long drink and drug binges.

'I stayed there [Everton] four years, until my contract finished, but after that I stayed in Liverpool for another year. I didn't want to leave because my kid was there. I was only young, I was 29.

'After my contract [had expired], I was staying in Liverpool city centre with a friend. We would go out partying just to get away from reality. Thursday, Friday, Saturday, Sunday – we were partying. It was an escape from reality.'

That reality: a failed marriage and two children living hundreds of miles away in Italy, the dissolution of his subsequent relationship, the difficulties of his third child being born with a serious illness, and the realisation that a football career which had initially promised so much had ultimately faded sharply, with just two Premier League appearances in his final two years at Everton.

'I called my manager and said, "Get me back to Holland, I'm going to die here."'

* * *

Van der Meyde arrived at Everton in the summer of 2005. David Moyes, who was in charge of the Merseyside club at the time, was a long-time admirer of the winger, having tried to sign him from Ajax some years before. The fee Everton paid Inter for his services was officially undisclosed, although *The Independent* reported it to be somewhere in the region of £2.1m – a sign of how his career had already begun to slide, as at 25 his market value should have been much higher.

On a personal level, the money was good, seeing the Dutchman double the salary he earned with Inter to £30,000 per week. However, it was only a bizarre twist of circumstances that saw Van der Meyde elect for a Premier League move, with his preferred destination, Monaco in the French Ligue 1, unable to accommodate his wife's extraordinary animal collection.

'I went to Monaco and they were offering a lot of money,' Van der Meyde recalls. 'I went there with my agent to look around and it was beautiful. They showed me an apartment and said, "This apartment is for you. You don't have to pay." Beautiful.

'Then I phoned my wife and said, "Listen, I'm going to sign for this club. It's beautiful here and they are offering a lot of money." But she said, "No, don't go there because the animals can't go." She had 11 horses, a camel, zebras. The whole garden was full.

'When I played at Inter I had a big field in my garden and it was full of animals. People would come on a Sunday to feed them. So I didn't sign for Monaco because of the animals. One week later, it was Everton. Liverpool's a little bit different to Monaco, eh? Fucking hell.'

Injured when he signed, Van der Meyde's Everton career was off to an inauspicious beginning, but his commitment, something which was continually questioned throughout his time in England, was, he feels, unimpeachable. The obvious logistical difficulty of transporting what amounted to a small zoo's worth of wildlife meant his wife initially stayed behind in Italy, leaving Van der Meyde to focus intently upon his recovery from injury while living in a hotel for three months.

In addition to his wife and two young children, he also moved a family of friends over from Italy, hiring the husband as a chef and the wife as an au pair, while their teenage son – who had stayed for a time with Van der Meyde as company while he was living in a Liverpool hotel – and daughter came, too, continuing their schooling in England. Rather than further settle the winger in his new surroundings, however, the arriving support network inadvertently sparked a chain of events that contributed heavily towards his four years with Everton becoming fraught with turmoil.

'After my wife came, the boy was turning 16 years old and I took him to a strip club – "I'll give you a present." I put him on the stage and had six girls dancing around his chair.'

It was while at the gentlemen's club that Van der Meyde first laid eyes on a dancer, Lisa, whom he describes as 'beautiful, like Jordan, amazing. I thought I would just go out with her one time. I wasn't planning to stay with her. But we went out together and it was really good; I felt really good. I fell in love with her.'

His injury, he thought, provided the perfect cover for a surreptitious affair with his new lover. He rented a city-centre apartment without his wife's knowledge, and he would stay there for weeks on end with Lisa, under the guise of taking himself away from the family home to focus fully on his recovery.

'I said to my wife, "I'm injured, I have to go to a hotel for a week," because I wanted to stay with the other girl. I went home every day to see my wife and the kids and to get clothes, and then I'd go back to the hotel. It went on for one week, two weeks, three weeks.

'My wife was thinking, "What the fuck is he doing? He's been gone three weeks now."'

Of course, it wasn't long before his wife's suspicions were aroused, and, with the help of a private investigator, Van der Meyde's second life was exposed. The hired detective initially attempted to trail him as he travelled between his spacious luxury home on the outskirts of Liverpool to the 'hotel' he claimed to be holed up at, alone, recuperating, but the winger's vehicular velocity proved to mirror the flank fleetness of his Ajax pomp – too fast for anyone hoping to keep apace. The employ of an electronic tracking device, however, fixed to his car on the next laundry run home, did the trick.

'I woke up one morning to my phone ringing. It was my wife. She said, "How's your new girlfriend?" I said, "What are you talking about?" She told me exactly what my girlfriend was wearing at that moment. I said, "You're right. How the fuck do you know?"' The detective was stood watching from an opposite apartment block, looking into the window of Van der Meyde's secret love hideout and describing the scene to his wife.

'I thought, "Ok, I've been caught, I have to accept the consequences."'

There were to be no second chances, no reparations or reconciliation; trust had been broken beyond repair. Van der Meyde and his wife had met in Holland. While he was a homebody with no great desire for broadening his horizons beyond the walls of the Amsterdam Arena, she, harbouring ambitions of becoming an air stewardess, could not wait to flee the country for pastures new. She'd loved Italy, the Milan life, and resolved to return with their two young children upon learning of her husband's infidelity.

'That was the worst thing I've ever done in my life: I left my kids,' Van der Meyde says, instantly transported back to that moment of regret, eyes welling as he pictures the scene. 'I was a real bastard. I was thinking, "What have I done?" I was holding them before they got in the car to go to the airport, they were only three and five years old. I was crying and they were looking at me. I still remember that look: "Why are you crying?"

'I drove home saying, "What the fuck have I done?" But the strange thing was, I was also in love with the other girl – if you're in love, you do strange things. I left my kids for somebody else. It was my own fault. For the kids, it was such a shame.'

Despite the tumult of his personal life, matters on the pitch began promisingly for Van der Meyde once he had returned to fitness in late October. He started six games in succession for the Toffees and, although lacking the kind of sharpness that comes only with a sustained run of matches, showed glimpses of the old magic, impressing with the potency of his crossing.

English football has always reserved a certain fondness for wingers. On the bog pitches of the not-too-distant past, the central areas were often rendered muddy quagmires by weather conditions and overuse, so it was a common tactic to work the ball out to the greener pastures of the flanks at the earliest opportunity, allowing the speedy wingers to carry it forward and relentlessly aim high balls towards burly, granite-headed centre-forwards. Some of the most revered stars of English football history earned their keep out wide, from Sir Stanley Matthews to George Best to Ryan Giggs. Although there were no pretentions of Van der Meyde, at this stage of his career, reaching such heights, he seemed an ideal stylistic fit for the Premier League, the division not yet reimagined through the lens of Pep Guardiola's possession-heavy positional play, or the dynamic counter-pressing of Jürgen Klopp and Mauricio Pochettino. Moyes's side operated with a simpler, more traditional remit, and there was a genuine desire among the Goodison Park faithful to see Van der Meyde succeed.

'I think there was more hope, rather than expectation,' remembers David Prentice of the *Liverpool Echo*, who has covered football in the city, and at Goodison in particular, for more than 30 years. 'People had been aware of what a good player he had been for Inter, and obviously for the national team, but also very aware that it had gone wrong for quite some time. And Everton got him for quite a modest fee, which made people wonder why that was.

'There was a hope that maybe he'd recapture the heights he'd earlier had. I know fans were desperate for him to succeed whenever he played. The fans realised how good he had been and were really keen for him to do well.

'Even very minor things: when Everton played Middlesbrough early on, he put a corner in for James Beattie to score, and the fans were really thrilled, thinking that could be a taste of things to come.'

That early run was as good as it ever got for Van der Meyde at Everton, though. He would only once start back-to-back Premier League games again, against West Ham United and Portsmouth in March of the 2006/07 season, and he would make only two league appearances across his final two campaigns with the club.

Many of the issues, it seems, stemmed simply from boredom, and the creeping darkness that came with too much time to think. After the last of his six games in a row from October to December 2005, Van der Meyde sustained a serious Achilles injury in training, the day before Everton were due to play Manchester United at Old Trafford.

Sidelined for six months and instructed not to run, and to turn up to the training ground only to receive sports massages and work in the gym, without the distraction of football, he was confronted with the reality of how his career, his life, had slid.

'At this time, I was getting bored. I was out for six months which meant I couldn't go to the World Cup with Holland. Everything was dark. My kids were away, I was injured, I wasn't happy, I couldn't play football – I was falling from a mountain into a black hole. But I was just pretending everything was cool for my family back in Holland, because I was famous back home. My granddad was always so proud of me. I was saying, "I'm fine. I'm just not playing; everything is cool." But I was not cool; I was getting crazy.'

Fit again by March, he returned to action, albeit only briefly, making just five more appearances the rest of that season. Now, the verve of his wing play, the ferocity of his runs and the consistency of his deliveries were no longer prevalent. Rumours of his penchant for the nightlife had begun to circulate, having been spotted in one too many nightclubs at inopportune times, and too regularly spied in a state of inebriation around the city. Van der Meyde has always strenuously denied being an alcoholic, contesting he never developed a dependency and that drinking, for him, was about escape through socialising, but that was the accusation levelled at him. 'Of course I went out, but I only went out when we were on a day off,' he told the *Liverpool Echo* in 2012. 'I never went out when we had training the next day or whatever. I was never doing stuff like that. But it all started to live its own life. And everybody was following each other, you know, speaking bullshit, and all that.'

Early in his second season at Everton, Van der Meyde was admitted to hospital, reporting breathing problems, claiming to have had his drink spiked in a bar. Months before, his home had been burgled while he was playing in a pre-season friendly against Athletic Bilbao, with the perpetrators stealing a Ferrari, eight Rolex watches, a Mini Cooper and his beloved, nine-week-old bulldog Mac – the dog and the Ferrari (sans functioning windscreen) were found and returned. His first Merseyside derby, in March 2006, ended prematurely when he was sent off for a rash challenge on Liverpool midfielder Xabi Alonso. In August 2007, as the Toffees began the new season, the Dutchman was fined two weeks' wages for 'a breach of club discipline' after missing training; 'Andy has had numerous warnings about this type of thing and we won't tolerate it any longer,' said Moyes.

Controversy, it seemed, had become his shadow.

Van der Meyde freely admits that many of the issues that plagued his Everton career were of his own making, but amid the professional and personal turmoil lay a serious problem beyond his control. His third child, a daughter named Dolce, born in Liverpool to his new girlfriend Lisa following the breakdown of his marriage, was born with a stomach condition that left her fighting for her life for months at Liverpool's Alder Hey Children's Hospital.

'She had a problem with her stomach and had to have an operation the day after she was born,' Van der Meyde remembers. 'She was on a drip machine. She couldn't eat so she was being fed by a drip for twelve hours each day.

'I was going to training and then straight to the hospital, then home and bed – every day. I didn't want to be there any more. I was getting crazy. I was making fights with my girlfriend on purpose at the hospital because I had to get away.

'You sit in a little room, this millionaire, you want to play football but you have a bad relationship with the gaffer, you're falling out with your girlfriend and you have a sick baby. And I was still thinking about my other kids in Italy. I was playing it cool with the team – they knew something was going on but they didn't know what. I had these four things on my mind.' After months of treatment, Dolce pulled through; his relationship with Lisa did not.

Moyes, as Van der Meyde details, was less than sympathetic to his plight. In the pressure-cooker environment of top-level football, where managers' jobs are on the line on a weekly basis, compassion isn't always in bountiful supply. Moyes had been a fan of the winger dating back to his days as a youngster at Ajax, so there was obviously a belief in Van der Meyde's ability from the manager. But Van der Meyde, who has spoken of tearfully pleading with the Scotsman for a chance to play when he was on the fringes of the side, feels he was unfairly treated, and that a line was crossed.

'I came on the pitch one morning at training and the gaffer wouldn't speak to me. He just [pointed for me to go and train with the reserves]. The second team was there: boys 16 or 17 years old, five players and not even a goalkeeper. I had to train with them.

'The first team were training on the next pitch, playing 11 against 11. Moyes whistled for me to come over. It was a corner, I had to stand at the second post. Once that corner was taken: "Andy, you can go." A few minutes later, he whistled: "Andy, come." I had to stand in the wall while they took a free kick. It was mentally fucking with me. I wasn't concentrating and my head was everywhere.

'There was a team in London who wanted to take me on loan, but in Liverpool there is the best children's hospital [Alder Hey] and my daughter was there. [Moyes] said to me, "Go to London, you can play there." I said, "I don't want to go to London. My kid is in hospital; I want to stay here." He said to me, "It's always something with your kid. Always problems." From that moment on, I thought, "Fuck you. You speak like that about my kid? You can do whatever you want with me now." It was unbelievable.'

Arguably Van der Meyde's greatest contribution in an Everton shirt came in his penultimate game for the club, an FA Cup fourth-round replay at Goodison against arch-enemies Liverpool, in February 2009. A tense, mid-week evening encounter at the home of the Toffees was, if truth be told, desperately short of quality. Goalless after 90 minutes, the Dutchman was introduced for what the BBC's match report called 'a rare outing' for the 'outcast' at the beginning of the second half of extra time, replacing captain Phil Neville.

Just two minutes before the game would have been settled by a penalty shootout, Van der Meyde rolled back the years, breaking down the right and crossing for Dan Gosling, a midfielder signed from Plymouth Argyle the previous summer, who'd only turned 19 two days earlier, to confidently fire home a dramatic winner. The goal, infamously, was a momentary mystery to fans watching on television, as the live coverage inexplicably switched to an advert for breath mints as Gosling prepared to shoot, only cutting back to the action in time to see Goodison Park in elated eruption.

With his assist, Van der Meyde gave Everton fans a glimpse of what they had hoped to have seen on a more regular basis during his four years with the club, and made partial amends for his dismissal against Liverpool two seasons earlier.

The winger's participation in the match was as much a surprise to himself as anyone, by this time thoroughly surplus to requirements in Moyes's eyes, with just 11 minutes of Premier League game time under his belt all season. And even by his own standards, Van der Meyde's pre-match preparation had been far from ideal.

'The day before the game I had to train with the second team, I knew I wasn't in the team. But the night before the game, my dog was having babies. The whole night I was awake getting the babies out – I didn't sleep.

'The next morning, they called me: "Andy, you're in the team tonight." What? I hadn't slept. I thought, "It's ok, I'm not going to play anyway." I came on for the last half an hour. I got the ball and I crossed to Dan Gosling and he scored. The stadium exploded – that game was the most important game in the world for the supporters. It was surreal for me.'

Despite making just ten league appearances in Everton blue in his four seasons at the club, and despite the off-field drama that was a poorly kept secret around Liverpool throughout his stay in the city, Van der Meyde was always, and remains still, a popular figure among Everton fans, as David Prentice attests: 'Very much so, because I think they realised he did have this talent, and they were desperate for him to try and recapture it. There was also that thing about Everton fans: they are a curious bunch and they love an anti-hero – Duncan Ferguson being the main case in point, the man who failed a breathalyser test 48 hours before he scored in his first derby match, a man who had run-ins on the pitch and off the pitch. Fans adored him as a loveable rogue, and I think Andy was a similar kind of character. And on the very brief occasions that he did feature, they were desperate for him to succeed. But it didn't really work out.'

* * *

So prodigious a talent was Van der Meyde as a child that Ajax, the club he grew up supporting, cast their net further than their recruitment policy at the time ordinarily allowed. The Amsterdam side, world renowned as one of the finest nurturers of gifted young footballers, tended to limit their scouting zone to within a 50km radius of the Amsterdam Arena, yet they made special dispensation for Van der Meyde, 100km away in Arnhem, and snapped up the budding winger aged 12, ferrying him back and forth to five training sessions a week via minibus.

'I'd go to school at nine in the morning until 12 in the afternoon,' Van der Meyde remembers of those early days at Ajax, 'then they'd pick me up to go training, but they also picked all the other Ajax boys up so it took two hours to get there. When I got there, I'd train, do homework and then train again, then they would bring me home. I was getting home at ten o'clock every evening. I was getting very tired.'

It was then suggested by Co Adriaanse, Ajax's director of youth who would later go on to manage the first team and make Van der Meyde a regular starter aged just 20, that the family should relocate to Amsterdam. Van der Meyde and his mother moved into an apartment in the city provided by the club, leaving behind his father and two sisters. 'At that time, I was 14 years old,' he recalls. 'They knew already that I had a big talent and was a different kind of player.'

A first-team debut came at 18, a 1-0 Eredivisie win over Twente in November 1997, but early outings were sporadic and he struggled to assimilate to life among the senior pros, joining the side he'd made his bow against on a season-long loan for the 1999/2000 campaign.

'I was in the first team at 18 but I went to Twente because I wanted to leave; I didn't feel good in the team. I couldn't be myself. Normally, I'm talking and making jokes, but some of the players at that time were a bit snobby and I didn't like that. I wanted to move.'

At Twente, Van der Meyde was entrusted with a regular starting role, afforded the freedom to express himself while also learning vital lessons about the demands of the senior game. In 32 league appearances he scored twice and registered five assists, perfectly content with the Enschede club: 'I wanted to play and Twente was a warm, beautiful club with good supporters; I wanted to stay there. But I had to go back to Ajax and it didn't go well, I wasn't happy.'

Upon his return to Amsterdam, Adriaanse had taken charge of first-team affairs, and the Dutch coach's militant methods didn't jive with Van der Meyde, whose season with Twente had shown he performs best in opposite conditions, when allowed a longer leash.

'Adriaanse was a very strict coach, no jokes or anything; if you stood still in training you would have to go to the sidelines and do 20 push-ups – it was like the military. A lot of players didn't like that.'

Adriaanse didn't last long, though, replaced in the summer of 2001 by Ronald Koeman, the legendary Dutch international sweeper who'd starred in Holland's 1988 European Championship triumph and fired Barcelona to their first-ever European Cup, powering home a trademark free kick to see off Sampdoria in stoppage time of the Wembley final. Koeman, who would go on to manage Valencia and Everton among others, was embarking upon his first major managerial role, having served as assistant manager with the Dutch national team and Barcelona, before cutting his teeth in a single season in charge of Vitesse. Discontent and with an offer on the table from Blackburn Rovers, Van der Meyde was minded to quit his boyhood club, but the new boss convinced him to stay.

'When Koeman came in he said, "Andy, come here." And I thought he was going to say I could leave for Blackburn, but he said, "Don't go. I want you to stay. We'll give you a new contract and you'll play left-wing." "How come? I've got no left leg; it's chocolate." But he said, "It's ok, you'll go inside and then shoot on goal." And I got a lot of confidence from him, which is important for a player, that confidence from the gaffer.

'Koeman was one of the first [to use inverted wingers]. They started to do it and, okay, I was a left-winger, and I enjoyed it. I would score more but I could also cross to the back post, whip it in.'

And whip it in he did, enjoying stellar form which saw him net career-high returns for league goals of five and then 11, also reaching double figures for assists in 2002/03, while a youthful, vibrant Ajax side claimed the Eredivisie title the season before.

It was an exciting time for the club, as a host of young academy graduates, led by Van der Meyde and the likes of Rafael van der Vaart and Wesley Sneijder, were complemented by youthful imports such as Zlatan Ibrahimović, signed as a teenager from Swedish side Malmö, and Romanian defender Cristian Chivu – three of whom, incidentally, would go on to play for Internazionale, with Van der Vaart the exception.

Van der Meyde remembers being struck by the radiance of Sneijder's potential in particular: 'They were a little bit younger. I was in the first team and I saw Sneijder play in the second team, and I knew: "This boy ... wow." I wanted him in the first team right away. He had two great feet and could pass the ball, so for me it was easy: I make the run and the ball comes. And he knew as well: he's going to go there; he'd play me through and no one could catch me – I was quite fast at that time.'

Having grown up idolising Dennis Bergkamp and Marc Overmars, studied at the feet of Jari Litmanen – 'the best player I ever played with' – and Michael Laudrup – who 'taught me how to score' – Van der Meyde was now a key part of the most promising Ajax squad since Louis van Gaal's 1995 Champions League winners. And he'd recently become a senior international, scoring against the USA on his Netherlands debut. Leaving Ajax couldn't have been further from his mind.

Footballers are ultimately commodities, though, their image a marketing gold mine and their playing registration potentially worth millions to the club that owns it. Although this, of course, often works in a player's favour, making millionaires of the most marketable thanks to sponsorship deals and image rights, it also makes them hostage to the mechanisms at play in world football, collateral of the food-chain dynamic undeniably determining a club's business ethos, and the objects of desire in a global transfer market increasingly resembling an arms race.

By the end of the 2002/03 season, 23-year-old Van der Meyde's stock had never been higher, and Ajax decided to cash in.

'I was good here and I didn't want to leave Holland. My wife and I had just bought a house in Amsterdam and I had a one-month-old baby. I started to play in the new pre-season. We were training in the Arena and the trainer said to me, "Andy, you have to go upstairs to the technical director."

'He came with me and we walked inside the technical director's office. They said, "Congratulations, Inter have just bought you." I didn't know anything about it. They just sold me like that. Koeman said, "Yes, but only if he wants to go."

'I was an Ajax supporter and they sent me away like that. I didn't even know Inter had interest in me. At that moment I was in the room, Arie van Eijden [Ajax general manager] and Leo Beenhakker [Ajax technical director] were on the phone to my agent: "We've agreed an £8m deal; Andy can go now." So I went downstairs, collected my stuff and left the stadium. Two days later, my agent was in Milan to negotiate personal terms. It was unbelievable. I didn't even want to go from Holland.'

Sold by Ajax, where he had been happy, comfortable and playing well, Van der Meyde arrived in Milan to find Inter in a period of disarray, the very moment, perhaps, that marked the beginning of his career's slow denouement.

Argentinian tactician Héctor Cúper, who had previously guided Valencia to back-to-back Champions League finals, was the head coach, but he was not a popular figure, enjoying difficult relationships with many of the side's stars.

Cúper had campaigned for the club to sign wingers to enable him to use a 3-4-3 formation. Lacking the autonomy to select his own men for the roles, Cúper was provided compatriot Kily González, from former club Valencia, and Van der Meyde. Having come from an environment where he had the full support of his manager, the Dutchman found himself in a very different situation at the San Siro.

'I came on the training pitch and went up to the gaffer to shake his hand. He shook my hand, looked at me and said, "Who the fuck are you?" He didn't even know, because the technical director bought the players.'

Despite that embarrassment, Inter began the season well, and Van der Meyde was in fine form, scoring a stunning strike in a Champions League group stage victory over Arsenal at Highbury, celebrated in trademark style, bent to one knee, firing an imaginary arrow into the crowd.

That celebration was seldom seen again, however, as Van der Meyde's form deteriorated along with his team's, crumbling to a 5-1 thrashing at the San Siro in the return fixture against Arsenal. Cúper was sacked in October of 2003, replaced by Alberto Zaccheroni, and Van der Meyde found himself on the fringes of the side. Inter rallied to finish fourth in Serie A, securing qualification for the following season's Champions League, although the former Ajax man played little part. He still had enough stock banked at international level to earn selection for that summer's European Championship, playing in all but one of Holland's fixture's en route to a semi-final exit at the hands of hosts Portugal.

Van der Meyde returned from the Euros to find Roberto Mancini had been installed as the new Inter manager, and his preference for a winger-less 4-3-1-2 formation meant the writing was on the wall for the Dutchman.

'Mancini came, and he bought a lot of players; in one season we had 40 players, so I didn't play any more. It was difficult.

'After a while you know you're not going to play, so you start pretending you're sick or injured, "Yeah, leave me alone." I had to travel a lot and not play. I started to get a bit fat from all the pasta, too.

'We only trained 45 minutes a day because we had a lot of games, so I had to train myself, and I wasn't used to that. Italian players, they would train for 45 minutes and then go to the gym or go running. I was like, "What the fuck are they doing?" because it wasn't like that in Holland – you train with the whole group and the gaffer and then he tells you to stop, and you'd train an hour and 20 minutes, an hour and a half.

'The second year I wasn't playing and I wasn't taking it seriously any more. I could do what I wanted. I met girls and did stupid things. Football fans in Italy almost want to cry when they meet you, no matter who they support. It's different to Holland or England. I went to clubs and they'd put me in VIP, they'd get rid of whoever was already in there. I wasn't playing, so I was getting bored and I wanted to go out – that was my last few months in Italy.'

Nima Tavallaey, a journalist and expert on all things Inter having founded the website *sempreinter.com*, reflects on the difficult situation Van der Meyde walked into: 'He came to a club in turmoil. After the spending spree of the 90s, that [former Inter chairman Massimo] Moratti had done without having anything other than a UEFA Cup to show for it, money was running out. Although Moratti spent heavily, the club's structure was not in place yet. That season completely fell apart.

'That was the time when the Dutch youth were the best in the world. And Van der Meyde was one of the best players at Ajax, he really was, but he never really gelled; he always looked uncomfortable. There were some poor performances as well. He gave some poor performances in big matches, when he was supposed to be the player to lift the team, but he never really did.

'For me, he's always been one of those classic Inter disappointments, where they start as a very talented player and one that was regarded as a huge talent in Europe, and then completely and utterly flopped.'

* * *

After leaving Liverpool, and with it a life of drug and alcohol binges that threatened both his health and his sanity, Van der Meyde returned to Amsterdam, where his mother and sisters still lived.

'I could relax,' his shoulders sink back as he remembers the feeling. 'For one time in my life I was relaxed. Everything dropped from me.'

His thoughts soon turned to a footballing comeback, and he began training with the Ajax reserves, an arrangement brokered by his agent, in order to recover fitness and gauge what remained of the natural gifts that once made him one of Europe's most-coveted players.

After just three days back in the old routine, he received a call from Fred Rutten, the former Schalke and Feyenoord manager who was in charge of Twente when Van der Meyde was a budding winger on loan from Ajax. Having fallen out of love with the game post-Everton, and therefore out of the loop with its movements, Van der Meyde initially misunderstood the magnitude of the proposition being put to him.

'He called me and said, "Hey, Andy, how are you? I want you to come and play for me again." I said, "Yeah, nice, I'll come back to Twente again." He said, "No, no – I'm the manager of PSV now." Wow. But you have Ajax, PSV and Feyenoord, the three big rivals. OK, PSV is not so bad, but if I go to Feyenoord [the Ajax fans] would kill me.'

The hardcore section of the PSV support were not overly thrilled with the prospect of Van der Meyde turning out for their team, having caught wind of a rumour that he had a tattoo of the Ajax crest on his leg, and a group of them turned up at the training ground determined to find out whether it was true.

'We went to the changing room and these four guys asked if I had an Ajax tattoo; I said no. I dropped my trousers to show them. "Do you want me to drop my underpants also?" "No, no, no, it's cool. Now you are welcome." They didn't want me to sign because I was from Ajax.'

The truth is he did have an Ajax tattoo, as well as an Everton one, but had both covered up with new tattoos during his year out of the game, desperate to rid himself of any reminders of football.

Without having kicked a ball in anger since leaving Everton, and indulging in activities hardly conducive to physical fitness in the year prior, Van der Meyde arrived at PSV overweight and shorn of his trademark floppy locks, barely recognisable to Dutch football fans old enough to remember his Ajax pomp.

'I went there and people were like, "Who is that fat bald guy?" They couldn't see it was me. But I ran two times a day for three weeks, in the woods – I didn't touch the ball, only running, running, running. After that I was really fit. I started playing games with the second team of PSV, then I played for PSV against Ajax and I fell – the same injury again, boom, over. I could have signed for three years at PSV but my career was over. I was only 30 when I stopped playing football.'

'Then a team in Azerbaijan, Tony Adams was their gaffer, they called to say they wanted to buy me. "You can sign for three years and make good money." I said, "Listen, I'm at home with my mother, my sisters, my friends in Amsterdam – fuck the money, I'm staying here." It was the best decision for me ever.'

Barring a short stint in the Third Division with WKE in 2011, that was Van Der Meyde finished with football. He has some coaching qualifications but doesn't see a return to the training field in his future, and is instead contemplating becoming an agent, an idea seeded by Paul Stretford, Wayne Rooney's agent, who recognises Van der Meyde as an affable character retaining high-level connections within football.

Although he retired at 30, perhaps the saddest indictment of Van der Meyde's lost potential is the fact that he was already seven years beyond his peak by then, never able to recapture the form of those stellar few seasons with Ajax.

The 'chaos theory' branch of mathematics defines the 'butterfly effect' as 'the phenomenon whereby a minute, localised change in a complex system can have large effects elsewhere', i.e. the air displacement caused by a butterfly fluttering its wings in Rio de Janeiro could trigger a chain of events that alters the weather in Chicago. In Van der Meyde's case, it seems his coerced departure from Ajax in 2003 eventually led to a tsunami of mishaps, mistakes and misfortune.

The Long Goodbye

A BUDDING football career ruined by injuries is always a tragic tale. When the requisite talent, work ethic and resilience of personality are all in place to allow for the riches, glory and fame of life as an elite footballer, only to be cut down callously before ambitions are truly realised, it is a difficult hand to accept being dealt.

With a single, career-ending injury, however, comes a degree of closure, a brutal wake-up call that offers no alternative but to shut one chapter and move on to another. But what about when serious yet recoverable setbacks just keep coming, relentless and unforgiving? Progress is checked and plans put on ice, but the end goal of fulfilling a life's dream remains in sight, a taunting carrot dangled just out of reach, which ultimately proves to be a crushing façade.

Football history holds many such stories, with some, like former Bayern Munich and Manchester United midfielder Owen Hargreaves, for example, still managing to fill merciful patches of good health with major club and international honours, a two-time Champions League winner with World Cup experience. Others, like former Wolverhampton Wanderers goalkeeper Matt Murray, are unluckier still.

In fact, it's difficult to think of a player who has suffered worse persistent misfortune with injuries than Murray. Before his first-team debut for Wolves, while still a teenager, he had suffered serious knee problems and gone before a surgeon's knife on multiple occasions.

There was no respite once established in the Wolves side either, with whole seasons passing him by as he recovered from ligament tears, tendon ruptures and broken bones, in knees, feet and shoulders.

Murray was still only 36 years old when I spoke to him, an age at which it is common for goalkeepers to still be playing at a high level, yet it had been more than eight years since his official retirement, nine since his last appearance, and a decade since he was last able to complete a full 90-minute match.

'I cried in the ambulance,' Murray said, remembering the final injury that proved to be the straw that broke the camel's back. It was a patella tendon tear, sustained in just his third game with Hereford United in League One in November 2008, having been sent on loan to Edgar Street to regain match sharpness after yet more knee trouble. 'They said, "Do you want gas and air?" I said, "I'm not in pain. I'm just gutted."

'It's so scary because you rely on your body. My second baby had just been born. My landlord that I lived with for six years of my life when I was a young boy had just had a stroke. My nanna was in hospital and she died. And my knee has just gone. It was all these emotions.

'My step-dad followed the ambulance to the hospital. I remember ringing Robbie Keane from the ambulance, because he was my mate from back in the day. I said, "Keano, I think I'm done." I just couldn't get back.'

* * *

'Although he played only one Premier League game in his career, conceding five at Blackburn, I have no hesitation in saying that he would have been regarded as the outstanding English goalkeeper of his generation had he stayed free from injury. Joe Hart was inferior,' says Sky Sports journalist Adam Bate, who offers insight into Murray's immense gifts both from the perspective of someone who covers the game for a living and as a football fan who grew up supporting Wolves.

'Matt Murray is the best goalkeeper I have seen play for Wolves,' Bate continues. 'He had good reflexes and memorably saved a penalty in the Championship play-off final in 2003, but what really set him apart from other goalkeepers was his command of the area. He would routinely claim corners, free kicks and long throws with ease and it would take so much pressure off the defence.

'Though his kicking was below average, I do not recall a single error leading to a goal, while he saved the side on countless occasions. Perhaps the simplest way to encapsulate his level of performance is that he really played only two proper seasons of football in his career. The first of those saw Wolves win promotion to the Premier League for the first time, with Murray named as the club's Young Player of the Year. The second saw him drag a very average team to reach the play-offs again – this time being named in the PFA Team of the Year.'

It was clear to anyone who saw Murray on his ascent, regularly disrupted though it was, that here was a goalkeeper of serious, elite-level potential, a shoo-in for senior international recognition and destined for a long career at Premier League level, whether with Wolves or elsewhere.

Chris Turner was a youth-team coach with Wolves when Murray began to progress through the ranks, and he is especially well placed to pass comment on the goalkeeper's talent, having stood between the sticks for Sheffield Wednesday, Sunderland and Manchester United in an 18-year playing career. After 25 years in coaching, Turner now works for Port Vale as a marketing manager. I asked him for a few words on what he saw in the teenage Murray during their time together at the Molineux club.

'He could have played internationally – no danger,' Turner says assertively. 'He was just hit by knee injuries. Massive bad luck.' The former coach was also quick to highlight Murray's kind nature: 'But I love the lad. I see him now on Sky, he's a very presentable lad and a good lad to know.'

Bate, too, was keen to stress Murray's personability, confirming the 6ft 5in keeper's gentle-giant reputation, widely regarded as one of the game's good guys. 'On a personal level, Matt is one of the nicest people in football,' Bate says. 'It can feel a cheap line to say that, but Matt's reputation is out of the ordinary. There are thousands of people in Wolverhampton who are happy to share memories of his kindness and generosity. At Sky, it is a similar story. He is someone who will go that extra mile to help out, even when, on the face of it, there is nothing in it for him.'

As we sat discussing his career, the ups and downs, the lessons learned, Murray, softly spoken and empathetic, came across perfectly as the kind of person you want to root for. Thoughtful, intelligent and endearing, the plight of his injury-besieged career served only to emphasise that fate is indeed a cruel mistress, with no notion of what is fair or deserved.

* * *

It's hard to believe when looking at him now, but there were fears Murray would never reach the requisite height and physical stature to keep goal at a high level. On an almost yearly basis in his early teens, the young goalkeeper was considered for release from the Wolves youth set-up. While his reflexes were always impressive and his thirst for development unquestionable, he was simply too small. Furthermore, Murray is adopted, so there were no parents to look to for clues over whether genetics would play a part in an eventual growth spurt. When it was time to put forward players for England selection, Murray was always overlooked in favour of positional rival Steve Spittle, who stood well over 6ft as a 14-year-old.

However, such fears were allayed the year Murray turned 16, shooting up to 6ft 3in shortly after completing his GCSEs, and thus a certainty for a scholarship, later penning a five-year professional contract on his 17th birthday after already spending time around the first-team squad.

It was only a desire to play alongside his older brother that led to Murray becoming a goalkeeper in the first place, too. Growing up in Lichfield in the West Midlands, where he currently lives, just a stone's throw from the coffee shop we met up at, he always favoured an outfield role, but was only allowed to play in the same team as his brother, a year his elder, if he went in goal.

What this allowed, though, was the opportunity for the young Murray to emulate his hero, long-time Everton keeper Neville Southall. A lifelong Everton fan thanks to the influence of his step-father, a Wallasey native, the budding custodian would even try to replicate the Welsh legend's distinctive look: 'I had the kits. I used to roll my socks down and had the shin pads showing, but with my skinny legs it didn't look too good.'

Word quickly got around the local Lichfield youth leagues, and managers of rival clubs would attempt to prise the young shot-stopper away with offers of top-of-the-range kits and the latest goalkeeper gloves on the market. But Murray just wanted to play with his big brother: 'We'd sometimes lose 7-0 but I loved it, absolutely loved it.

'The guy who asked me to come wasn't a scout at Wolves, he was an apprentice at Wolves who used to coach us. He used to see me playing all the time and said, "I think you should come to Wolves." Obviously, he knew my age as well. The fact that I was a year below but was still regarded as one of the best keepers in the league was a plus. I joined Wolves at the age of nine.'

Martin Thomas, a former Welsh international goalkeeper who now works for the FA developing goalkeepers at under-21 level, began coaching at Wolves when Murray was around 14. And despite the youngster's lack of size at the time, Thomas instantly recognised his potential. 'His expression is, I was "a catcher, not a snatcher",' Murray remembers. 'So we had this goalie who was 6ft 4in, Steve Spittle. [Thomas] walked in after one training session and said, "Yeah, there's a goalie there, but not the one you think. The goalie's the small one who can fly around the goal, catch it, is good technically, and he'll grow into himself."

'He was a massive influence. I remember being embarrassed as a young kid, saying to him, "I bet you are an amazing dad." I just thought he was amazing: his manner, everything. I just got it. I understood how to play my position.'

When Chris Turner arrived at the club, Murray had already sprung up physically, looking every bit a first-team star in the making. 'Matt was just totally outstanding,' says Turner. 'Massive physical presence in the goal. He had a great character and loved to work hard in training, loved to learn about the game. And his attitude was top-drawer.

'I did hear the story that at one stage they were worried whether he was going to make it, whether he was going to be big enough. But I knew straight away, the boy has got to be coming to the club as a scholarship goalkeeper, and I saw him progress. Then after I left, he broke into the first team.'

By the age of 19, standing 6ft 5½in and weighing over 90kg, Murray filled his goal imposingly, while maintaining all of his natural speed and responsiveness. However, having grown so rapidly in such a short space of time, he feels his body 'never got the chance to settle', contributing to a slew of knee and other joint problems before even breaking into the first team.

'I was already having all these injuries and that was a problem. I've struggled with my knees. There was talk of them shutting me down at the time and strengthening up. Hindsight is a wonderful thing. I do believe that was a big problem.

'I don't feel when I was young coming through they looked at maturation. If I look at the lad I was competing against when we were 14, he was 6ft 4in, had a full beard and looked like a man. I was 5ft 8in. My voice didn't break until I was 15. I was technically OK and quite athletic, but I was a boy competing against a man.

'All the work we did, we just did the same. A lot of the lads were physically more advanced than me. Now I'm doing my coaching badges and that's something that they are very, very keen to look at on the badges. It's about maturation. So the young men, the young lads are doing the right work for how they are growing, their growing pains, their strength and development. That is vital. I look back now and think, "If I was playing now, I don't think I would have had a lot of the injuries."

'I got a bad knee injury when I was about 14 or 15, playing against Port Vale. Back then, through nobody's fault, you just used to go home, chill, and when you felt you could play again you went back, whereas you should build back all the imbalances, and do all the gym work and the strengthening.

'Then I had Osgood-Schlatter and patella tendonitis. When I was young, 16 or 17, they were just opening me up. Operation after operation. So by the time I was 18, I'd had an operation on my Osgood-Schlatter, two operations on my patella tendon, an operation on my cruciate. I'd been opened up so many times.'

With his size no longer an issue, Murray began to gain recognition as one of the country's hottest goalkeeping prospects at around the age of 16. He was selected for the England under-16s, where he worked with former Three Lions keeper

Peter Bonetti, and started training with the Wolves first team, appearing on the bench occasionally.

A loan spell with Kingstonian in October 2000, when he was 19, was designed to offer a taste of regular senior football, preparing the young goalkeeper for what, by that stage, looked to be his destiny – the No.1 spot at Molineux. However, just 20 minutes into his first outing for the Kingston-upon-Thames lower-league outfit, he suffered a cruciate knee injury. More months of rehabilitation ensued.

Wolves boss Mark McGee had been a big admirer of Murray's, offering the teenager the chance to learn at the feet of experienced first-teamer Mike Stowell in training sessions and had clearly earmarked him for big things. But with results on the slide, McGee was sacked in November 1998, replaced by assistant Colin Lee, who took the mantle of overseeing Murray's careful progress, arranging loans to clubs lower down the football pyramid, such as the fateful temporary spell with Kingstonian. But Lee's eventual replacement, Dave Jones, who took charge in January of 2001, opted for a less sympathetic approach, demanding more from a young player he clearly felt had begun to enjoy his burgeoning reputation a little too much.

'Dave Jones came in and I'd been injured, struggled out on loan with injuries, and he really gave me a rocket,' Murray recalls. 'I've never been pasted like that around an office in my life. He proper gave it to me.

'He was just saying I was a goalkeeper with potential, living the life of chilling with Robbie Keane and Joleon Lescott, but I hadn't actually done anything myself. No one knew my name. He said, "Is anyone going to know your name or are you just going to be hanging on with them? You're going out with them, but they've played; you've got a game on Tuesday in the reserves. Next time you are in front of me I'll be paying you up. I don't care if you've got two years on your contract." He hammered me. It was tough love.'

The frank, one-way discussion in Jones's office might have been uncomfortable, but it served to light a fire under Murray. In the months that followed, with the aid of coaches Terry Connor and Bobby Mimms, he worked tirelessly to regain his fitness and prove to his manager that his reputation as the country's brightest young goalkeeper was merited.

'I got in and around the first team. [Jones] was bringing in keeper after keeper on trial, but I was doing well in the reserves. He didn't let me go away in the summer after they had said I was going to go away to Sweden on loan.

'That pre-season I worked really hard. I didn't concede a goal in pre-season. Then Oakesy [first-choice goalkeeper Michael Oakes] got injured and he gave me my chance. I played 48 games that year, got promoted and played for the England under-21s. That's when people really started saying, "This keeper can play."'

Murray's form that season was one of the driving factors behind Wolves' run to the final of the Division One play-offs at Cardiff's Millennium Stadium. He had kept clean sheets in 19 of the 47 games he'd started for the West Midlanders following Oakes's injury, and he'd claim a 20th as Jones's side overcame a strong Sheffield United outfit to earn promotion to the Premier League.

Wolves were 3-0 winners in Cardiff, but the game was not as one-sided as the scoreline would suggest. The men in old gold raced to a 3-0 half-time lead and rode their luck as the Blades threw everything into their comeback efforts.

In the first half, with the score at 2-0, Murray produced the first of what would go on to be a string of world-class saves, and it was brought about by one of his own players when he reacted stunningly to claw away captain Paul Ince's goal-bound header.

He even played a part in two of the goals. The first, a 20-yard rocket by Irish international Mark Kennedy, came from a long goal kick that Nathan Blake flicked on. And the third, finished off from close range by striker Kenny Miller, was again the result of defensive chaos caused by a long Murray clearance.

Into the second period, Wolves were under siege. When defender Paul Butler was adjudged to have handled in the area, Murray bailed his side out by saving Michael Brown's spot kick. Interestingly, the goalkeeper's penalty save seemed to stem as much from winning a psychological battle with the United midfielder as it did from any feat of reflex reaction.

The Wolves No.13 – Oakes still owned the No.1 jersey having started the season as first-choice keeper – stood a step to the right of the centre of his goal, showing Brown a wider target to the goalkeeper's left, inviting him to shoot that way. The penalty taker obliged, falling into Murray's trap.

After Murray acrobatically tipped a powerfully struck Michael Tonge free kick on to the post, ITV commentator Peter Drury exclaimed, 'Here is a Premiership goalkeeper in the making.' Just weeks after his 22nd birthday, Murray was named man of the match in the most intense, high-profile and high-pressure game of his career.

Murray says, 'It was a whirlwind season. Near enough everything went right for me: I'm playing with my mates – Lee Naylor, Joleon Lescott, Adam Proudlock; I'm in the England under-21s, playing with Wolves, winning and keeping clean sheets.

'Dave Jones gave me a new deal, a good new deal – I suddenly went on to decent money. Life was good. I remember walking down the steps of the Millennium Stadium and thinking, all the media want to speak to me: "How does it feel to be a Premier League goalie?" It's easy.'

It was an outstanding performance – and, indeed, season – for Murray, the kind that should have served as a springboard for a thriving top-flight and international career, yet it would ultimately prove to be his zenith.

'Then I got injured.'

* * *

Hernia and foot problems meant Murray played just one Premier League game in the 2003/04 season, a 5-1 thumping at the hands of Blackburn Rovers at Ewood Park. As Arsène Wenger's Arsenal became the 'Invincibles', remaining unbeaten through all 38 games, Wolves limped out of the division, finishing rock bottom, although level on points with relegation companions Leeds United and Leicester City, and only six adrift of Everton in 18th place. Had they been able to rely on the gifts of their best goalkeeper, perhaps things might have worked out differently. Instead, persistent injuries allowed Murray to make only seven senior outings for Wolves in the three seasons that followed their 2003 play-off triumph.

Murray feels that some of the issues he began to suffer with at this juncture were preventable, or at least could have been dealt with a lot better. Major injuries often start when smaller problems compound or aren't managed correctly; the former Wolves keeper certainly believes this is what he experienced for a period.

'I had the hernia problem. I just got sent away and when I came back I was struggling with it. I wanted to work on it but the physio told me just to rest up.

'Unfortunately, Kempy [Wolves physio Steve Kemp] wasn't there then, it was another physio, who I loved to bits but he should have had me in doing core work. And I loved practising my crosses, but I overdid in and got a stress fracture in my foot.

'I felt a pain in my foot and I went to see a specialist. He sort of rubbished it. I played a game against Manchester United in the reserves and I got the worst pain ever and my foot opened right up. That cost me about 18 months to two years of my career, nearly cost me my career.

'I stress-fractured my navicular through jumping, jumping, jumping. I had to have it pinned. I had bone from my hip put in my foot. It cracked again, had to put more bone in there again. If that operation hadn't have worked, that would have been me done at 23 – they'd have had to fuse my whole foot together. All because that specialist said, "Stand up and down on your toes ... Nah, there's nothing wrong with you." Barry, the physio, had taken me there – he hadn't done anything wrong. But that specialist, he cost me a lot of my career. I've still got foot problems now because of it.'

Named on the bench for a handful of Premier League fixtures, including a trip to Old Trafford to face Manchester United, Murray was only listed as a substitute out of obligation and a lack of other options, and was never truly available to play. In the fleeting, merciful moments when his body approached a workable level of fitness, the niggles persisted – the hernia problem, operated on in the off-season, was still bothering him when he started against Blackburn. That then led to muscular problems in his back, going into spasm while on international duty in Croatia with the under-21s. By this stage, injuries were being stacked on top of injuries.

'I came back after that foot operation, played a couple of games – Millwall in the FA Cup, clean sheet. We beat West Ham 4-2 and I felt it go in the warm-up. I thought, "I can't pull out now." So I played the game, but I was in bits. Got back in and they looked at my foot. They sent me for a scan. I was there with my step-dad and it had opened right back up. I had to get more surgery.'

* * *

The dark clouds parted for a sustained period during the 2007/08 season, with an injury-free Murray able to play 47 times. Once again, his consistent run of games highlighted what a remarkable goalkeeper the 26-year-old was, despite having largely missed out on crucial years of his development in his early 20s. With Murray in the side, Wolves reached the play-offs and he was named in the PFA Championship Team of the season. He might have been able to guide his team to the top flight once again were it not for a serious shoulder injury, suffered the day before Wolves were set to face local rivals West Bromwich Albion in the semi-finals.

Murray recalls, 'I broke my shoulder the day before [in training]. They said, "Just one more cross." I remember taking it and the young lad bottled it because I'd come flying through. I went over his back, landed down and cracked my shoulder. It was a cross I'd taken 100 times.

'I was in all summer to work through that, came back and was again doing extra work. But I trod on the back of my goal and popped my cruciate. Again. Same knee.' His miserable misfortune was unrelenting.

Ben Thornley, the one-time Manchester United prodigy, whose own injury torment flattened his career trajectory, spoke of the difficulty of showing up to the training ground every morning only to skulk into the gym to keep plugging away on the path to recovery. Watching your peers pass by on their way to doing what they love, what you love and what you wish you could be doing, takes a toll mentally. Envy and self-pity can easily, and understandably, begin to fester. This is a plight Murray became all too familiar with throughout his career.

'I know exactly how that feels,' he says. 'Robbie Keane was the year above me – and I would never wish him not to have had [the career he's had] – but you look at him and think, "What a player." Joleon Lescott, he worked really hard to overcome his injuries and look at his career. Lee Naylor never had an operation. Keith Andrews went on to play at a high level. All the lads that I played with, or lads in the England under-16s – Gareth Barry, Joe Cole – they are all going on and doing things, getting in the under-21s, all doing their thing.

'At the Wolves training ground, you used to have to go straight out to train or go right to the gym, which overlooked the training ground. And some lads used to moan: "Ah, I don't want to train today," and you're thinking, "I'd give anything to just go out there and train." Stuff you took for granted, you really wished you had. I would say turning right was tough.

'Look, you never wished your mates not to have it, but you're envious because you're thinking about what might have been.'

* * *

Murray never played for the Wolves first team again after injuring his shoulder on the eve of the 2006/07 Championship play-offs semi-final against West Brom. Having recovered from the broken shoulder and rehabilitated after two operations to repair a subsequent torn ACL, he joined Hereford on loan in the third tier in November 2008. It was a bid to regain match sharpness and prepare to battle fellow academy graduate Wayne Hennessey for the No.1 spot at Wolves.

'When I did my cruciate I worked really hard to get back. I went out on loan to Hereford the year [Wolves] went up under Mick [McCarthy]. I was going to play a few games. The first game was one of the best games I've ever played in my life. Loved it. Hereford were like, "Oh, this is amazing." This was League One. I only trained with them one day a week. My ex-wife was pregnant. I was like, "Yeah, I'm back at it now. I've got a year on my contract, I'm on it. I'm going to get back in the team here. I'm going to push Hennessey; I'm going to push [Carl] Ikeme."

'I played the first two games [at Hereford]: brilliant. The third game: struck a back-pass and had a full rupture of my patella tendon. I'd had no problems with that knee since I was 18. And when I was on the stretcher then, I knew it. I couldn't believe it. That was horrible. Scary.'

At 27, after a decade of constant, battering setbacks, Murray was ready to throw in the towel. 'I knew I was gone then. I knew, when I did that, because of the cruciate, foot and then that. I thought, "This is going to take a hell of a lot …"

'My kneecap was up here somewhere. They have to straighten your leg,' Murray winces in recollection of the pain. 'I'm not going to lie, I cried in the ambulance.'

Yet, after regrouping and processing his latest road block, Murray resolved to fight back to fitness once again. Almost exactly one year after being stretchered off at Edgar Street, he was lacing up his boots and donning the gloves for a final push at resurrecting a career that had by now long appeared lost. Just 23 minutes into his comeback in a reserve fixture, though, feeling as though his knee was threatening to malfunction yet again, Murray was substituted. That would be his last ever appearance in a Wolves shirt. The following August, aged 29 and with just 100 senior games for Wolves to his name, he announced his retirement.

'They tried twice with the knee that finished me,' he remembers of learning his final attempts at recovery had been futile. 'And on the day they told me, I knew it was coming. But when you actually hear it, it's such a mixture of emotions. You feel relief that you don't have to go through this any more. I haven't got to explain this to anyone any more. I haven't got to go through operations, all this pain and heartache. But, at the same time, it's your dream over. It's what I've always loved, so now what am I going to do?

'They say your dream isn't your children's dream. If I had no children, maybe I would have gone on a little bit more, risked letting my insurance money go and risked having knee replacements. But the specialist said to me, "Look, you've done everything you can, you've had a great career. I don't think you can go on training at the top level." And he was a great specialist.

He made me feel like my knee was the only knee he was looking at. He said to me, "Do you want to be able to walk with your little kids? I have to say to you, as a duty of care, you won't play to that level, in my honest opinion, and you'll be in a really bad way if you try to, so I would call it a day. If it was my son and my knee, I'd call it a day." He took the decision away from me.

'It was tough, though.'

Murray has kept himself busy post-retirement, juggling coaching four days a week with Barnsley and working with the Nike Academy alongside his TV work for Sky and radio commentary. Focused and driven, he confesses an ambition of someday managing Wolves. But despite appearing extremely well adjusted and able to lucidly contextualise the struggles of his playing career, he admits it hasn't always been easy. Even someone as thoughtful and reasonable as Murray is forced to grapple demons and overcome self-doubt when dealing with what was ultimately a career marked out by potential left largely unfulfilled, and through no wrongdoing of his own.

'When it is not your fault, you get angry – that is the emotion. And life isn't fair. You have to sit down with your psychologist and they tell you life isn't fair. Why has [Wolves goalkeeper] Carl Ikeme got leukaemia? That's not fair. Why did some other kid break his leg?

'You've got to look at what your blessings are: "I've got healthy children; I've got this and that." If you don't become a footballer again, can you cope with it? If someone takes all your money, can you deal with it? And you actually go, "Do you know what, I can." But at the time you feel like you can't, and you start projecting. You start worrying about things that might never happen – you start catastrophizing.

'The PFA is fantastic: you can ring them and they will help you. The Wolves club doctors: unbelievable. There were people at Wolves – counsellors, psychologists – who were there.

'Wolves were fantastic to me. Some clubs might not have been, but I can only talk about my experience. They gave me an ambassadorial role. They helped me fill my time. And they honoured my contract – they didn't have to; they could have paid me for six months but they paid me for ten out of the 11.

[CEO] Jez Moxey and the Wolves fans were fantastic. The Wolves players were fantastic. My family were unbelievable. So there was a lot of help in place, but you have to go and be honest and speak to people. But it was still hard times. There were some really, really hard times. It's tough.'

The psychological struggles Murray speaks of are in keeping with this book's core theme: what's left when the dream is taken away? It's a question of identity. What is a footballer when no longer a footballer? It's a riddle with no answer. Or, more accurately, a question that each individual in such circumstances must come to answer in their own, unique way, in their own time.

'I get asked to play in charity games but I can't even do it – my body hurts that much. It was like when I broke my shoulder. The West Brom fans were giving me banter, which is fair enough. But when they are singing, "Murray, how's your arm?" that is the bit that people don't understand: it's your dream. It is like saying to a DJ, "You can't play music any more." We love football. You'd play football anyway [regardless of being paid]. So when you can't do it ...

'You work all week and your adrenaline at the end of that week is the match – 90 minutes, boom. The risk, the excitement: a minute away from being a failure, conceding your worst goal or getting an injury, but at the same time you are a minute away from being a hero.

'And when you are winning and you're doing all that stuff, it's the best feeling; it's like a drug. But then suddenly you have got to replace that drug with something else. So you bang weights all week, but you can't play. Then what am I going to do? Am I going to gamble? Am I going to drink? What am I going to do? That's why footballers end up in so much trouble. You've got nothing to replace that feeling with.'

Murray seems to have found his peace through constant forward motion, compartmentalising his previous life and homing in on new goals, finding new crafts to master. He had already begun preparing for a career in the media and coaching as his playing days were winding down, commentating for local radio and leading training sessions for young students at a college in nearby Telford. That doesn't mean he never pauses to look back, though.

'You're not Matt the footballer any more. Suddenly it's a very daunting world, because all I had ever written, from 16 years of age, was: "Best wishes, Matt Murray." Now you're retired, you're done, see you later. I was going to play until I was 35, 36, not retire when I was 29. It is daunting. And there are very few players who earn enough to never work again. And even if you do, what then? Even if you get to 35, that is a lot of life left to live. It's very daunting.'

Worn-Out Tools

'**I** KNEW from 19 that this wasn't going to last. I was already preparing myself for it mentally.'

There's a matter-of-factness to Lionel Morgan, a comfortable self-honesty that is instantly apparent. Now in his mid-30s, he was one of the most gifted English footballers of his generation as a teen. He is under no illusion about the ability he possessed as a fast, tricky winger breaking through at Wimbledon, and anyone who witnessed him in full flight will attest to his prodigal gifts. It is that same assured ability to self-analyse, however, that brought Morgan to the realisation, with shattering clarity, that his body was not going to allow him a sustained career in the game.

'I'd been injured for so long, anyway – coming back, getting injured again. I knew it was going to happen,' he explains.

Injuries are a fact of life for a footballer. Some are lucky enough to avoid the need for surgical intervention throughout an entire career, others battle niggles, strains and pulls from week to week, season to season. And an unlucky few find themselves on first-name terms with knee specialists, star-servicing surgeons or expert physicians. Morgan's, though, is a rarer case still, having been forced into retirement aged just 21.

Having retired so early, with little more than 30 senior appearances under his belt – none of which came in the top flight – beyond the most avid Wimbledon fans who remained regular attendees at Selhurst Park through the club's dark final years before morphing into the Milton Keynes Dons in 2004, few will be aware of just how promising a prospect Morgan was.

Playing outside the Premier League in an era before YouTube, and when the Championship did not receive blanket coverage, footage of the young winger in action is preciously scarce. A rare opportunity to showcase his gifts to a wider audience came in November 2001. It was an England under-19s outing shown live on Sky Sports. The Young Lions took on Georgia as part of their qualification campaign for the European Under-19 Championship, and Morgan was the star of the show. His electrifying performance on the right wing in England's 4-1 rout of their visitors at York City's Bootham Crescent ground saw the young Wimbledon star named man of the match. Sky's co-commentator for the game, Nigel Spackman, a former Liverpool midfielder, likened Morgan to his ex-Anfield colleague John Barnes.

It was high praise, which served to add a wider hype to a young player whom most within the game knew to possess elite potential, but Morgan insists he wasn't even at his best against Georgia. 'It was just another game,' he recalls during our meeting near Islington Town Hall in north London, a few miles from where he grew up in Tottenham. 'It wasn't anywhere near my best game for England, it was just one that was televised.'

Indeed, it was an England appearance that almost never came to be. Still making his way back to fitness from yet another injury, Morgan had only recently returned to training, and hadn't played meaningfully for three months. As such, the call-up from England under-19s boss Les Reed was something of a surprise. In the days before he was due to meet up with his international team-mates, he had been suffering from flu.

'I was blowing by half-time, I was so tired,' he remembers, not that it stopped him outshining a fine crop of England hopefuls which included the likes of Glen Johnson, Jermaine Jenas and Dean Ashton.

Journalist Andy Brassell may be more known for his in-depth coverage of European football for *The Guardian* and TalkSport, but, around the turn of the millennium, he was a long-suffering Wimbledon fan and dedicated match-goer.

'People were talking about him for a while before he came through,' Brassell says, recalling the excited whispers that circulated around Selhurst Park, heralding Morgan's first-team breakthrough. 'There was a lot of excitement around him.

'I think it was his full debut, against Rotherham at Selhurst Park in the Championship, which was the first time we got to see a full game of his, and he was really good. Someone who's a left-footer of quality always catches the eye a little bit more. He had pace and balance. I thought he was very mature as well. People were expecting a lot of him.'

At the time, Wimbledon were a club in crisis. Having fallen out of the Premier League, financial struggles were taking their toll. There was a growing discontent among the fans, as rumblings of a potential move to Milton Keynes, some 60 miles away, caused a rift between the club and many of its supporters. While for some the emergence of a player of Morgan's quality, a youngster with genuine international pedigree, would have served as a timely reminder of the hope, entertainment and escapism football can offer, the winger's development will have been confined to an afterthought for many, as graver issues took precedence.

'If you asked a lot of Wimbledon fans what happened to him,' Brassell suggests, 'some would say, "Oh yeah, he had to retire early," but a lot would say, "I have no idea what happened to him," because events at the club overtook looking at his progress. It was a time when the football was a sideshow.'

The structural mess at Wimbledon was epitomised by the loan of Danish under-21 international David Neilsen to Norwich City during the 2001/02 season. In their haste to reduce the wage bill by shipping out the striker, Wimbledon had neglected to include a clause in the loan agreement that precluded him from playing against them. Inevitably, with the next fixture being against Norwich in the Championship, Neilsen scored against his parent club in a 2-1 victory for the Canaries at Carrow Road.

Former Arsenal midfielder Stewart Robson was Morgan's youth-team coach at Wimbledon, before later progressing to take charge of the reserves and taking a handful of his best youngsters, most notably Morgan, along with him. Speaking to a disconnect between the first-team level, overseen by manager Joe Kinnear, and the young players being produced by the club's prolific academy, Robson highlights Wimbledon's calamitous leadership by outlining how the club's most gifted starlets weren't valued at all by the hierarchy.

'What worried me about the whole thing was, when I went there, Jobi McAnuff [a talented midfielder who would go on to play more than 100 times for the club] wasn't even given a contract. It was, "Well, he goes to college so he can come along every so often and play with us, but we don't think he's going to be good enough." And Lionel Morgan wasn't even mentioned, so I don't know what they were looking for – they were two exceptional players.'

Robson certainly recognised the abilities of the players under his tutelage, though, and Morgan speaks glowingly of the man he describes as 'an intense character' and 'one of the best coaches that I've seen'. Asked whether he believes Morgan would have become a full England international were it not for his cruel injuries, Robson is unequivocal: 'Yes, I do. He's as talented a player as I've worked with. He could do things that other players couldn't do. He had everything you would want from an attacking player: he could kick with both feet – although he was predominantly left-footed – he was quick, powerful, great skill, good vision.

'I remember we played against Aston Villa away and we went 2-0 down very early,' Robson continues, detailing one of Morgan's finer displays at youth level. 'We were on a very good run and the players knew what I was asking of them, and I wasn't very pleased that we were 2-0 down. But we won the game 5-2, and [Morgan] scored two magnificent goals and set up a couple of others.

'Right off the back of that I think Aston Villa contacted his agent, or contacted somebody he knew, and tried to get him to go there. People were beginning to see what a talent he was. The talk wasn't about Neil Jenkins any more, who people had been talking about beforehand, it was now about Lionel Morgan.'

The word was out.

* * *

Although he grew up virtually in the shadow of White Hart Lane, with stray shots from games with his school team often striking the outside of the stadium, and he was born into a family of Tottenham Hotspur supporters, Morgan chose to support Arsenal. 'Even though I was born and raised in Tottenham, the club didn't reflect the community; I never felt a proper connection,' he explains, instead adopting Gunners goalscorer Ian Wright as his childhood football idol.

His first football mentor was Clasford Stirling, founder of a youth football club on Broadwater Farm, a London housing estate that became synonymous with urban decay following rising crime rates and riots in the 1980s. Stirling started his Broadwater United coaching academy in the mid-80s in an effort to bring purpose and structure to the lives of vulnerable young people in the area through football, kids for whom crime and violence were all-too-familiar facts – and in some cases ways – of life.

Stirling was awarded an MBE in 2007 for his work, a kind of undercover social worker and surrogate disciplinarian. And it would not be a stretch to suggest his academy in some way contributed to Broadwater now owning the lowest crime rate in the London borough of Haringey, seeing a 20 per cent reduction in crime between 2013 and 2016.

Stirling's son Jude has enjoyed a 16-year career as a professional footballer, while Jobi McAnuff is another Broadwater alum. Morgan points to falling under Stirling's auspices as the time his football became more structured. 'That's when it became a bit more serious,' he says, 'because Clasford was a disciplinarian. It doesn't matter what age you are, if you come through his door, you are going to do things properly.

'It's about competing, it's about winning. It wasn't about just taking part. And that was from the age of eight. It was serious business, and that's fine. I know nowadays people try to get away from that – it's just about taking part and all that kind of stuff. And I think that's fine as well; there should be a place for that. But I also think there should be a space for some serious football development and creating the right sort of mentalities. That's what happened at Broadwater Farm, and that's what made me fall in love with football – just wanting to win and not being ashamed of playing to win.'

Morgan went on to star for a team born out of a merger between the Broadwater side he was playing for and another club in Hertfordshire, again run by Stirling, called Valley Youth. And it was while playing for Valley Youth, typically impressive with his close control and dribbling ability, that he caught the eye of Wimbledon scouts.

'Jobi and Jude were a year above and were already there, so it was just a natural thing for me to go in. By eight or nine I was at Wimbledon.'

They didn't wear red with white sleeves, nor did they have a prolific striker in a No.8 shirt, so the Dons didn't resonate with the eight-year-old Morgan, whose football knowledge, understandably given his age, didn't extend far beyond Wright and Arsenal. Wimbledon did, however, offer a glimpse into what could be a bright future for the young winger. Picked up by a Premier League club, training once a week at a satellite centre in north London, his potential was evident and family and friends couldn't help but wonder where his talent could take him.

Such giddiness is often what sets young players at academies up for a bitter fall. The reality is less than half of one per cent of kids within a club's academy at under-9s level eventually make it into the first team, but donning the kit and representing a Premier League club can be intoxicating. Not so for Morgan, who, it appears, has always possessed the calm level-headedness he exudes today, sat back in his chair, even-toned and considered beneath the screech of coffee machines.

'I got to the age of 14 and I was at a crossroads in my mind. You speak to a load of kids now and from the age of eight they'll tell you they want to be a footballer. I wasn't thinking like that at all. Until I got to the age of 15, I never thought I was going to be a professional footballer. It was just something I liked doing and I was good at.'

* * *

Wimbledon were relegated from the Premier League at the end of the 1999/2000 season, ending a 14-year run in the top tier of English football. It's not uncommon for relegated sides to bounce straight back up into the Premier League after one campaign in the Championship. In fact, since the play-offs were introduced in 1987, around a quarter of teams demoted from the top flight have done just that. But the Dons never seemed likely to add to that statistic. And fans, it appeared, held little hope, evidenced by the plummeting attendances of their final Premier League term – just 8,248 spectators watched Wimbledon's 2-0 defeat of Sheffield Wednesday in April 2000, the lowest-attended match in the division that season. Their relegation, confirmed by a final-game loss to Southampton at the Dell, came 12 years to the day from the club's greatest moment, the 1988 FA Cup Final victory over Liverpool.

Dropping down to the First Division (the second tier hadn't yet been re-banded as the Championship) meant several stars were offloaded to balance the books, with striker John Hartson – a £7.5m record signing just 18 months earlier – sold to Coventry City mid-season, and Carl Cort joining Newcastle United. Such departures and an almost non-existent transfer budget necessitated first-team chances being given to young players, who otherwise would likely have remained in the reserves had Wimbledon still been in the Premier League. Morgan was the most notable of these budding hopefuls.

'I remember going back to pre-season training making a conscious effort in my mind that I'm going to get in this team. It meant dislodging some good players, but I didn't care. I got that from Stewart Robson: "You're the best player; get in that team."'

A drab 0-0 draw with Watford at Selhurst Park on 26 August, the third game of the season, again attended by few more than 8,000, was wholly unremarkable but for the fact it offered Wimbledon fans a first glimpse of a scrawny yet obviously gifted 17-year-old winger. In a forgettable match, Morgan provided inspiration, confidently taking on his marker and creating the game's best chance, crossing for Hartson – who would have already left the club for Rangers were it not for fitness concerns scuppering the summer switch – to head straight at goalkeeper Espen Baardsen.

'When Terry [Burton, the manager] told me on the Friday that I would be starting, there was that little bit of excitement, nerves,' Morgan recalls. 'It was good, playing against Watford.

The speed of everything was like nothing I'd experienced before. Championship football at that time was helter-skelter. Just being able to cope with it physically, that is the main thing.'

He went on to make a further five first-team appearances that season, splitting his time between the seniors, reserves and under-19s. He became more frequently involved in the first team the following season, with Wimbledon still in the second flight following an eighth-place finish in 2000/01. Despite the club's impending turmoil, Morgan gives great credit to the team spirit at Wimbledon at the time in aiding his transition into the first-team squad, with experienced heads like Neil Ardley, Michael Thomas, Gareth Ainsworth, Kenny Cunningham and Marcus Gayle all on hand to dispense wisdom.

'Kevin Cooper, the left-winger, used to say to me, "Kid, my hamstring is going to get a bit tight in the 80th minute. I'll pull up so we can get you on." And he would. We had so much help at Wimbledon from the senior pros.'

A first senior goal came in March 2002, a stunning long-range free kick labelled 'Beckham-esque' by assistant manager Stuart Murdoch, the only goal of a home win over Rotherham United. Morgan says, 'Neil Ardley was our free-kick taker, but he said, "This one is a bit too far out for me." I think it was about 30 yards from goal; 25 yards and it would have been him who would take it. It was what I practised at the training ground: bam, and it went in.'

By this point, though, injuries were already plaguing the teenage wide man, causing him to miss months at a time, recuperating from ankle complaints and recurring knee issues.

'The first injury I had of any note was when I fractured my ankle playing in a game I shouldn't have been playing in. I was playing in the reserves and under-19s, but then there was this under-17s game, and there was no other game on in the week so they said, "Just go and play in that game." So I did. I was out three months.

'I got my first knee injury at 17, which was a cartilage injury. I'd already made my debut under Terry Burton at 17 in the Championship.' Persistent cartilage problems brought Morgan under the knife on several occasions, each time trimming away at the troublesome meniscus. 'I probably had that six or seven times, so it was just bone on bone, rubbing away. You've got a limited timescale then.'

The most serious of Morgan's knee injuries occurred in April 2002, just days after his free-kick goal against Rotherham. He suffered a torn anterior cruciate ligament (ACL) in a 2-0 victory over Crewe Alexandra at Selhurst Park. The injury required two operations and left him sidelined for seven months.

'I went abroad to get that [operation] done, in Austria, because one of the players who had that done, Damien Francis, he went to Austria. But there were some complications with Damien. Our [regular club] surgeon, Dr Fairbank, he wasn't happy: "Why are you sending him to Austria when I've been doing your operations for years?" I ended up having to go back to him because I ended up with an infection. I didn't know this at the time but Damien had had the exact same problem, so there must have been an issue [with the surgery in Austria].

'The guy was a bit of a rogue. I remember him being a bit eccentric. It was a beautiful hospital, so clean it was like a laboratory. I just remember him coming in, everyone was dressed in white, like you'd expect, and he was wearing a checked shirt like he'd just come off the mountains. He said, "Right, I'm just going to relieve the pressure in your knee." And he just stuck a needle in it, bam! There was blood spilling out all over this beautiful white place. It was weird.

'I came back from that and I'd only been home for a day, but I knew something wasn't right; it just didn't feel right. The pain wasn't surgery pain, it was like a burning sensation. I ended up in hospital over here for two weeks. Part of my knee, where the screw was, there was a hole where the muscle couldn't regenerate. It wasn't just a case of putting a skin graft over it, they had to use a special machine that helps to regenerate muscle tissue.

'I didn't know at the time how serious it was, because I think people at the club and the physios don't want to put these things in your mind, so it was only later that I realised this could have been really dangerous – I could have lost my leg.'

Setback was followed by setback. Young footballers need continuity to progress, regular playing time and the chance to develop a deeper understanding of the game through trial and error. Morgan's body was denying him that opportunity. When the ACL healed, the cartilage problems returned, requiring two further operations, in late 2002 and then again in April 2003.

While often injuries are a matter of pure bad luck, being in the wrong place at the wrong time to sustain an impact injury, or twisting sharply or accelerating too quickly, tearing muscles and straining ligaments, Morgan feels he did his recovery prospects no favours by rushing to get back to fitness. 'If you're not a professional sportsperson, you probably take a year off to recover from this kind of injury, but as an athlete it's six to nine months. This is where sometimes I think footballers need saving from themselves, because they want to go out and play.

'You're at the training ground every day, showing up at eight o'clock, leaving in the evening. Everyone else is turning up, training, having a laugh and playing matches. But every day you're in and working hard; literally ticking off the days. Our physio, Paul Hunter, was one of the best. Every day we'd be ticking off little milestones. But I probably came back a little too early, given the manager at the time wanted me back in the team.

'I'm not blaming anyone for anything – it's football; they want players back as quick as they can, and you want to be back as quick as you can. But sometimes you might break down.'

* * *

Although injuries were interrupting his development, Morgan was still catching the eye. Whether it was for the England youth teams or with Wimbledon in the First Division, whenever he took to the field, it was clear to see that here was a player of immense potential.

Wimbledon looked increasingly unlikely to earn a Premier League return, finishing eighth, ninth and tenth in their first three seasons in the second tier, but Morgan belonged in the top flight. His ascension seemed to be merely a matter of time.

Tottenham were long-time admirers of the winger who had honed his skills a stone's throw from their White Hart Lane ground. Their interest was firm enough to result in a bid for the player in February 2002, a few weeks prior to his first senior goal and subsequent ACL injury. The Spurs interest came hot on the heels of Jermaine Jenas, a colleague of Morgan's in the England set-up and a comparable contemporary in terms of talent level, joining Newcastle United from Nottingham Forest, where he had been captain, for £5m. Using the Jenas deal as a benchmark, David Pleat, Tottenham's director of football, sounded out Morgan's old coach, Stuart Robson, who had since left Wimbledon, to get the low-down on his target. '[Pleat] phoned me up and said he was thinking about offering £7m to Wimbledon for him,' Robson recalls. 'He said, "You know him, you've worked with him, what do you think?" I told him all the good things but I said, "You just have to be slightly aware that he's had one or two knee injuries, so I'd do your homework there. Then if you are going to buy him, I'd be prepared to pay more but on a playing percentage, just to cover yourselves." In David Pleat's words, "Newcastle have just paid £5m for Jermaine Jenas and I think Lionel Morgan's a better player." And I said, "So do I."'

Tottenham's structured offer was rebuffed by Wimbledon, who clearly thought Morgan's value would only rise with the greater exposure he was due to receive. However, injuries were not the only barrier to progression Morgan was facing at the time. As he remembers it, a delicate political game was being played out, born out of the club's dire financial circumstances.

'Some people said it was my contract – if I played a certain amount of games my money would have gone up,' he says. 'These were some of the little pitfalls that were getting in the way. There were questions about, if I were to play those games and earn that kind of money would my attitude change? All these little things that were just getting in the way of someone playing football. It was stupid.

'The way I looked at it, even at 17 at the time, Forest were smart: play this kid [Jenas], make him captain and his value goes up. It wasn't quite the same [at Wimbledon]. I was quite annoyed. I remember going into the office and having a massive argument after, because the chairman had accepted the bid [from Tottenham], it was done. But then at the last second it wasn't happening. I was really angry.'

Spurs would return for Morgan, though, with a bid finally accepted as Wimbledon slipped into administration in June 2003 following Morgan's successful recovery from double knee surgery. A neat career circle was being drawn, a switch to the club he grew up alongside, the team supported by his family yet he'd 'never felt a proper connection' with, were set to make him part of their future. But his body, once again, threw a spanner in the works. Morgan failed his Spurs medical, scrapping the deal. He left with the promise that they would come back for him again if he could prove his fitness over a sustained period. Just three games into the 2003/04 season he injured his knee in training, necessitating two more operations. The Premier League would remain a dream unfulfilled.

'I remember going for a medical at Spurs when finally a bid had been accepted, and I failed the medical. And I heard the whispers: "He's never going to pass a medical." That was when I knew that was it, I wasn't going to play football really. I was 20 at the time. I knew time was ticking away for me.'

* * *

Wimbledon were relegated at the end of the 2003/04 campaign, having finished bottom of the First Division with just eight wins to their name all season. The club controversially left Crystal Palace's Selhurst Park, where they had been ground-sharing with the Eagles for 12 years, and began playing their home games at the National Hockey Stadium in Milton Keynes in September of 2003.

With attendances averaging just 4,750, swamped in off-field controversy and on-field gloom, the club was at its lowest ebb. Throughout the season, administrators sold off any player who could fetch a cash return, meaning Morgan had to watch on as fellow academy graduates progressed upwards: Nigel Reo-Coker and Jobi McAnuff joined West Ham United in the Premier League, and Mikele Leigertwood signed for soon-to-be-promoted Crystal Palace.

Morgan remained, but he played just three more senior games for Wimbledon, his season ended by injury in October. As the club was brought out of administration at the end of the campaign and re-branded as the Milton Keynes Dons, his contract expired. Without a renewal offer, he underwent trials at a handful of clubs, with several showing interest if he could prove his fitness. He never could. Morgan retired at the age of 21.

'I went to Crystal Palace first,' Morgan remembers, pausing for a sip of coffee and straightening himself in his chair. 'Iain Dowie was in charge and Jon Goodman was fitness coach. They said, "Look, if you get fit there's a contract here for you." I was there with his fitness coaches for about six months, trying to get fit. Physically, I was as fit as I ever had been, but the knee just wasn't up to it, although it had got better.

'Then I left Palace to go to Watford, because Terry Burton was there under Ray Lewington. I knew Ray because both his sons, Craig and Dean, I had played with at Wimbledon. I'd felt better so I thought, "I'm going to go there and give it a go." But it just never happened for me. My knees ... And that was it.

'I wasn't going to keep trying. That's the part where you can really do some damage to yourself, when you keep chasing something that's not going to happen.'

Perhaps the constant struggles with injuries actually helped soften the eventual blow of having to call time on a career that had promised so much. Succumbing to such a drawn-out inevitability must have felt like breathing out, a release of tension, the book finally closed on a negative chapter.

'That's life. I've always had that realism. That's what it is: life goes on. I saw it as a chance to get out. At that point, I wasn't missing football. I wasn't really upset. I was relieved more than anything, just to get away from it all and doing something else.'

That something else, initially, was coaching, as Morgan threw himself into completing the relevant qualifications, going back to his roots at Broadwater Farm before taking an assistant manager's position at Wingate & Finchley in the Isthmian League, England's seventh tier. That role was short-lived, however, with Morgan finding working with younger players more rewarding, leading him to creating his own academy and becoming an agent.

'I ended up working for the company that used to look after me. When I look back now, it was the right thing at the wrong time. I didn't really want to be around football to be honest, going to games and talking to people; hassle – that's how I saw it. Then Jobi [McAnuff] came to me and said, "Let's just do our own thing." We did that for a period of time with some relative success.'

Together with McAnuff, he founded Infinite Sports Management, enjoying a measure of success in taking care of hopeful young players. The pair's experience of the trials and tribulations of life in a professional club's academy stood them in good stead, able to speak authoritatively and honestly with their clients. Honesty, as Morgan found, isn't always the policy of choice in a football agent's world, however.

'In order to succeed in that world you've got to compromise on quite a few things about yourself, which I wasn't prepared to do. What did it for me was losing a player because I'd told his dad the truth, which he hated. If I had told the lie it would have been alright, and I knew that before going into the meeting. But I didn't. That's when I knew this thing isn't for me. So now I coach. I've got my own coaching company called Rising Stars. I do workshops for Show Racism the Red Card, I've got my own charity, which is something I really enjoy.'

Despite giving the clear impression that what he went through as a footballer shaped the man he has become, testing and reinforcing the positive personality traits he possesses, Morgan is circumspect when considering a future in the game for his eight-year-old son: 'I've got a boy who has been on trial at lots of different places, and I think, "Do I actually want him going through this whole journey?" I'm not sure I do. It's a small percentage of kids [who make it professionally]. And now, the focus, it's so cut-throat. I kind of don't really want him in that environment.

'It's too professional now, at such a young age. I think that environment only works for a certain amount of kids, and I think it's about peaking at the right time: being the best at 15 is all that matters; being the best at eight doesn't mean a thing. Coming through at Wimbledon, from the age of eight to 16, there was not one other player who was still there. For a number of reasons, they didn't make it. Luck is a massive thing. Timing is everything.

'It's genetics, it's luck, it's hard work, it's talent, it's being in the right place at the right time, working with the right manager and the player having the right mentality. Resilience, dealing with disappointments, injuries, patience – so many factors that players have got to deal with. It's tough. But the rewards are so high that people and parents stick with it.'

Reflecting now upon his football career, Morgan is impressively open and speaks lucidly about his experiences, without a hint of sadness or regret. But he admits watching his playing prospects drift towards the horizon wasn't always easy to deal with.

'For me, I couldn't watch a game for two or three years – I could not watch a football match. You're seeing more and more now the influence of the PFA, getting involved with wellbeing. Back then it probably wasn't something that was here, or at least I wasn't sure that it was there. The profile of that side of the PFA wasn't something I knew about, whereas now they are a lot more proactive; they'd probably come to you.

'At the same time, I remember people like Bobby Barnes [from the PFA] being at the training ground, he'd always say the right thing. But I never knew what they did. They always said, "We're here for you guys," but what did that mean?

'Now you've got people like Michael Bennett doing some great work with mental health and trying to break down that stigma, for players to come out and speak about the problems they have.

'I was fine with it until someone came to me saying, "Ah, your injury ... You could have been this ..." That's the last thing you want to hear. So I stayed away from football. It's not that I didn't love football – I love football, I watch football at home, I go to Arsenal and I love it. But I didn't want to speak to anyone about football.

'And in the end, that's part of the problem, isn't it?'

A Tale of Two Strikers

THE FA Youth Cup is one of football's oldest and most prestigious youth tournaments. Founded in 1952, more than 400 teams enter each year, with the knockout tournament acting as a springboard for many a budding career. In the past, the Youth Cup has helped launch the careers of George Best, John Barnes, Michael Owen and Manchester United's still-revered 'Class of '92' team which included Ryan Giggs, David Beckham, Gary Neville et al.

Of the 2002 vintage, posterity remembers Wayne Rooney as the pre-determined future star. Everton lost to Aston Villa in the final that year, defeated 4-2 across two legs, but their 16-year-old forward stood out throughout the tournament. Rooney went on to become the Premier League's youngest goalscorer the following year, before taking international football by storm at Euro 2004. A record-breaking move to Manchester United that summer led to 12 years of fulfilment of his vast potential, winning every possible trophy and departing English football for a move to Major League Soccer in 2018 – after a brief homecoming with Everton – as both United's and England's all-time leading scorer.

The *Birmingham Mail*'s reporting of the 2002 FA Youth Cup Final, though, dubbed the face-off between Villa and Everton as the 'Tale of Two Strikers,' reflecting how Rooney shared equal billing with Villa's own teenage prodigy Stefan Moore. Indeed, Moore, who captained the winning side and whose younger brother Luke also lined up in the game, outshone Rooney across the two-leg final, scoring twice and being named man of the match in the 4-1 first-leg victory, then lifting the cup in the return fixture at Villa Park.

A spectacular goal on his first-team debut, a midweek Premier League game against Charlton Athletic under the Villa Park floodlights just four months after his Youth Cup heroics, appeared to point to a bright future at senior level. But Moore's Villa career quickly petered and he slid sharply down the leagues. In his 20s, he started a taxi firm in Warwickshire to supplement his income from non-league football. While Rooney still had World Cups and major European finals to look forward to in the 2010s, Moore was seeking opportunities between the fifth and ninth tiers of English football. His last top-flight appearance came two months after his 21st birthday, by which point the prospect of him ever making good on the promise of his teenage years had all but faded.

The Youth Cup Final is naturally the first topic I raise when I sit down with Moore for our interview. He's now in his third spell with the National League North's Leamington, this time, at 34, in a player-coach capacity. We meet at the club's training ground and hole up in a kitchenette-cum-trophy room behind the clubhouse bar, overlooked by the forbidding spectre of a silver bust of a former chairman occupying pride of place on the trophy shelf.

'He was a great player and obviously went on to do great things,' Moore says of Rooney, without a hint of envy. 'Did I fulfil my potential? No, there's no doubt about that.'

The truth is Rooney was a generational talent, a player for whom a career at the very highest level of the game was, barring serious injury or something equally as unforeseen and unfortunate, as close to a certainty as football permits. No one at the time would have gone so far as to suggest Moore's ceiling was as high as Rooney's, but their subsequent paths weren't supposed to diverge so drastically.

'The Moore brothers obviously have potential,' said Villa's Youth Cup-winning coach Tony McAndrew immediately after the final triumph in 2002, reflecting the high hopes held for the Birmingham club's two prized, home-grown prodigies. 'At the moment, you would think they can play in the Premier [League].'

Jimmy O'Connor played as a centre-back for Villa throughout their 2002 Youth Cup run. In addition to Moore's talent, O'Connor remembers being struck by his captain's maturity and reassuring temperament. 'That FA Youth Cup stands out a lot with Stef, who was our skipper,' he says. 'A lot of us were first years, so we were a year younger. They were big games. The nerves were there and excitement, but a lot of the lads hadn't played in decent stadiums yet, in front of big crowds.

'I always remember thinking how calm Stef was throughout that run,' continues O'Connor, who currently plays for Kidderminster Harriers, coincidentally one of Moore's former clubs. '[He was] a real calming influence on the lads. He was a real leader at that time. His calmness showed, and the further we went in that tournament, it rubbed off on us more, in particular that final.'

Chris Nee of the acclaimed football website *In Bed With Maradona* remembers the building sense of anticipation among Aston Villa fans about this emerging young generation, of whom Moore was front and centre. 'It was something we were aware of as supporters,' Nee says of the under-18s side's cup run. 'Any time your team gets to the semi-final of any competition, you start to pick up a bit of interest. That group of players was catching the imagination.'

The season after the Youth Cup victory, the one in which Moore made his first-team debut, was a particularly grim one for Villa. Graham Taylor had returned to the club as manager in February 2001, replacing John Gregory, with hopes high that the former England boss could fend off the stagnation beginning to set in at Villa Park. Taylor's previous spell in charge had seen Villa finish second in the old First Division in 1989/90, with the manager impressing enough to be named Bobby Robson's successor with England after the 1990 World Cup.

There was to be no restoring of former glories, though. In the 13 Premier League games Taylor oversaw at the back end of the 2001/02 season, Villa picked up just three wins. Much of the following term was spent staving off the very real threat of relegation, eventually finishing 16th, just three points outside the drop zone.

Villa's dismal form served only to exacerbate fans' yearning for this group of promising youngsters to break through. The 18-year-old Moore was hailed as the light at the end of the tunnel, the local lad – a lifelong Villa fan, no less – poised to reinvigorate the club.

'The way the final played out meant that any expectations we had of Stefan went through the roof, possibly unfairly,' Nee continues. 'There were a lot of players kicking around our youth system who weren't up to scratch, and the fact he stood out nationally worked against him in the sense he was [seen as] the cure for any ills we had at the time. You can imagine that would be difficult for any kid to take on.'

* * *

Any young player either preparing to play against Aston Villa's under-age teams in the late 90s or joining the club's academy will have quickly become aware of Stefan Moore. The teenager from Erdington, who grew up just two miles from Villa Park, was the coming man of an academy which was enjoying a particularly fruitful few years, having nurtured the likes of Lee Hendrie, Gareth Barry and Darius Vassell. Opposition players were being briefed of the threat Moore posed, and he was held up as beacon, a standard bearer, for fellow Villa hopefuls.

A year younger than Moore, Jimmy O'Connor joined Villa's youth set-up in 1997. 'When you first go there, certain players stand out right from an early age,' he says. 'Luke and Stef – Stef in particular – was kind of the poster boy for the rest of the lads to look up to, one of the standout players you looked up to and thought, "He's got a real chance." I heard about him more than I played with him, that's how high [he was rated]. I'm talking [age] 12, 13.'

Scouted as a nine-year-old playing for local side Romulus, a buzz had already begun to develop around the gifted youngster before he joined Villa; he even turned down advances from Wolverhampton Wanderers in the confidence his beloved home-town club would soon come calling.

'I always felt at home,' Moore says of his early experiences with Villa. 'They made me feel comfortable and at home. I remember in the six-weeks' holidays, probably from when I was about 12, 13, I used to just stay in a hotel and go to the training ground all the time – even when my group weren't in. They just wanted me around the place.

'I had the feeling I was liked, do you know what I mean? I was looked after. In the youth team, two or three people have a chance to get into the first team. They probably thought I had a chance. At that age you don't think, "Oh, I'm going to play [in the first team]." Obviously that's your dream, but I don't think you really see it. When you're in the youth team you don't understand what it takes. When you leave school, that's when it starts to become men's football. You're playing on a Sunday, it's fun with your friends, until you leave school. That's when it's, "Here we go, now I'm in the real world." Then I trained with the first team a few times when I was 17 and I thought, "I'm doing alright here." So you just get a bit more comfortable and you think you've got a chance.'

The men who oversaw Villa's academy and youth teams at the time – former Liverpool player Kevin MacDonald, ex-Middlesbrough defender Tony McAndrew and Villa legend Gordon Cowans, a European Cup winner with the club and ten-cap England international – ran a tight ship. Discipline was the order of the day, and although he didn't always see eye-to-eye with his coaches Moore is quick to praise their influence.

'The youth coaches were very good, they kept people grounded. When I moved away from Villa and saw the way other youth coaching went on, it wasn't the same. I don't think you could've had three better people. At the time, I really struggled with our relationship,' Moore says of Youth Cup coach McAndrew. 'But as time has gone on, I've realised that was down to me and how I was being – he only wanted the best for me. He was very strict; you didn't get away with anything. You speak to anyone from that era of Aston Villa. You didn't really clash with Tony – he won. He is the coach, he wins. I think that's the way it should be, because the rewards are that big.'

Almost two decades on, in 2017, the Premier League were called to investigate allegations of bullying levelled at Kevin MacDonald, who was still a prominent member of the Aston Villa coaching set-up. Parents of a young player in the club's academy complained of 'bullying, aggressive behaviour, and unacceptable language by Mr MacDonald'. The Premier League commissioned an independent review which found 'a lack of focus on player welfare' at Villa and advised the club on how to improve its practices. At time of writing, fresh bullying allegations from another former player have led to Villa 'reassigning' MacDonald from his role as under-23 manager and suspending the coach pending a full investigation.

In October 2001 Villa deemed Moore ready to begin his transition into senior football, albeit not at Premier League level. He was sent on loan to Chesterfield in the Second Division, with whom he made his senior career debut in a 1-0 defeat to Blackpool a month after his 18th birthday. By his own admission, though, he struggled to adapt to life in the third tier – 'I thought, "Wow, this is men's football."' – and remained goalless through his three-game, one-month spell with the Derbyshire club before being recalled by Villa.

'I went back to Villa and we had the FA Youth Cup Final. They said, "You have to come back and play in that." That was a big turning point for me, if I'm honest. I was captain and I grew up a lot. After that, when we won the FA Youth Cup, Graham Taylor was so good with the young players. I'd be in the reserve-team dressing room, getting changed or whatever, and he'd come in and just sit in the corner. He wouldn't always speak – he'd speak sometimes, he'd listen to the lads. You could tell he was desperate to get some of the young players in the team.'

* * *

Fed by Juan Pablo Ángel 40 yards from goal, he turns and, without hesitation, breaks forward towards the Charlton goal at high speed. Confronted outside the penalty area by Richard Rufus, the away side's experienced, wily centre-half, he flicks the ball to his opponent's left before running around the defender's right side to collect it.

Four seconds after receiving the ball, he's now 15 yards out, without a defender in sight and faced down by the Charlton goalkeeper Dean Kiely. He knows what to do. He knows what he will do. And he knows he will score. Opening his body to create the perfect angle, he slides the ball into the far corner, tantalisingly kissing the keeper's left glove on its way in. Just eight minutes after rising from the bench to make his Premier

League debut, 18-year-old Stefan Moore has his first Aston Villa goal.

He runs to the corner of Villa Park where the Holte End and the Doug Ellis Stand meet, clutching the club's crest, beneath which reads the simple motto: 'Prepared.' This was a moment Moore had been preparing for all his life, and the Villa faithful, roused by the strike that settled an otherwise unremarkable 2-0 midweek win, wore expressions which suggest they too had anticipated this young player's ascension.

Jimmy O'Connor was among a handful of young Villa players watching on from the stands as Moore marked his arrival at first-team level. 'I remember all the lads celebrating together,' he says. 'It was almost like one of us had cracked it. It was great to see, and from that moment on I really thought the sky was the limit for him. I thought he'd go on to play for Villa for years and years and become one of their all-time greats, that's how highly he was thought of.'

Moore had been involved with the first team before. Previous manager John Gregory had occasionally taken the youngster travelling with the squad to away games before he was even a regular at reserve level, and he had made substitute appearances in a couple of ties in the Intertoto Cup – a derided and now-defunct early season European competition which promised a place in the UEFA Cup for its winners – a few weeks before his Premier League bow against Charlton in September 2002. But it was that goal, the way he exuded such confidence and composure in its execution, that announced Moore as a teenage harbinger of a new, better era for Villa.

Quite some pressure for such a young man to shoulder, then? 'Nah, when you're young you don't feel it,' Moore insists. 'When you get older you start to think about things more. When you're a 17-, 18-year-old going to play, you don't even know what's going on, you're just going to play football. You haven't got any of the trimmings yet, you're just going to play football; just a young kid playing football. You're living your dream.'

Indeed, the day after his wonder-goal against Charlton, Moore was back in college, continuing to combine woodwork classes with full-time training at a Premier League club, before his coaches decided he was unlikely to ever need the fall-back option of carpentry and that football should be his sole focus.

His first-team opportunity seemingly came sooner than some within the club had expected, though. Eased into the fray during the Intertoto Cup, Moore found himself back with the reserves when the 2002/03 season began in earnest. But his performances in the second-string couldn't be ignored.

'The season started and [Taylor] went for more experienced players,' Moore remembers. 'It was probably about the third or fourth game of the season, we played Liverpool in a reserve game at Villa Park. Markus Babbel and Igor Bišćan played centre-half for Liverpool and I scored a hat-trick.

'I remember then Graham Taylor – we had six strikers at the time: Markus Allbäck, Dion Dublin, Juan Pablo Ángel, Vassell, Peter Crouch and me – he called us in and we had a meeting for the forwards. He said, "I wasn't expecting Stefan to be in the picture but he's here now. There's going to be five strikers involved on a matchday, fight it out between yourselves." And I thought from then, "Do you know what, he's going to give me a chance."'

Taylor certainly did give Moore a chance. The young striker finished the season with 13 Premier League appearances under his belt, although he wasn't able to add to his debut goal. He featured against such illustrious opposition as Manchester United and Liverpool before a minor knee injury temporarily halted his progress. While he was convalescing, however, the club rewarded him with a new three-and-a-half-year contract, a sign of the faith Villa had in their rising star.

The veteran manager was soon on his way out, though. Villa had only confirmed their Premier League survival on the final day of the 2002/03 season thanks to a victory over already-relegated Sunderland. The romantic return of Taylor hadn't worked; he was replaced in the summer of 2003 by former Leeds United boss David O'Leary.

Villa improved quickly under O'Leary, eventually finishing sixth. But the reset button had been pressed on Moore's progress. The new manager put his faith in more experienced players, and an ankle injury, which required surgery, meant more time on the sidelines for the young striker. He made just eight Premier League appearances in 2003/04 and only one, his last for the club, a 1-0 defeat to Manchester United, the season after.

'I had the operation in January, but two months before that I'd tried to get back,' Moore recalls of the point at which his Villa career began to unravel. 'What happened was David O'Leary came in and he had a lot of players in the first team, a lot of seniors. I didn't even go on pre-season tour with the first team. He'd dropped me straight out.

'It probably took me ten games of the [2003/04] season to get back around the first team, get on the bench and start to come on again.'

A goal against Blackburn Rovers in December 2003 brought Moore back into the reckoning, earning a run of four straight starts. But then came the ankle injury.

'We were playing Arsenal next and I was meant to play. We trained, and the day before the game they said, "Do you want to have ten minutes of five-a-side?" I went up and landed on Ronny Johnsen's ankle. I went for a scan and they said, "You're out for two or three months." But I just couldn't get back.

'After that two or three months, I had another two or three months' rehab, then I had to have an operation. I went for the operation and, again, four months' rehab. It still wasn't right. I was having injections in my ankle. It probably took me nine months to get back. And once you've had an operation, everyone says you'll never feel the same again. I didn't realise it.

'You're always fighting against it; it'll never be how it was. Operations are sometimes the quickest way to get back, but you're never as good as you were. That's what happened: I had the operation and just really struggled then.'

It was at this point that Moore began to lose motivation. Downbeat by a longer-than-expected recovery from injury, he saw himself slip further down the pecking order and out of O'Leary's thinking, with Vassell, Ángel, loan signing Carlton Cole and even brother Luke usurping him.

'Obviously, you want to play football, don't get me wrong. But you're on a good contract. Life's pretty easy, if I'm honest. I think I'd gotten injured in the November, but it took me until

September of the following year to come back. And O'Leary said, "You're not really in my plans."

'I had two years left on my contract, so went on loan to Millwall. First game of the season, away to Plymouth, I pulled my thigh. I had a good chance, shot and pulled my thigh. The loan was meant to be for three months, but after six weeks I had to go back because my thigh wasn't right. It took me a while to get over that.

'I did struggle with injuries, getting over them and getting myself right. I've still got a little hole in my thigh.'

Moore made just one more appearance for Villa, coming off the bench in a defeat to Manchester United in December. Next came a loan to relegation-threatened Leicester City in the Championship for the remainder of the season. By the end of the 2004/05 season, at the age of 22, unwanted by O'Leary and disillusioned by how things had gone sour with his boyhood club, Moore agreed to the final year of his contract being settled and he joined Queens Park Rangers in the second tier on a free transfer.

'I think I hung around too long at Villa,' Moore reflects. 'As a young player, you need to go and play first-team football – men's football. Not this academy, under-23 stuff. Great technically but it doesn't matter. On a Saturday, when someone's livelihood is on the line to pay their bills at the end of the month, it's different. I was a Villa fan, I was at home, I was on good money. Life was pretty good, if I'm honest. But it didn't help my career at all.

'The rewards are that big now, nearly every player has got their own personal trainer. I never did any extra. I trained what they said and that was it. Now people finish training and go and see their personal trainer on the night. Look at the rewards: three years ago, the average wage in the Premier League was £45,000 [per week]. The rewards are that big that people work harder for it.

'I didn't really do any extra, or in the summer. I look back and I work harder now than I did then. I wouldn't go back and change anything because I had a good time.

'You can blame the manager if you want but you've got to make it happen. Other people made it happen, I never. I just never did it. Listen, I'm proud of what I did in football. Could I have done a lot more? Yes. Did I underachieve? Yes. Reasons for that? I did have an injury but people do have injuries, you get over that.'

* * *

After the promise of his debut and early displays with the first team, injury troubles and an inability to find a consistency of performance meant it wasn't long before the sentiment that followed his rise to senior football began to fade. 'I think it just came down to his injuries,' Chris Nee says, remembering how the high hopes of Moore quickly faded among fans. 'There was an extended period of injury that made me doubt him a little bit, and the lack of form in between injuries.'

No one would have predicted just how far and how quickly Moore would fall, though. Less than a month after his 25th birthday, the former England under-19 international and FA Youth Cup star was playing non-league football. Just five months before Moore dropped out of the Football League, never to make it back, Wayne Rooney, the other star of the 2002 Youth Cup Final, had helped Manchester United secure a Premier League and Champions League double.

To his surprise, upon joining QPR Moore found he had developed a negative reputation among managers. By his own admission, he could have worked harder to make a success of his time at Villa, but he was never a disruptive influence. The Chinese whispers were spreading, though.

After playing regularly in his first season with QPR, Moore had been sent on loan to Port Vale to begin the 2006/07 campaign in order to regain fitness after yet another injury. When he returned, John Gregory, his former Villa boss, had taken over at Loftus Road, QPR's third manager in seven months.

'He came in on the first day I was back and said, "I've heard your attitude is all wrong. I don't really want you around the place. I'll pay you off,"' Moore remembers of his meeting with the new manager. 'I hadn't seen John Gregory for years. He'd just gone off what people had told him about my attitude and that I don't want to be around the place. I don't know where it came from, I haven't got a clue.'

It transpired that QPR didn't have the money to pay Moore off, so he stayed and ended up winning Gregory over, forcing his way back into the team at the end of the season. But Italian businessman Flavio Briatore's purchase of the club ultimately led to Gregory's sacking in October, eventually being replaced by Luigi De Canio. Moore was an outcast again.

'Come January, they'd bought quite a few more players and just offered me a payoff. I thought, "It's not working out for me, I might as well go."'

Next came the *Sliding Doors* moment of Moore's post-Aston Villa career, and what he describes as his 'biggest mistake'. Stuart Gray, whom Moore had worked with at Villa, wanted to take the forward to Northampton Town. Moore instead opted for a trial with Melbourne Victory in the Australian A-League – 'I went to Australia for three weeks. Great life, but the football was terrible ... It didn't work out.' Upon his return, Gray's interest remained firm, but this time Moore rejected Northampton in favour of a move closer to home, joining Walsall in March 2008.

Despite scoring just four minutes into his debut, Moore soon fell out with manager Richard Money and left Walsall at the end of the season, having played just five games. 'I just didn't get on with him,' he says of his relationship with Money. 'We had a little discussion; it wasn't very pleasant. I never played again that season. That was my decision in football: I should've gone to Northampton.'

Ahead of the 2008/09 season, the offers were no longer coming in as they once had. At 25, he was viewed as a busted flush, a lost talent, with no side in England's top four divisions willing to take a chance on him. He spent the season with Kidderminster in the Conference, before joining Halesowen Town on a part-time basis, two divisions further down the football pyramid.

'I fell out of love with football. I hated going to work. I was thinking, "What am I doing here?" I wasn't even playing. Kidderminster were flying at the time. I was questioning why I was doing it.'

He'd had to go an awfully long way to find it, but Moore finally rediscovered his scoring touch with Halesowen, netting

42 times in 52 games for the West Midlands side. This resurgence led to interest from upwardly mobile Crawley Town, who would shortly go on to earn promotion to League Two as Conference champions while embarking on a remarkable run to the fifth round of the FA Cup. Moore was desperate to make the move.

'They offered Halesowen £25,000 for me. They wouldn't take it. I was like, "You have to." I ended up putting something in the paper and getting fined two weeks' money for it. That was my last chance. I was 27. They were on the up. That was my last chance to get back into the Football League. After that I thought, "I'm never going to be a full-time player again."'

* * *

'My game nowadays is I go home and away with a team in non-league Midlands football,' says Chris Nee, 'so the name Stefan Moore is fairly regularly mentioned around me these days, or was a few years ago.

'He's been knocking around various clubs. When you drop as far as he's dropped, you become a bit of a name in non-league football. He still carries the label of "former Premier League goalscorer Stefan Moore" around here.'

When we met, Moore was in his 11th season at non-league level, encompassing spells with Kidderminster, Halesowen, St Neots Town, Brackley Town, three stints with Leamington, Solihull Moors and, since our interview, a move to Redditch United which lasted only weeks before a switch to Tamworth.

'When I dropped down [to non-league level], I just went,' Moore says. 'A lot of people drop down and come back up. I went down to non-league. After I didn't get the Crawley move, I knew that was it then. I was 26, 27. That's when I set up a business. I set up a taxi firm.'

As his football career became only a part-time concern, Moore recognised the need to supplement his declining income. He and a friend began a taxi business, with Moore prepared to 'do whatever it takes' to make it a success, even manning the phone lines and driving the cabs.

'I just needed to work. I'd never had a full-time job, that was my first. I had a friend who was an electrician who said he didn't want to work all his life, so we tried something. His dad was a taxi driver, so we thought, "Let's give it a go." I didn't know what I was going to do, but we did alright. It was hard and different – a culture shock. But you get out and do what you've got to do.

'By the end we had 70 cars, we did well. Someone wanted to take it off our hands so we sold up. It was something I could do alongside my football. I was playing part-time, training Tuesday and Thursday then playing Saturday. It worked out quite well.'

Moore's story is one of bad luck, bad timing and bad decisions. But it is also a tale of lost love. As the disappointments began to mount up quickly, he became browbeaten and disenchanted. He recognises that he could have done more and that people could have in turn done more to help him fulfil his vast potential.

'The setbacks get to you in the end. I've always believed that I could do it, that I could score goals if I played. But I think there is more to football. People used to say to me, "You haven't tried today." And I'd think I had. But have you really tried? I needed someone questioning me. There was no one who really did that. No manager worked me out.

'It's all about winning games rather than improving,' he continues, picking up on an under-appreciated pitfall of the game's most gifted youngsters: those who are thrust into senior football at an early age enter an environment in which results are the only currency; this often means they receive less one-on-one coaching and personal development work than less-talented peers who remain at youth level for an extra two or three years.

'That is the thing in England that I think is terrible: not enough managers make you a better player. I spoke to my brother about this. Only one manager he says has ever made him a better player: Brendan Rodgers. One manager. How can that be? Because they want to win on a Saturday. They don't give a shit about you. They can't. Because if they don't win, they get sacked.'

A father of three, Moore has a son currently on Aston Villa's books. Despite the harsh lessons football had doled out to him, he is keen for his son to pursue his own ambitions within the game. 'I wanted him to go for it,' he says. 'I think it's a good upbringing with good discipline, you get to see the world. It keeps the kids out of trouble and gives them a sense of direction. Oh, there's a lot of pressure, yeah. But if he wasn't training with Villa he'd be playing football anyway. I think it's good. It sets you up for life.'

If his son is at one end of the spectrum, in the infancy of his life in football, Moore is at the other, with retirement a creeping inevitability. Luke Moore, two and a half years Stefan's junior, is already out of the game, having retired at 30. Although many considered the younger Moore brother an inferior talent to his older sibling, Luke was able to sustain a high-level career for much longer, playing in the Premier League and the Championship for Aston Villa, West Bromwich Albion and Swansea City. He retired in 2015 after two years in Major League Soccer with Chivas USA and Toronto. Seeing the ease with which his younger brother stepped away from the game, coupled with his own experiences, has given Moore a healthy perspective on the prospect of life post-football.

'Let's be honest, you're 35, you've got a lot of years left to live,' he says. 'A lot of life. My brother retired at 30. He's got a great life. He just packed it in, doesn't want to play. He got offered deals. He just said, "I don't need to do this every day. There's plenty more to life." Which there is. You live in this bubble, but there's a big world out there, a lot of things to do.

'You'll always have that love for football, but should it be your whole life? It is for some people. I love playing and the buzz of a Saturday, but it's all the work you've got to do to get there. It's a job. People wouldn't understand that. Players haven't seen the other side yet until they drop out. A lot of people struggle when they haven't got that structure.'

In closing, I ask Moore what it takes for a hotly tipped young footballer to go on and achieve everything expected of them; what goes into the making of a Wayne Rooney, and how could his own fall have been avoided? As someone who has experienced both sides of the coin, the rapid rise and the dream debut followed by a sudden and unforgiving descent, it is a question he is as well placed as anyone to answer, and he does so lucidly.

'You need to be in the right place at the right time. Graham Taylor liked me. He saw something in me and he pushed me in there. Maybe I shouldn't have been in there, maybe I should, but he put me in there. There could've been another manager who wasn't sure about me and preferred somebody else.

'Don't get me wrong, you'll always have a Wayne Rooney – he's outrageous. He was always a step ahead of everyone and that was always going to happen. But everyone else: it all has to fall in place for you to get to where you want to be. The fans just love football and just think, "He must be better than him because he's playing." But that's not the way it works in football. That's not the world we live in.

'And it's a business, remember.'

Virtual Reality Bites

THE Football Manager video game franchise has come a long way since its humble beginnings in 1992 under its previous moniker Championship Manager. Starting life as an innovative soccer management simulator, which was devised by brothers Paul and Oliver Collyer and written in their Shropshire bedroom, Football Manager is now a global brand. It boasts a worldwide network of 1,300 scouts in 51 regions, keeping in-depth and up-to-date records and statistics on 350,000 real-life footballers at 42,000 clubs, from budding 15-year-olds in the game's remotest outposts to superstars like Cristiano Ronaldo and Lionel Messi.

Football Manager has consumed the lives of many of its devotees, been the subject of numerous books and infiltrated professional football as clubs have sought to use the game's extensive player database as a scouting tool. Indeed, in 2017 football magazine *FC Business* named Miles Jacobson, director of Football Manager developers Sports Interactive, as football's 47th most powerful man.

With a new version released every year, the first thought of most of the game's players is to seek out the 'wonderkids' of the latest release, the young players who, when purchased in-game, can be developed into world-class stars. And there is no footballer more synonymous with Football Manager's – or, more accurately, Championship Manager's – wonderkid label than Cherno Samba.

In the early 2000s, before a split between developers Sports Interactive and Eidos led to the game being rebranded, Samba was the teenage sensation every Championship Manager player snapped up from Millwall as their first port of call when loading the game. The striker came to guarantee goals in the game, invariably developing into one of the best players in the world by his early 20s and usually guiding England and whichever club won the race for his signature to major honours.

In reality, Samba's playing career never reached such heights. A product of Millwall's academy, he was released by the south London club aged 19, without ever appearing for the first team. A nomadic career took him to Spain, Greece and Finland between short spells back in English football. And the England youth international ultimately elected to represent Gambia, the country of his birth. He retired aged 29 after breaking his ankle while on trial with non-league Southport.

There is a consensus, then, that the Championship Manager scouts were wildly wide of the mark in their assessment of the teenage Samba, that he was mistakenly billed as English football's brightest hope yet in reality he just wasn't very good. This revisionist line of thinking, though, is simply untrue.

Samba was indeed an elite prospect once upon a time, courted by the likes of Manchester United, Liverpool and Leeds United while at Millwall. He was such a prolific scorer at youth level that his return of 132 goals in 32 games for his school, St Joseph's Academy in Blackheath, south London, broke a schoolboy scoring record held by Liverpool and England star Michael Owen.

It was the breakdown of a proposed move to Liverpool, in fact, that set Samba's budding career off track, aged just 14.

'It was just through banging the goals in for Millwall,' Samba says, beginning his story at the point Liverpool's interest in him was piqued, breaking to sip from his large latte in a busy coffee shop opposite Euston Station. 'And also, I got into the England set-up and was playing a year above my age – so I was 14 playing in the under-15s. I think it was against Northern Ireland that after the game everything went berserk. What got everyone talking was my England debut, and after that we played against Wales. That's when I got man of the match. I scored one and set up two. That's when it was just blown out of all proportions.

'It was a good feeling. It was, "Yeah, this is what it's about and this is what I want."'

Although a Millwall fan, Samba had a soft spot for Manchester United, English football's dominant force in the 1990s and early 2000s. Despite the Red Devils' best attempts to woo him, however, it was Liverpool who convinced the gifted teen to sign for them, thanks to the employ of a secret weapon: a personal call from Michael Owen.

'Gérard Houllier had asked me who my favourite player was,' Samba's smile beams at the memory. 'I'd always looked up to Michael, and I had taken his youth scoring record. I'd always looked at the way he scored and tried to imitate him. So when Gérard Houllier asked me, I said Michael, and they got him to call me.

'I'll never forget that, I always tell the story. I was on the school bus and Michael called me. My mates on the bus didn't believe it was Michael Owen: "You lot, be quiet, I'm talking to Michael Owen!" – "Shut up, Chern." I had to put it on loudspeaker for a little bit.

'He said Liverpool was "a great club, they'll look after you. It'd be a privilege to play alongside you." Just all these nice things. And you can imagine, the whole bus went absolutely mad. And for me, that was my mind made up.

'I went to Liverpool and Michael took me around. He was a really nice guy, really down to earth. And I fell in love with the club, even though I had been a United fan as well. He was about 18, 19. He'd just burst on to the scene.'

So it was decided, Samba would leave Millwall for Liverpool, swapping a middling First Division club for a side with designs on challenging Arsenal and Manchester United for the Premier League title, and a club with a track record of giving opportunities to players from their academy – Jamie Carragher, Robbie Fowler and Michael Owen showed there was a pathway to the senior ranks. But the two clubs couldn't agree a fee; Liverpool were prepared to pay as much as £1m for the prodigal striker, a significant fee for that time period, but Millwall demanded double.

'They just didn't agree. I think at the time Jermaine Pennant left Notts County for Arsenal for £1.5m, which was a record [fee paid for an under-16 player] and if I would have gone it would have been a new record. But they just couldn't agree.

'The funny thing is, I didn't know anything about [the deal collapsing] – my mum knew about it, my dad knew about it, my agent knew about it, but I didn't.

'I remember one time we were sitting in the office – me, my agent, Gérard Houllier and my mum and dad – and we were waiting for a fax to come through, but I didn't think anything of it; I thought everything was going to be fine. Then, two or three weeks later, I noticed my mum was really down, and that's when my dad took me in the kitchen and said, "I need to speak to you. Your mum's a bit heartbroken at the moment because obviously your move didn't happen." I said, "What? You knew for weeks and you are only telling me now?" I just burst into tears and fell on the floor crying.

'I didn't want to play football again. And I stopped playing for six months. I'd go out with my mates and play in the park, but I didn't want to go back to Millwall. My parents, friends and family said, "Look, this is your career; don't throw it away. Just go back." To Millwall's credit, the chairman, Theo Paphitis' – Samba, at this point, makes his feelings towards Paphitis clear with a swing of a clenched fist – 'and the sporting director came to meet with me and asked me to come back. So I listened to my mum and dad, to my agent and Theo, and went back, but my heart wasn't in it.

'Once that deal didn't go through, I lost appetite for the game. That's when I thought, "I'm here to secure a life for me and my family." Can you imagine thinking that at 14? All I thought about was how I could be sorted out after football financially.'

* * *

South London has long been a hotbed of footballing talent. Indeed, in 2016 an article in *The Guardian* detailed how 14 per cent of the English players in the Premier League at the time hailed from within a ten-square-mile patch of south London. And in the late 1990s, the production line was churning out budding footballers en masse. 'I've got a video of a match when we were in Year 7,' says Osei Sankofa, a former England youth international team-mate of Samba's, 'when we were 11 years old: the 22 players on that pitch all went on to be a pro at some level of the game.'

Still, surrounded by such a plethora of talented young men, Samba stood out. Sankofa came through the ranks at Charlton Athletic, local rivals of Samba's Millwall, and he remembers the sheer physical force the young Samba possessed: 'Physically, the game was too easy for him – he was playing men against boys when he was ten years old, and no one could stop him,' Sankofa says. 'The size he is now, he was that big at 11 years old. That puts you at a massive advantage.

'The way Millwall used to play as well – it was a physical, up-and-at-you kind of game. They intimidated a lot of teams. Because he was so big, and because the whole team was so big, they used to steamroll everybody.

'It wasn't a surprise that he got touted around, but probably a surprise that he didn't get signed, because of the impact he had on schoolboy football; he's still a legend today for what he did ten, 15 years ago.'

Samba is frank in his own assessment of his ability versus his peers as a pre- and early teen. 'I was scoring four, five, six goals a game,' he says. 'We had the likes of Kieran Richardson, Anton Ferdinand, those sort of players [in the area] who all went on to do really well through their careers, so you can imagine the standard was good, but I was miles above everyone else, to be honest.'

'Football's subjective, but numbers don't lie,' says Kevin George, a former Charlton, Millwall and West Ham United youth player, who now works with professional clubs as a human performance consultant, 'and Cherno was getting 40 goals a season. You can't be no good and do that. He was playing for England as well – and not only that, he was keeping Wayne Rooney out of the team.

'If you look at that, you can't say he wasn't a good player. I thought he was really good.'

Samba, who says football was in his blood thanks to his dad playing as a goalkeeper, moved to England from Gambia aged six and remembers football being a constant in his life, acting as an integration aid with the local kids.

'I think it was when I was ten or 11 that I started getting all the attention,' Samba says, picking up his story. 'I had scouts and agents coming to watch our school team. I thought, "Hmm, what's this all about?" But then I thought, "You know what, I might make a career out of this." So that was when I started taking it seriously, but not to the point where I was thinking of it as a career, just that this is something I want to do if it works out.'

Samba joined Millwall at the age of 11 and eventually signed his first professional contract with the club at 17. But the word was already out about his talent and potential upside, making him a prime target for sponsors aiming to get in on the ground floor with a player who could soon be elevated to the elite professional level. The attention and the money thrust upon him while so young, Samba feels, saw him fall foul of the too-much-too-soon culture that pervades youth football at the highest level.

'I think Nike approached me when I was 14, when I'd just burst on to the scene. I used to go to Nike Town, the shop would close and I'd just be able to get anything I wanted. You can imagine, at 14, 15, I'd get all my mates and come out with six or seven grand's worth of stuff, carrying it back on the bus in bags. I was getting so much stuff. I used to get vouchers and there'd be £1000 on each voucher. I sorted my mates out with trainers, tops, all sorts of things.

'I believe [footballers] are spoilt in this country. When I turned 17 I went to a Peugeot showroom and bought a car for £11,000 in cash, just like that. That was from my earnings at Millwall.

'Looking back now, I wouldn't do that. I wish I was protected enough to not do that. And I wish I was given a smaller amount of money at that age, because what happens is by the time you're 19, 20, 21 the football is out of the window – all you're thinking about is the money. That's why you have so many players now who get to 21 and they don't have a club, they're fading out of the game.

'For part of it, I blame myself. If I knew then what I know now, I wouldn't go and buy that car for £11,000. I would be more humble. At 17, as soon as I passed my test: "I want that car, how much is it? £11,000? I'll have it."'

Samba, having viewed football as a means to an end following the collapse of his Liverpool move, felt at this stage as though he had 'made it'. 'Of course. I already felt like that when I was 15. And this is what happens in football now.'

* * *

By 19, Samba's progress had stalled. Although still regularly selected for England youth squads, he hadn't made a breakthrough at senior club level and looked increasingly unlikely to do so. It was 2004 and Dennis Wise was Millwall manager. While he enjoyed working with Wise's assistant Ray Wilkins, who had passed away days before we met – 'Bless his soul,' Samba says of the roundly liked and admired Wilkins, 'he was a nice man.' – the young striker didn't envisage a first-team opportunity under the manager.

'I wasn't getting any game time, so I don't think they were going to renew my contract.' He was, he admits, earning more than many of Millwall's first-team regulars. 'And I wanted to leave anyway. I thought it was time to go out there and try something else.'

'That's when Spain came about. I had a few choices and I could have stayed [in England], but I just wanted to get out of here. I wanted to go and test the water. I was sick of it all and there was too much going on. My heart wasn't here any more, so that's why I went to Spain.'

Samba joined Second Division side Cádiz in the summer of 2004. His first season in Spain was interrupted by a meniscus injury, and he was sent out on loan to Málaga's B team for the 2005/06 campaign, before then returning to England to sign for Plymouth Argyle.

But, regardless of continuing struggles with establishing himself at first-team level, Samba speaks fondly of his time in Spain. Having insisted upon regular tuition, he became fluent in Spanish within eight months, and on the pitch he felt his skills were put to better use than ever before.

'It was the best time of my football career. Those two years that I had in Spain were the best of my life. I loved the place, loved the culture, the food, the weather. And, more importantly,

I loved the style of football. They appreciated me. I loved every single minute of being in Spain.

'My strength was coming deep, picking up the ball and attacking defenders. Over here [in England], I was a little bit restricted. I remember my first game in Spain, they played three up front, so I was on the right. I was doing doggies, running back and helping out in defence. I was coming back and forth because that was what I was used to: bang, bang, bang.

'But in the second half, the manager took me off. I was sat in the changing room thinking, "What is he doing?" Because I was helping out in defence, doing my job. The next day he called me into his office and said, "Samba, what are you doing? You're a striker, you're technical: stay up there, do your thing. Defenders are for defending." I just kissed him and gave him a hug; it was happy days, man. But I came back here again after and I'd lost that [defensive work], so I had to learn it all again.'

Samba penned a two-year contract with Plymouth, working under their eccentric manager Ian Holloway. He was handed a league debut in an away fixture against Coventry City on 30 September and marked the occasion by scoring the game's only goal.

'I'll never forget that,' he says of his first goal in senior English football. 'It was a good goal. I felt, "Yes, I'm back now." This was what I wanted. I was injury-free, I was fine.'

He didn't score again in a further 12 appearances with Plymouth, though, and was on the move when his contract expired in 2008. Samba was 23; the best offer he received came from nine-time Finnish champions FC Haka. 'I knew at that time it was all about securing my family,' he says. 'They turned out to meet my terms and I went over.'

His second European excursion proved less enjoyable than the first, however, as he found Finland 'too much of a different culture. They're more laid back. And the level of football was not the best.'

While in Finland, recognising any chance of senior England selection was long gone, Samba elected to represent Gambia at international level. 'Gambia had wanted me to play for them for 15 years, but I was playing in the youth team for England.

'I was playing in Norway (for FK Tønsberg). When you have the likes of Wayne Rooney, Michael Owen, Darren Bent playing Premier League football week in, week out, what chance have I got? That's what made me decide to play for Gambia.' He would accumulate four caps for the country of his birth, scoring once.

After leaving Haka in 2009, Samba hopped on a merry-go-round of trials, trying out unsuccessfully with Portsmouth and Norwich City before joining Panetolikos in the Greek second tier. 'By then I was a journeyman,' he admits of his meandering career path. 'It was a beautiful place, in the north of Greece. It was good. The same sort of Mediterranean life as Spain – weather was good, food was good. The football was alright, but nowhere near as good as Spain, obviously. I enjoyed myself there. But then I got injured again – hamstring.'

Returning from Greece in 2010, it was back on the trial trail for Samba – 'I was just trying to get a contract somewhere.' He eventually secured a move to Norwegian side FK Tønsberg in 2012, but left after a year when the club fell upon hard times financially and could no longer afford his wages.

More trials. The last of which, with non-league Southport, saw Samba suffer a broken ankle in training. He recovered enough to accept a post as player-coach with Chase Town, but any passion he had left for the game had been drained from him. Still feeling the effects of his ankle injury, he decided enough was enough.

'I did a training session and I thought, "Nah, this is it for me." I spoke to my agent and said, "This is it." My body was telling me – my ankle wasn't right, and by this time I was 29, it'd take me six months to a year to fully recover. Already at the back of my mind I was thinking, "What's next?" I had started thinking that previously, anyway.

'Tears flowed down my eyes at that time, thinking, "Wow, what a journey. This is it."

Samba's playing career ended, mirroring the precise moment at which it had been knocked off course a decade and a half earlier, when he discovered his dream move to Liverpool had been cancelled – 'I just dropped on the floor, crying.'

* * *

Samba is a strikingly warm and gregarious soul. He bears no obvious bitterness for the way his time in football panned out, and through coaching young players he aspires to put his negative experiences to good use, helping emerging talents avoid the pitfalls that put paid to his own prospects.

Having studied for his UEFA A Licence – the second-highest coaching qualification recognised by European football's governing body – alongside Frank Lampard and Graeme Le Saux at Chelsea, Samba's ultimate aim is to manage Gambia at a World Cup or Africa Cup of Nations. 'That's my goal,' he says, 'but at the start I need to work in an academy here and gain experience, because you need that.'

Samba could be forgiven for, if not bearing resentment, at least having tired of the constant mention of Football Manager in connection with his name. He is, after all, most remembered for being unable to match the accomplishments of his virtual self. But no, he fully embraces his synonymy with the game and has even begun to work with its producers, making appearances at public events and featuring in an advertising campaign.

'I love it, actually,' he contests. 'When I was playing, I didn't like it, because I felt, "Bloody hell, just look at my footballing abilities; stop talking about this game." But looking at it now, it's part of me and part of my DNA; I can't get away from it.

'I always tell people, I'll be 91 with a walking stick and people will come to me saying, "Hey Cherno, Football Manager ..." I embrace it. It's had a lot to play in my career and I'm grateful. I love the attention, I love the fans. Without the fans, I'm no one.

'Some players in it – I don't want to mention names – they don't want [the attention], they don't want to talk about it. I'm happy with it. Every time I go out, people stop me and say, "Are you Cherno? Can I have a picture with you?" And I love it. Now it's come to a point where I'm doing some work with them. It's great.'

One point on which Samba will in part concede, however, is that perhaps his status in the game set the bar too high in reality. Even if he had been able to deliver more on his potential during his playing career, matching the achievements of Championship Manager 01/02's Cherno Samba would have been nearly impossible. That, surely, only served to set him up for disappointment.

'Yes and no. You've got to be mentally tough. You've got to have mental strength. There are always going to be distractions, not just in football but in life in general. It's up to the individual to say, "This is my goal, this is my path – I don't care about that."

'If Football Manager hyped me up to that extent, that shouldn't affect me. I should know what I want, what my goal is, and follow it.

'However, being so young at the time – I get it. There's a balance. It's a very difficult question to answer, because adults get distracted, let alone youngsters. I believe at 18 you are still not an adult. You're still a baby, so it does have an effect.'

Nineteen-year-old Ally Dick celebrates Tottenham's UEFA Cup triumph at Wembley in May 1984

Giuliano Maiorana poses alongside Alex Ferguson and Bryan Robson after signing for Manchester United. His relationship with the manager soon broke down

Ben Thornley (right) pictured alongside Class of '92 team-mates Phil Neville (top), Paul Scholes (left) and Gary Neville (bottom)

Danny Cadamarteri burst on to the scene at Everton in 1997

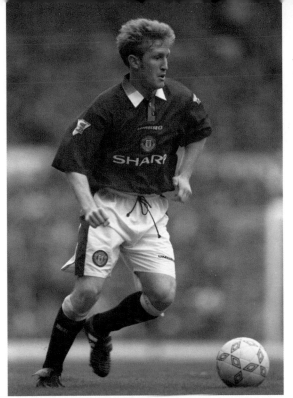

John Curtis in action in Manchester United's 7-0 win over Barnsley in October 1997

Wolves prodigy Ryan Green challenges Wimbledon's Lionel Morgan

Andy van der Meyde's move to Internazionale should have been a career highlight but instead it sparked his downward spiral

Matt Murray was the most gifted English goalkeeper of his generation but injuries forced him to retire at 29

Lionel Morgan was one of Englands's most-wanted wingers while a teenager at Wimbledon

Stefan Moore lifts the FA Youth Cup for Aston Villa in 2002 after overcoming Wayne Rooney's Everton

Cherno Samba was an England regular at youth level but he is more synonymous with the Championship Manager video game

Tottenham youngster Owen Price set a world record with a spectacular strike from the halfway line at Highbury

Fabio da Silva sees off Barcelona's Lionel Messi after starting the 2011 Champions League Final for Manchester United ahead of his brother Rafael

John Bostock remains the youngest player ever to play for both Crystal Palace and Tottenham

Adam Morgan celebrates scoring his first senior Liverpool goal in a friendly against Toronto in 2012

Price Tag

'**A**T THAT age, I wouldn't know what anxiety meant, but now I'm older I realise that was what I was having. You are more scared of making mistakes because of who you are meant to be.'

Owen Price's story makes for an interesting juxtaposition with Cherno Samba's from the previous chapter. The two players grew up as contemporaries in the south London youth football scene, with Price, hailing from Tooting, attending Ernest Bevin school, rivals of Samba's St Joseph's. Born less than two years apart, both were England regulars at youth level.

While Samba's career was thrown off track by the disillusionment he felt at the collapse of a transfer to Liverpool at the age of 14, Price got his dream move at the same age, joining the club he'd grown up supporting, Tottenham Hotspur.

Spurs paid £450,000 to sign the teenage Price from Charlton Athletic, a headline-grabbing sum for a player of his age in 2000, and the young winger soon discovered the personal cost of his price tag. 'It comes with so much pressure,' he explains. 'You don't realise. You feel like you've got to pull up trees every week; like people expect you to score hat-tricks every week.'

The anxiety Price endured after making the switch to Spurs was difficult to contend with. The publicised move raised his profile, and within a few months he was called up for the England Schoolboys squad; beyond a hotly tipped talent in his local community, he was now a player of note on the national scene, a reputation he felt constant pressure to justify.

The pressures affecting Price were not only internal, however. His transfer fee and elevated status became a source of jealousy, not from his peers – Price is quick to report that he received nothing but support and congratulations from fellow players – but from coaches.

'My manager at Charlton, when I was there, was really nice. When I left and we played Charlton and he was managing them, he was shouting, "He's shit." And I was thinking, "This guy is 40 years old." 'When I moved [to Tottenham], he was like, "Oh, he's shit, he's useless." I heard him on the sidelines when I was playing and he said it in the changing rooms. I'd played for them, so some of the boys were telling me. I couldn't work it out. You're a grown man and I'm 15.'

Osei Sankofa, a former England youth player who was in Charlton's academy at the same time as Price, shares his thoughts on the weight of expectation Price would have been subjected to after his Tottenham transfer: 'Half a million pounds for a 15-year-old is a scary sum of money even now, so back then it must have been a huge thing for him.

'When you have a reputation as being a particular player – or when you've played for England especially – people look at you and are looking to be instantly impressed by what you do. But I think it's important to remember, as a 14-year-old, you're a child. You've got all these expectations of all these adults who maybe didn't get to half the level you're at but are putting all this extra pressure on you.

'As a 14-, 15-year-old,' Sankofa continues, 'you've got nothing to gauge that against; you've got no coping mechanisms – you've got to get on with it as best you can. It wouldn't surprise me that that would be difficult.'

It wasn't just rival coaches for whom Price became a target of jealous vitriol, either. His own youth-team coach at Tottenham, he says, singled him out for similar treatment. 'I was getting paid more than him and he made it known that he was not happy with it,' Price told Kevin George, author of *Soccology: Inside the Hearts and Minds of the Professionals on the Pitch*. 'Whenever I made a mistake he would turn to my team-mates and say, "He shouldn't be getting that kind of money."'

While it seems reasonable for the coach, a former Spurs player, to take issue with one of his teenage charges earning more than him, any bitterness towards the player was wholly misplaced.

Price admits he began to bite back at his perceived mistreatment, reacting angrily when he felt the brunt of criticism. But he was still, along with striker Michael Malcom, the star player of the Spurs under-17 team crowned southern champions. Many of the players from that team were tipped for stardom, most notably Price and Malcolm, but Price feels the fact that none of this gifted crop were able to make in-roads at first-team level was in part due to the environment created by the academy-team manager.

'If I was wrong for the way I [acted], and he wasn't wrong, how come there were no stars [to come from that team]? Someone has to have done something wrong; it can't all be the players' fault. Sometimes you've got to look closer to home.

'You've not produced any stars from that team, and that was your job. If the coaches that are there now were there then, it would be a different story, because we could relate to them. I couldn't relate to the manager that we had. There were two generations between them and us. They'd get angry at the young generation, angry at the world.'

* * *

Price describes growing up on a council estate in Tooting, south London, spending every spare hour playing football inside a caged, multi-sport court. His talent was apparent from an early stage and he was picked for Millwall's School of Excellence before joining Charlton Athletic's academy at the age of 12.

'Obviously, at that age, no one knows how far that talent's going to go, but he was always a very good player,' says former Charlton team-mate Osei Sankofa. 'Everyone knew who he was, and everyone knew he was being talked about. We were both at Charlton at the same time. He played up from my age group a couple of times. He moved on to Tottenham very quickly after that.

'He was very special,' Sankofa enthuses. 'What set him out was his technique – technically, his ball-striking ability and ability to cross a ball at such a young age. He's small and stocky and he's been that size since he was 13 or 14, so he was able to generate huge power in his legs, which gave him a massive advantage when it came to longer passing, crossing the ball and free kicks.

'Traditionally, south London street players, you'd expect [to be] skilful, quick – and he wasn't slow – but the biggest thing about him was his technical ability.'

Standing out within a talent-rich school team at Ernest Bevin, Price was selected to represent south London and then Inner London Schoolboys as interest in him began to grow at club level.

That interest would reach fever pitch when at 14 he scored a spectacular, record-breaking goal in the final of a national schools tournament, held at Arsenal's Highbury stadium. With the ball rolled back to him from kick-off at the start of the game, Price employed the superlative ball-striking technique outlined by Sankofa to launch a goal-bound effort from the halfway line which sailed beyond the helpless goalkeeper and into the net.

The goal, which can be viewed on YouTube, was timed at 4.2 seconds, setting an officially recognised world record as the fastest goal ever scored in a cup final.

'I'd done it a few times before,' Price recalls, 'but not scored. The guy who took the centre, I said to him to lay it back. But he didn't lay it back; he stopped in there in the centre, so it was like a race for the ball – one of them was coming to shut me down. But it went well. I'd done it in the round before, but I don't know where it went.

'When I was at Charlton, we'd play a couple of games at the end of the season at The Valley, and we played one at Chelsea. So I'd played in other stadiums before, but Arsenal's felt different. It had history. As soon as you walked in, it was like going to a museum.'

Price had recently penned a sponsorship deal with Adidas, and he was wearing their flagship Predator boots for the first time during the final. At the time, in 2000, David Beckham was at the peak of his stardom and a teenager scoring a goal reminiscent of the Manchester United man's strike against Wimbledon four years earlier, wearing the same boots, heaped attention on Price as one of the country's hottest prospects.

There is a misconception, though, that Price's move to Tottenham came about because of his record goal, when in fact he had agreed to join Spurs before the final.

'When I was at Charlton there were a lot of clubs I was talking to. I was two days away from signing for [Aston] Villa. I'd found a school, a house – everything, I'd met the guys. The guy that brought me up there was a good friend of my uncle's – my uncle was my agent. The year before he'd taken Jlloyd Samuel up there, because Jlloyd was at Charlton. That was the path that I was taking.

'Just before that, I was at an FA Youth Cup match – I think it was against Arsenal – and in the team room was David Pleat [then Tottenham's director of football]. He got talking to my uncle, because my uncle was a scout at the time. He asked me who I was. We told him the story [of the planned Villa move] and he said, "Before you do that, come and play a game with us and see how it goes." And that's what we did.

'Fulham were one of the clubs I was talking to, and there was a scout from Man United I was talking to. There were quite a few clubs. Because [my uncle] had been in football, he knew what would be best for me. Once I went up to Tottenham to meet the guys, it just felt right, and I really didn't want to move away from home.'

* * *

In the summer of 2004, change was afoot at White Hart Lane. Jaques Santini, the former France national team coach, had been brought in as manager and Spurs signed 12 new first-team players. There was a particular emphasis on attracting and utilising young English talent at this time, as Sean Davies, Michael Carrick and goalkeeper Paul Robinson were all bought from Premier League rivals.

During pre-season that year, Price began to make an impression at senior level. 'We went away to Sweden; we played a couple of games,' Price remembers. 'And we played against Celtic at Celtic Park. That was my first experience of a full house. And that was my first experience of being in and around the first team. They'd chartered a flight and everything.

'When Santini came in there was a whole new set-up, but he didn't speak a word of English – not even "Hello" – so it was hard to get your point across. It was never going to last.'

A solid start to the 2004/05 campaign saw Spurs undefeated in their first six fixtures. But the style of play espoused by Santini was deemed too cautious by many Tottenham fans. Four of those opening six games were drawn and Spurs had mustered just four goals. After the final game of that initial run, a 0-0 draw with Chelsea at Stamford Bridge, the Blues' charismatic new manager, one José Mourinho, remarked, 'Tottenham might as well have put the team bus in front of their goal,' in reference to the away side's uber-defensive tactics. In that moment, Mourinho brought the term 'parking the bus' into common football parlance – a phrase now commonly directed at its creator in accusation of his own over-cautious approach.

A subsequent run of five defeats from six Premier League games led to Santini resigning in November. The Frenchman cited personal reasons for his departure, but it was widely speculated a fallout with sporting director Frank Arnesen was the real reason behind his exit.

Arnesen enjoyed a strong relationship with Santini's assistant, Martin Jol – although Arnesen is Danish, he was a flying winger for Ajax, the Netherlands' most famous club, during the peak of his playing career and thus felt a kinship with the Dutch coach. Jol was quickly appointed Santini's successor, a point at which Price feels his prospects diminished.

'Then the recruitment policy changed,' Price says. 'It's almost like they'd got bigger fish to fry [than developing young players]. Although I was bought for a lot, the money changed and it wasn't seen as so much.'

Still, though, Jol had been sufficiently impressed by what he'd seen of Price in pre-season to promise to hold off signing Crystal Palace's Wayne Routledge – another teenage right-winger and an England team-mate of Price's – who had been identified as a target, if Price continued to develop as hoped.

'And then I broke my leg.'

Price was playing in an FA Youth Cup tie against West Bromwich Albion when, in a challenge with an opposing player, he suffered a fractured tibia and fibula in his right leg. It was his 18th birthday.

'I tried to stand on it and it went completely,' he remembers. 'That set me back. It took me longer than expected to recover.

'It's almost like when you're injured, you're forgotten about, because you're no use to anyone, and that's how they make you feel.'

Routledge was signed the following summer, as was Leeds United's Aaron Lennon, another English right-winger who was two years younger than Price.

'When they signed Routledge, they tried to send me on loan to Stevenage. At the time, Stevenage were in the Conference. In my head, I was thinking, "Are they doing this to try and get rid of me, or are they doing this as a test?"

'I wanted to speak to the club before they sent me out on loan. Then they said there'd been a change of plan and they wanted to send me to Heybridge Swifts. I'd never even heard of Heybridge Swifts.

'I've always thought you can tell what a club thinks of you by where they send you on loan. Like Chelsea, they have some players on loan in the Championship and some in the Conference, and they're the same age – or the best ones go to Vitesse Arnhem, like Mason Mount – so you can almost tell what they think of you. I thought, "I can't see me getting a chance [at Spurs]." I went and spoke to them. I had to go to the academy director, Peter Suddaby.

'I was starting to lose faith; I could see no light at the end of the tunnel at this point. I was moping around. I thought it was best [to leave]. They'd just signed Routledge and I knew they were going to sign Lennon. Routledge was my age; Lennon was younger than me – the writing was on the wall. That's the frustrating thing: you've played with them and against them, you know they're not better than you.'

The lengthy road to recovery from injury only added to Price's disillusionment. In addition to the physical trial of healing and working back to fitness, as a young player without the security of an established reputation at senior level, anxiety and self-doubt sets in.

'When you're injured, it's like the world's passing you by – you're stuck in a rut and you see people progressing. Although it wasn't a million years ago, the technology they've got now probably could have shaved two months off my [recovery time] compared to what I had.

'Then you start to question yourself, thinking, "Am I the same player?" And it was partly because I didn't have the backing of the club to help get me through. We literally had a window you could see training through while I was in the gym – it was horrible. I played for England at under-15s, -16s and -17s, then I broke my leg at 18. You see all the players you played with kicking on and you wonder what could have been. You get disillusioned when you see those people kicking on and you still don't see a light at the end of your tunnel.'

Seeing no ready path to the first team, Price negotiated his release from Tottenham in January 2006. With the payoff he received for the remaining two years of his contract, he invested in property to secure his financial future. His self-belief was shattered, though.

'My confidence was low,' Price admits. 'I didn't want to go trialling around other clubs. I was thinking, "I don't want to go on trial because what if they don't want me? Then I've got to go to another club, and another club." Football is a small world, they'd be saying, "Oh, is he coming to you now? He was with me last week." And that was something I didn't want.

'I decided the best thing for me was to go away.'

The scout who had tried to take Price to Aston Villa as a 14-year-old set him up with GIF Sundsvall in Sweden, who were managed by Englishman Dave Wilson. After a successful trial, Price was offered a permanent deal, staying with the club for a year before six-month spells with Finland's TPS – where he worked under former Bolton Wanderers and Hibernian striker Mixu Paatelainen – and Ljungskile SK of Sweden.

Of his Scandinavian adventure, Price says, 'It was one of the best things I've done, experience-wise. I had one of my best seasons out there.'

He returned to England in 2008 and after a trial with Deportivo La Coruña in Spain had spells in non-league with

Northwich Victoria, Farnborough, Hythe Town and Greenwich Borough.

Still only 31 when we met, Price hasn't fully closed the door on his playing career, but his focus now is on giving back to the game and, like Cherno Samba, helping others learn from his difficult experiences.

'I do one-on-one coaching with young kids, players who have come out of academies, trying to get them back in. Before you can be a good footballer, you have to be a good human, so it's all about making them good people as well, giving them life skills. I don't think enough coaches back then worked on that kind of stuff. People don't realise the mentality you've got to have to play one single game, especially in the Premier League. People don't realise what it takes, and the sacrifice.'

For all the vast and varying life and footballing lessons Price has accumulated since, and for how his experiences at Tottenham, playing abroad, coaching and becoming a father have reshaped him as a person, does that price tag from when he was a 14-year-old still follow him?

'Always. That's all people know about me. People think they know you without knowing you.'

Degree of Separation

I T'S a dream commonly held but one very seldom realised. All over the world, as football-loving siblings grow up side by side, they picture themselves playing in tandem for their favourite team, someday together pulling on that cherished shirt, stepping out side by side into that hallowed arena.

Of the millions upon millions who harbour such an ambition, it becomes reality for an incredibly select few. The chances of any aspiring footballer making a career at the top level are slim enough, so for two from the same family to do so, and within the same team, is to overcome odds so tiny it would make predicting the winning lottery numbers seem as straightforward as remembering one's date of birth.

In this regard, however, Manchester United, the 20-time English champions with a genuine claim to being regarded as the world's biggest club, have history. In total, 11 sets of brothers have represented the Red Devils, stretching back to their humble beginnings as Newton Heath in the late 19th century. Realistically, there was a far greater statistical likelihood of two brothers playing in the same side in those early years, when clubs were local concerns, represented by the best and brightest of the local community. But as the game evolved, and as scouting networks spanned the globe and exorbitant fees were splashed on securing the finest talent from far and wide, the odds began to stack up against aspiring siblings. So when Jimmy and Brian Greenhoff became Old Trafford regulars in the 1970s, and the Neville brothers, Gary and Phil, repeated the feat for club and country in the 1990s and 2000s, it was a much rarer occurrence.

In 2008 two teenager brothers from Petrópolis, a mountain town an hour outside Rio de Janeiro, signed for United, hailing from a location so far from Manchester that even their wildest dreams could not have pictured them under the glare of the Old Trafford floodlights. Fábio and Rafael da Silva, identical twins aged 18 – so alike, indeed, that manager Sir Alex Ferguson could only tell the pair apart by the fact that Fábio wore a wedding ring – became the first pair of brothers from outside the UK to represent the club.

Although identical in appearance, their first-team prospects at Old Trafford proved to be very different. Rafael, a right-back, found himself an immediate contender to assume a position ageing club captain Gary Neville was poised to vacate – between the start of the 2007/08 season until his eventual retirement in 2011, the long-time United No.2 made just 36 Premier League appearances. Left-back Fábio, however, faced the ultimately insurmountable task of supplanting a prime Patrice Evra, arguably the best left-back in the world at the time, and the Brazilian's hopes of doing so were hampered further by a shoulder injury that would require surgery, robbing him of the chance to make the kind of first impression his brother made at Old Trafford.

In the end, Fábio would depart Old Trafford in August 2013 with just 56 first-team appearances under his belt, first signing with Cardiff City, then Middlesbrough in England's second tier. Rafael was a long-time mainstay of the United back four and racked up 169 appearances for the club before joining Lyon in 2015. The two brothers' diverging fortunes with the Red Devils expose a rarely considered dynamic: one twin brother watching the other fulfil the dual dream while his own prospects fade gives rise to a confusing and conflicting set of emotions.

'Me and my brother have a relationship like no one realises; we are so close together,' Fábio begins, prefacing his explanation of how he fought to prevent envy from becoming a bedfellow of the pride he felt for his sibling. 'Of course, I am so happy for everything that is happening to him. I'm not playing regularly but I'm still very happy for him.

'We knew it wasn't going to be easy. We knew that, at 18 years old, coming to Man United, not speaking the language, it's never easy. We were 18 but we left home when we were 11; we were mature for that age.'

What made Fábio's predicament doubly hard to reconcile with was the fact that before they joined United he was regarded as the brighter prospect of the two. Having started his footballing life as a striker in Fluminense's youth ranks, he retained an eye for goal even after being redeployed at left-back, scoring ten times in 13 appearances for Brazil's under-17 side, a team he captained. 'I'm not going to lie, I lost confidence a bit,' Fábio resumes, maintaining a fixed gaze as we sit in an empty press room at Middlesbrough's training ground. 'When we came over, everyone spoke about me: "Oh, Fábio is the good one from them both." I had been the captain, scoring goals. Everyone was saying, "This boy, he is going to be better than the other one."

'It's never easy, even when it's your brother. I dealt with that and I tried my best, but it wasn't easy to replace Patrice at that time. It was in and out. I had some confidence. I reached the national team. But I had some bad moments, no confidence. But,' he concludes philosophically, 'that's football. That's life.'

Although they tended to play on opposite sides of defence, Fábio, being right-footed, was also a selection consideration for right-back, meaning he was occasionally in direct competition with Rafael. A particularly significant instance of this came during the 2010/11 season, when a purple patch towards the back end of the campaign saw Fábio start six of United's final ten league games ahead of Rafael at right-back. Had they been competitive growing up? 'Always,' asserts Fábio. But this time was different: now they were competing with one another for a starting place in the Champions League Final at Wembley against the great Barcelona team of Lionel Messi, Xavi and Andrés Iniesta. Fábio got the nod; Rafael didn't even make the bench.

'It was different, to be honest with you, competing like that. [Rafael] had been on the bench two years earlier for the Champions League Final in Rome. I think he wanted to play so much in that final [in 2011].

'To see that frustration ... Of course, he was happy for me to play, but for it to actually come from you [that he missed out] ...'

It was bitter-sweet. 'Yeah. Because it's your dream too, but to see him like that, it's sad. But the other side: I'm over the moon. I'm going to play in the final of the Champions League. I dreamed of that when I was ten years old. Even five years old. To play in that final. That was the best Barcelona team ever.'

* * *

The 2005 Nike Premier Cup, an under-15s youth tournament held in Hong Kong, proved to be the springboard for Fábio and Rafael's careers – 'It started then: "Oh, these two boys ..."' Fábio remembers of the growing hype.

Ordinarily, only teams who had an endorsement deal with Nike were entered into the competition, but it is Fábio's understanding that, having been alerted to the wealth of talent within the Brazilian side – including the twins – scouts from Manchester United arranged for Adidas-sponsored Fluminense to receive an invite. And Fluminense duly claimed the cup, beating Paris Saint-Germain 1-0 in the final.

After the tournament, the Da Silva twins were invited for a trial with United, along with Fluminense team-mates Arthur – a defender now based in India – and Maicon 'Bolt' – a winger nicknamed after sprint king Usain Bolt, who currently plays for Antalyaspor in the Turkish top flight. Only the brothers impressed enough to inspire greater interest from the English club.

The Da Silvas also received a lucrative offer from Arsenal at this time, but, feeling they owed a debt of loyalty to Fluminense, they left it for their club to decide whose offer to accept. Fluminense made a deal with United, arranging for the gifted siblings to move to Manchester when they turned 18. The initial plan was to loan the pair out to a continental side, both to gain experience and to accumulate enough appearances to satisfy British work permit regulations relating to the employment of non-EU players. The discovery that the boys held Portuguese passports through their grandfather's heritage, however, fast-tracked them into the Red Devils' first-team set-up.

Facing a difficult transition, and despite Fábio being already married, the Da Silvas lived together for the entirety of their time at United, even when Rafael was also married a few years after their arrival. The club set the Brazilian duo up with a house and an English tutor, but having each other, living side by side, made their assimilation to their new life '100 per cent' easier, as Fábio sees it.

'It's tough. People don't realise how hard it is, because the culture is so completely different. If you grew up in Brazil and you only know Brazil, it's completely different. When we arrived at United, in Manchester, we couldn't speak one word of English – not even "water". We didn't come from a poor family, but our schooling level wasn't great, so we didn't learn English. For us, it was hard, but we learned so much.'

Lessons were also gleaned from the failure of older brother Luiz Henrique, seven years the twins' senior, to settle in Europe and make the most of his opportunity when signed by Italian side Brescia at 17. A precociously talented midfielder, Luiz, in the eyes of his younger brother, lacked the required focus and professionalism to forge a sustained career in Serie A.

'He came on his own,' Fábio recalls. 'He came to Brescia. He was very young. I'm not meant to say it but my brother is more talented than us. Actually, everyone said that in Brazil, from our city. But he came young. Me and [Rafael], we came to play football. My other brother had other things. [Luiz] is my brother but I'm here to tell the truth: my brother is not really focussed on football. To be professional and to reach a high level, you have to be focussed 100 per cent on football.'

So, arriving in Manchester, Fábio and Rafael had learned how not to do things, courtesy of Luiz. And their older brother, who moved to England with them and trained with semi-professional sides Altrincham and Radcliffe Borough, encouraged them not to make the same mistakes he made. 'Oh, yeah. He pushed us to be professional. If you ask Rafael, he'd say the same thing.

'I'm not going to say we came from a very poor family, but you have a difficulty of life living in Brazil. We didn't have money. My dad and mama never let us starve – they worked very hard. To see what happened with my brother was actually very frustrating. You see some things you don't want to see, so you want to do it for you, and for your family more. It frustrated my mum and dad to see that my older brother wasn't professional.

'When he was at Brescia, the club were already talking about bringing us over. But my older brother didn't want to stay there. We were ten or 11 years old. We were just joining Fluminense, and Brescia said, "If you're going to stay here bring your brothers as well for the academy." But my brother was not focussed. He was crying, homesick.'

When the Da Silva twins arrived in Manchester, owing to his remarkable scoring record at youth level with Brazil given his full-back position, Fábio was preceded by slightly more hype than Rafael, although both, while identical in appearance – so much so that Fábio was once booked for a foul Rafael had committed in a League Cup tie against Barnsley – offered different strengths.

René Meulensteen was a first-team coach at United from 2007 to 2013, and he remembers his first impression of the pair: 'They were slightly different. Fábio was more of a fluid footballer. They were both right-footed, but because I think Fábio was more of a talented player, he was capable of playing on the left as well.

'They had grown up in Brazil and been educated to play as wing-backs, rather than full-backs, which was a transition for them. Rafael was that sort of no-nonsense, quick, aggressive, tenacious defender who still had qualities going forward; Fábio was more the sort of gentle type. Maybe gentle is not the right word, but more of a fluid footballer, who could play in different positions as well.'

The 'fluid' skills that Fábio possessed, along with his eye for goal, were honed further up the pitch, having begun his footballing life as a striker before being moved back to join his brother in defence. 'At Fluminense,' Fábio remembers, 'when we were 11, my brother started to play right-back because the coach there at the time said, "I think you're a right-back." But he kept me as a striker for maybe another year. So my brother moved to right-back, and after a year or maybe nine months, I go to left-back.

'In the beginning, I liked to score goals, so I thought it was going to be hard for me to score goals. But we did anything the coach said, whatever he thought was going to be good for us.'

This ability to follow instructions to the letter, having complete trust in, and deference to, their manager was a trait the Da Silvas shared, and one that was perhaps the most valued among their arsenal of attributes.

'If you speak with people [who have worked with me] that is one of the things they are going to say,' Fábio says. 'That's one of the best attributes of me and my brother. If a coach says something to us, we're going to do exactly what he says. The coach normally likes that.'

Such tactical discipline was the driving factor behind Ferguson famously deploying the pair in midfield for an FA Cup quarter-final against Arsenal, with eyebrows being raised when the team sheet showed Fábio on the left wing, Rafael right, and a central-midfield pairing of youngster Darron Gibson and versatile defender John O'Shea. *The Telegraph*'s Jim White was present at Old Trafford that day and he recalls his surprise: 'I said, "We're doomed here." [But] it was clear as soon as the game started there was a tactical reason they were there.'

That reason, as Meulensteen has detailed, was to cut off the supplyline to playmaker Cesc Fàbregas by applying relentless pressure on the Arsenal full-backs, Bacary Sagna and Kieran Gibbs; stop Fàbregas, the theory ran, and you stop Arsenal. United won 2-0, with Fábio scoring his second goal for the club just two weeks after opening his account for United in a 4-0 Premier League win over Wigan Athletic.

There was an inevitable buzz surrounding United's signing of two such highly regarded full-backs, not least because they hailed from Brazil, the motherland of exciting, attack-minded full-backs – Fábio names Roberto Carlos and Marcelo as his inspirations, the latter especially, whom he describes as 'magic; so technical,' and who was a teenager in the Fluminense first team when the Da Silvas were beginning to alert global scouts. But beyond any technical gifts, it was the Da Silva twins' work ethic and unfaltering application that quickly saw them revered inside Old Trafford.

'You wouldn't say they were the quickest,' *SB Nation*'s Andi Thomas reasons, 'but they were quick, and basically they seemed very well put together and very resilient; if they got kicked, they would get back up; if something went wrong they would carry on at the same speed and try to fix it.

'I remember one of the earlier bits about them referring to them as terriers or whippets or some kind of particularly tenacious dog. There was that kind of thing about them: they were always very hard-working, very yappy almost, in a complimentary way.

'It was exactly what you want from youth-team prospects. They were so obviously keen to get about the pitch and do what they were there to do. You wouldn't confuse it with arrogance, or even necessarily a kind of overwhelming confidence, it was just a desire to be involved in the football that was going on around them. It was quite heart-warming.

'As a United fan, I felt like I desperately wanted them to succeed. And it helps that it's quite a funny story to have two identical twins playing opposing sides of the pitch for United, and they've both got these kind of cherubic curls in their hair. There was one point where it looked like they were both going to play on the same wing and just overlap each other all the way down the pitch, which would have been quite a sight – "Is my TV broken?"'

* * *

'When we were 15, we went to the first trial,' Fábio says, detailing he and his brother's earliest Manchester movements. 'My brother went first and straight away he trained with Ferguson and the first team – at 15! When Ferguson falls in love with someone, it's just ... and with my brother it was like this: "I want this boy and I want his brother here as well." So I started to come over every three to six months.'

Complications out of their control disadvantaged the brothers in the infancy of their United careers, with a regime change at Fluminense complicating, and almost compromising, the deal, leaving the twins in limbo for six months. 'From January 2008 to July 2008 was very tough because we couldn't play football. And then you are already six months without playing football, games or anything [when starting at United], so we struggled a little bit. In January we came to stay in the first team, but we were not training very well because we had no match fitness. So we then trained a few days [with the first team] and a few days with the under-23s.'

By the time pre-season warm-up fixtures for the 2008/09 campaign came around, Rafael had regained sharpness and was raring to go, impressing on the field with the first team. Fábio, however, could only watch on, a shoulder injury that required surgery keeping him out for five months – 'For me it was a setback,' he confesses, before highlighting the biggest roadblock to his longevity at United: 'And to have Patrice [Evra] in front of me as well ...'

In 2008 France international Evra was arguably the best left-back in the world, a Champions League winner who would go on to accumulate 82 caps for his country and monopolise the left side of the United backline between 2006 and 2014. As undeniably gifted as Fábio was, displacing Evra was a practically unwinnable battle for the then-teenager, even without a shoulder injury.

Rafael, by contrast, enjoyed a virtually clear pathway to regular first-team football. Long-time right-back and club captain Gary Neville was well into his 30s, battling the effects of age and injuries as his career wound down towards retirement in 2011.

'Patrice was so consistent,' Fábio says, confiding that the Frenchman was at once the perfect role model and an insurmountable positional rival. 'He was amazing. At that time, yes, I think he was the best left-back in the world. From there, I was in and out, in and out. But my brother was more consistent. He started to play every game.'

'Yes, that was it: Patrice Evra,' says René Meulensteen when I ask if the world-class French full-back's presence was the main reason behind Fábio's inability to truly establish himself at Old Trafford. 'And there was no discussion about that, because Patrice was naturally left-footed, was a big character in the team, a big character in the dressing room. He was always fit; never injured, never suspended. He was a very reliable character that Ferguson could count on, week in, week out. For a young boy to break in in that position is very, very difficult.

'It was a bit unlucky for Fábio,' Meulensteen continues, 'because at the beginning he got forced to play on the left-hand side, whereas naturally he was a right-footed player. I could also see different positions for Fábio. I could have also seen him as a tandem, with Rafael at right-back and Fábio right-wing or right-midfield, because Rafael could have bombed forward, Fábio could have played a bit more inside.

'But, again, [there was] competition in those positions: we had [Antonio] Valencia, we had Nani at the time, even Cristiano Ronaldo, so it was very hard. Those two young boys broke into one of the best teams United ever had; to then try and establish yourself is obviously very, very difficult.'

Meulensteen then goes on to give a peek behind the curtain at how any hopeful at United was assessed: 'Every game you play is an exam, because you're under the magnifying glass – 99.9 per cent of the games are broadcast on TV, so there is no hiding place. Sometimes, if you are a young player, that can become a bit of a burden. Every position, you look at the player and ask: "Is this player making a difference, to enable Manchester United to win the Premier League or to get to the Champions League final?" If the answer is no, it's simple: they're not good enough.

'The difference is, to be able to succeed at the highest level, which is Man United, you have to have an unbelievable level of consistency in your game, to perform week in, week out, and most likely two times a week, at the very highest level. And then you get a cocktail, a combination of things: the quality that you need, but you need intelligence for the game – can you make the right decisions at the right times? Can you make the right decisions in high-profile games? Can you make the right decisions in pressure situations? What is your mental quality? To be able to relax after a game and get your mind on to the next one. All those things come into it. That is different from the top level to any other level.'

* * *

His run of regular games at the tail end of the 2010/11 season – and indeed his starting berth in the Champions League Final – proved to be a false dawn for Fábio, who featured in just 246 top-flight minutes throughout the following campaign, with a mid-season Achilles tendon rupture being a contributing factor.

In July of 2012 Fábio was sent to Queens Park Rangers on loan for the coming season. The fact that United signed Dutch left-back Alexander Büttner to assume the role of Evra's understudy the very next month was a clear indicator that Fábio had not been sent to Loftus Road simply to recover form and fitness ahead of a triumphant return to Old Trafford, and that rather he was now viewed as surplus to requirements.

'There aren't many players who leave United on loan for a season and then come back to the first team,' Andi Thomas suggests. '[David] Beckham had that early loan with Preston, but that was before he was really on the first-team radar, whereas Fábio came in, drifted out and then went on loan to QPR. That was the signal that it probably wasn't going to happen for him.'

QPR hardly offered the kind of settled, stable environment in which the Brazilian could right his wayward trajectory, either. After barely surviving their first season back in the Premier League the year before, they would finish rock bottom in 2012/13, while Fábio watched Rafael feature regularly as United strolled to another title. Sir Alex Ferguson retired at the end of the season, replaced by David Moyes, but the new manager offered no new dawn for Fábio.

'Things didn't go very well on loan,' admits Fábio. 'I went back to Man United and it was the same thing: play a game, miss four or five out, play another game. I felt I wanted to play football, even if I had to go down [below the Premier League]. I just wanted to enjoy myself.

'For me, personally, I don't want to be in the shadow of anyone; I just want to be myself and express myself. [United] wanted to give me another two-year contract, but I said, "No, it's time to go." Ole Solskjær [then Cardiff City manager] came to my house asking me to join. I said yes. I really liked Ole. I played with him and I worked with him as well when he was under-23 coach [at United]. He wanted me there. I said, "Yeah, let's go. I'm ready for a challenge."'

Although it had been on the cards from the moment he was sent on loan to QPR a year earlier, leaving United still stung. Fábio knew he had no option but to take a step backwards before he could set his sights on a return to the elite level, and this wasn't an easy pill to swallow.

'When you leave a big club like Man United, you tend to lose confidence,' he admits. 'You tend to feel like everything you do is not good enough. I've played in a Champions League Final. I've played many games for Man United.

'Normally, you start from a small club and get to a big club. But in my case, the way I started, I dropped a bit when I moved to other clubs [after leaving United]. It's quite frustrating in some points. But for me, from my point of view, I take it as a challenge, like everything I do in my life: [I do it] for my family, to improve myself every single day. So that's what I put in my mind, every training session and every day.

'You can't let what has happened in the past consume you. "I was in a Champions League final, now I'm in the Championship. That's not good enough." No. You have to live your life every single day and set challenges for yourself. It's not easy to play in the Championship. You have to be tough. You have to be strong. So you have to put this in your mind and that's what I did.'

One might think one of the more upsetting aspects of Fábio's departure from United was that it separated him from his twin brother for the first time in their lives. But Fábio insists he and Rafael – who himself left the Old Trafford club to sign for Lyon in France in 2015 – had long since readied themselves for what they saw as an inevitable parting.

'When we were 13 or 14, we already started to prepare for that, because we knew we played in the same position – because I played right-back as well – it wasn't going to be easy to stay in the same team forever, like my mum and dad had always dreamed.

'We had prepared ourselves for a long time. When it happened, I won't say it was better, but the first year when I left Man United [to join QPR on loan in 2012], my brother was one of the best Man United players.

'I think because we look up to each other so much, sometimes we forget about ourselves a bit.'

Cardiff were in the middle of their first season in the Premier League when he joined in January 2014, but relegation was a near certainty. He stayed with the Bluebirds for two seasons in the second tier before returning to the Premier League with Middlesbrough, although Boro, too, were playing Championship football by the time of Fábio's second season with the club.

We met just days before Middlesbrough were due to face Aston Villa in the Championship play-offs – the winner of the two-leg semi would contest a lucrative Premier League promotion at Wembley later in the month. Although Fábio had been out of the side in the months since Tony Pulis's appointment as manager, he was desperate to return to the top flight and spoke of how he gained a new appreciation for winning post-United.

'It's different in a good way. You don't want to draw games or lose games, but it's a challenge. In Manchester, we weren't happy to win things any more, we were just sad when we lost. No one was happy when we won. Of course it's good to win, but when you win so many things, you come to expect it. And when you lose, everyone's sad. It's different when you win with another team: the winning means more – you celebrate.'

There was to be no celebrating for Middlesbrough, though – they lost out to Villa, who were then beaten in the showpiece final by Fulham.

But Fábio would be playing top-flight football the following season: shortly after our interview, in which he confirmed he'd penned a contract extension with Boro, he surprisingly signed for Nantes in France's Ligue 1.

Earlier, I'd asked what it might be like for Fábio and Rafael to line up opposite one another, having never played against each other at any point before: 'It would be very strange. It would be good, though.'

All eyes on Nantes vs Lyon.

Keeping the Faith

HERE are a number of factors that determine when a footballer is given a professional debut in a competitive game, of which talent is only one. The needs of the team, more often than not, dictate opportunity. A sudden spate of injuries can see a youngster quickly elevated, as can a string of fixtures in close proximity, or a manager looking to appease fans or make a point to an underperforming veteran. Regardless of the circumstances, though, most players have experienced their first taste of first-team action by their late teens; some have to wait until they pass 20, while a particularly gifted few break through as young as 16 or 17. Fewer still make their senior bow at 15, with the likes of Pelé, Diego Maradona, Neymar and Sergio Agüero all beginning their careers at this absurdly early age.

John Bostock also belongs to this exclusive club.

In October 2007, during a Championship fixture against Watford at Selhurst Park, Bostock replaced Ben Watson with 20 minutes to play to make his Crystal Palace debut. He was 15 years and 287 days old. This made the London-born midfielder the 17th-youngest player in the history of English professional football, and he remains the youngest player ever to appear for Crystal Palace's first team.

'I had an inkling that I was going to be involved,' says Bostock, still just 26 years old and playing for Lens in the French second tier when we spoke. 'I came home from school and my dad had a phone call saying, "John, you are going to be in the squad tonight." I tried to get a little sleep in but I couldn't sleep, I was so buzzing.

'I came to the stadium and I think at the time I wasn't technically allowed to be in the dressing room because I was so young. I couldn't be in a men's dressing room, so I won't say if I was or wasn't,' he laughs. 'My family came to the game and watched. To make your debut in front of your family at your own stadium was just immense.'

And they are a family of die-hard Palace fans, with Bostock owning a Selhurst Park season ticket from the age of five; he describes having been part of the club's academy, let alone playing for the first team, as 'an honour'.

'It was a Tuesday game,' he says, continuing to recount his professional debut, 'so I had to go back to school the next day. It was mayhem. There were photographers at the door. I think because I had good family around me I could really enjoy it. I didn't feel like I had to endure it. I enjoyed it because it was something I had worked for; it wasn't like it just came over night. You work from the age of five and six to make your debut. OK, for it to happen so young was an extra bonus. But it became a reality and it was so nice to enjoy that period.'

'He didn't look out of place, did he?' grinned Palace manager Neil Warnock after the game, a 2-0 victory in which the teenage newcomer lit up the closing stages with assured passes and chest-out confidence. 'I don't know yet how far he can go, but you've seen what he can do. I had to have a word with him at the end because there was a bit of showboating. He probably played a bit too much "football" in places,' Warnock joked, 'but we will soon knock that out of him.'

Warnock had been so impressed by the teenager, who was combining a high-level football career with his GCSE studies, that he handed him his first start just a week later, in an away trip to Cardiff City.

Bostock says, 'It was funny because I was starting in midfield at 15 years old, and to see some of the players I was up against, like [Jimmy Floyd] Hasselbaink and Robbie Fowler, two absolute legends. So to play against those guys was really enjoyable. I remember after that game I got home at like two or three o'clock and had school the next day. It was a very surreal experience.'

Bostock's arrival into the first-team fold came sooner than most would have expected, and the maturity and assuredness with which he handled his step up, both from a technical and psychological standpoint, was hugely impressive. Palace weren't getting carried away, though; they had a long-term vision for the youngster and he played just two more first-team games that season. 'John's better playing 100 games with us over two or three years than being number 20 pick at Chelsea or Manchester United, isn't he?' said Warnock after the Watford game. 'And we'll keep his feet on the floor.'

Although every move Bostock has subsequently made has been executed with feet and ego firmly grounded, he chose not to stick to Palace's plan, joining Tottenham Hotspur the following summer in what transpired to be an acrimonious split from his boyhood club. Still only 16, he became Spurs' youngest-ever player, another record he still holds. But circumstances beyond his control set him off on a European odyssey which is only now seeing him deliver on the promise he showed more than a decade earlier.

* * *

Even before his debut at 15, Bostock was renowned as a special prospect. Aged six, his father took him to an open trial with Crystal Palace. Despite initially being told he was too young to participate, he ended up being one of only two players signed from a group he estimates to have numbered 200 at the trial day.

Word started to spread of this precocious talent on Palace's books, first around London, then nationally, with Arsenal, Chelsea and Manchester United all designing to poach him from Palace. At 14, the mighty Barcelona, who were champions of Europe at the time, made an offer for the youngster.

'Of course, of course,' Bostock says, admitting he was tempted by a move to the Camp Nou, where he would have joined Barça's famous La Masia talent factory. 'Everybody knows Barcelona is like a footballing dream. But I had some very good options in London and my family decided, for now, it'd be best if I chose to develop in London. That was the thinking back then. But yeah, of course, that was a surreal moment.'

Seeing the steady flow of Palace youth products making their way into the first team from the club's own prolific academy reassured Bostock that he was in good hands.

'I think you could see, like Ben Watson and Tom Soares, those players who were maybe one or two generations older than me, you could always see that if you were good you were going to play at Palace. It was clear to see that there was a route through to the first team.

'My generation was really good. There was Victor Moses, Nathaniel Clyne, Sean Scannell. It was a good team. You could see that if you were patient and worked hard you would get in the first team. That was always something to hold on to at Palace.

'The Chelsea system,' he continues, 'is a whole different evolution of the development pathway. I think the way they have gone about it is, "We'll give you a chance, but it won't be here." Whereas Palace have proven themselves over the last 15 or 20 years to have one of the best academies in the country for producing players and giving them a chance. Maybe Southampton pip Palace to the number-one spot, but Palace have always been known for producing really good players.

'When you are a young player and you realise there is a route into the first team, I think it gives you that little bit more desire to get there, because you know that if you do the business there is not a blockage there.'

That being said, once Bostock reached the first team, he didn't necessarily feel there was a coherent plan laid out for his development. The majority of super-talented teenagers who make early breakthroughs at senior level impress via speed, athleticism and daring, with holes in their tactical understanding and discipline. Bostock was different: he was a 15-year-old boy with the game intelligence and vision of a much more experienced pro; in order to properly nurture his talent he had to be handled differently.

'It was every game as it comes, really,' he says, conceding there was no bespoke plan for his development at Selhurst Park. 'I had confidence from Neil Warnock. But then there was another coach at the time who I could tell didn't really think my style was suited to playing in the Championship, so he kind of made me know that. That made me a little bit confused as a young kid coming up to hear that. It was like you don't really know where you stand.

'Neil Warnock gave me a lot of confidence. I think every player that works under him will tell you how much of a good manager he is, especially as a man-manager. But I was just taking every game as it comes. Those sorts of situations don't come along every week or every year, in terms of trying to develop a 15-year-old kid who is already in the first team. I think we were all learning as we went along.'

An England under-16s regular from the age of 14, by 16 Bostock was captain of the under-17s, a year younger than most of his team-mates but, unlike his Three Lions colleagues, he had already made the step up to the men's game with his club. Developmentally, he was quickly outgrowing his peers. At the end of the 2007/08 season he decided he was ready for a new challenge, leaving second-tier Palace to sign for Tottenham in the Premier League.

'It was at a time of my life where a big decision had to be made: whether to stay at Palace or move elsewhere for my development. And the people around me and I thought that it was in my best interests to go to Spurs.

'A development plan was put in place. I was going to be training with the first team and playing the majority of matches with the reserves, while being given a few chances to play in the first team. It just sounded like that was the best move for me. That's the thinking at the time behind the move. All the right things were said.'

Spanish tactician Juande Ramos was Spurs manager at the time, but the deal was set up by the club's director of football, Damien Comolli. I spoke to Comolli about the process of identifying Bostock as a target and attracting him to Tottenham.

'I think we followed John for two years before signing him,' he said. 'A good two years of watching him on a regular basis.

'We were extremely attractive for young English or British players because we had a lot of them in the first team. They were queueing up to join us. We were getting quite a lot of calls from agents and fathers [of young players] saying, "We want to join you."

'We had the likes of [Aaron] Lennon, [Gareth] Bale and Chris Gunter getting into the first team. We were not only signing young, talented players, we were playing them. That's how we would have approached John and his dad.'

Leaving Palace, the club he grew up supporting and had played for since the age of six, wasn't a decision Bostock took lightly. 'Especially because of the way it happened,' he says, in reference to the bitter fallout that ensued. 'And also, when you are 15, you have a say, but you are very influenced by the people around you and what they say. You trust them. Nobody knows the future, nobody knows exactly what is going to happen, but you trust their judgment. Being a kid, you need to trust somebody. Somebody who knows more about you and can see the picture a little bit broader.

'I am still a Palace fan, I love the club. So yeah, to leave the way I did, it was a sour taste. But at the time it was a decision made in good faith. We thought it was the right time and the right one.'

The fact that Bostock was not yet 17 meant he wasn't old enough to have been tied down to a professional contract at Palace. Therefore, he was free to negotiate with any other club; if he agreed to a move and the two sides couldn't come to terms on a transfer fee, a Professional Football Compensation Committee (PFCC) tribunal decides how much the buying club should pay, and the figure they determine is non-negotiable. This is how it played out with Bostock's move to Spurs, with the PFCC deciding Tottenham should pay £700,000 for the midfielder, a figure which could have risen (but never did) to as much as £1.25m if conditional bonuses were triggered.

Simon Jordan, the outspoken Palace chairman at the time, was incensed. How, he reasoned, could a player wanted by Manchester United, Chelsea, Arsenal and Barcelona be worth such a paltry figure? Jordan, apoplectic, withdrew the Bostock family's Selhurst Park season tickets.

'He said, "They won't be coming to the stadium again; we'll take their tickets off them,"' Bostock remembers. 'From that day, we haven't been back to Selhurst Park. I went back once. I was on loan at Hull and we played at Selhurst Park, but I didn't get on in that game, I was on the bench. It was awful. I was so emotional and had tears in my eyes. It was an awful experience.

'But I understand how Simon Jordan felt, looking back,' he continues. 'He produced a young kid, and for whatever reason he felt that he hasn't got the money he wanted for him. Football is a beautiful game, but I also understand that if you own a club, the club is number one, not the players. I don't hold any ill feelings towards Simon Jordan whatsoever. You can't always control the way people react to certain decisions.'

I reached out to Jordan for comment on this saga, but the former Palace chairman politely declined, saying, 'I have no particular interest in commenting on John Bostock. All of my comments regarding this are well documented back in the day and a matter of public record.'

So instead we turn to some choice snippets from an interview Jordan gave to *The Telegraph* in June 2008, days after the tribunal's decision: 'For a tribunal to reward a purportedly bigger football club in Tottenham to take one of the most gifted young English players in the country for a sum of £700,000 is nothing short of scandalous ... The tribunal, in my view, are supposed to reflect the conditions of the transfer marketplace. And they came up with a figure of £700,000 for a player who has captained his country at under-17 level, who is perceived to be one of the best youngsters in the country ... We had a £900,000 offer from Chelsea when he was 14 which we turned down. It's beyond me and it makes me question why I bother with football.

'I have an academy who have produced a world-class footballer for someone else and got paid two-and-sixpence for it. We weren't unrealistic – we didn't try to be clever and put a value of £5m on the player.

'He was looked after for a long time with bespoke training specifically for his development. It was John Bostock's year next season at Palace and we weren't going to sign central midfielders because we wanted to clear a path for him. He'd have got into our team this year and established himself as a first-team player at a big club. I'm not so sure that's going to happen for him now.'

* * *

Bostock's controversial move to Spurs was confirmed on 30 May 2008, with the PFCC settling the dispute of his transfer fee shortly after. The 16-year-old playmaker was able to enjoy the summer break, looking ahead to new, greener pastures at White Hart Lane. However, a spanner was soon thrown into the works. Without a win in their opening eight Premier League fixtures of the 2008/09 season, Tottenham relieved manager Juande Ramos of his duties, along with many of his backroom staff and director of football Damien Comolli. Harry Redknapp was drafted in, abolishing the structure previously in place with technical guidance above the manager. He quickly turned results around, taking Spurs from rock bottom to an eventual eighth-place finish. But Bostock's whole development plan as devised by Comolli, his reason for leaving his beloved Palace and shunning other offers in favour of Spurs, had been wiped out.

Bostock was still given a first-team debut by Redknapp, coming off the bench in a UEFA Cup game against Dinamo Zagreb ten days short of his 17th birthday, enough to make him Tottenham's youngest-ever player (a record he took from Ally Dick, the subject of this book's first chapter). But it was one of only four appearances he would ever make for the club. Redknapp found Spurs in the relegation zone, so he hardly had the luxury of carefully blooding the club's young hopefuls; his was a rescue mission. Five months earlier, Spurs had been the right choice for Bostock's next step primarily because of the faith they put in young players. Now, the north London club had made a strategic 180, bringing in experienced heads Robbie Keane, Carlo Cudicini and Wilson Palacios during the January transfer window.

'They tried to get rid of Gareth Bale after I left, so that is the proof in the pudding that they tried to change strategy,' Comolli explains, 'until Daniel Levy put a stop to it and said, "This is not right."'

Bostock said, 'I joined Spurs with all the expectations around my name. I played four or five games in the reserves and I scored seven goals. I was training with the first team. So I thought, "I'm off to a blinder here." I went on pre-season tour with the first team. It just felt like it was a step of progress. I'm at a huge club in Spurs and there is a plan for my development here.

'Then Comolli left and Juande Ramos left. Harry Redknapp came in. He gave a few kids their debuts, and I was one of them, and I'll forever be grateful for that. He's a good manager with lots of experience. He knows how to bring kids through who he believes in. But, apart from the manager being there, there wasn't actually anybody there overseeing my development.

'What I mean by that is we had two great academy managers – Alex Inglethorpe, who is now at Liverpool, and John McDermott, the academy director, who is unbelievable. But in terms of somebody overseeing the process of me progressing – I'm talking about my loans, my next steps in my development, what would be in my best interests – I felt like that had been lost with Comolli leaving. There's nothing you can change. There were a lot of kids coming through and at that point I just felt like one of a number.'

The move that was supposed to have provided new challenges, a step-up in competition and the chance to test himself at a higher level ultimately saw Bostock forced to take developmental backward steps.

'The club saw that it was in my best interests to play back with the under-18s again. That just blew my confidence. I felt as though I'd already proved myself at that level a few years back. To go back there, where everyone is expecting you to be the best player by a country mile and perform every single week, that was a real tough test for me.'

Between November 2009 and his eventual Spurs exit in 2013, Bostock was loaned out five times, making just one senior appearance for his parent club in this time. While he initially welcomed the chance to go out and play first-team football elsewhere, rather than remain at under-18 and reserve level with Spurs, loan move after loan move left him in stasis. These temporary spells away from White Hart Lane robbed Bostock of continuity during crucial developmental years. He was played out of position more often than not, in a variety of leagues and under managers whose approaches and demands differed vastly.

He went from Brentford in League One to Hull City in the Championship, from Sheffield Wednesday in League One to Swindon in League Two, where he played under the eccentric and controversial Paolo Di Canio – 'I know that because I've worked under Di Canio, I can work under any manager in the whole world' – and finally to Toronto FC in Major League Soccer.

While there were moments in which Bostock demonstrated his immense talent during these spells – he scored a brace on his Brentford debut and a 30-yard rocket in his first game for Bradford – he never played more than 11 games during any of these loan periods.

'Having been sent on loan so many times,' Bostock remembers of this testing period of his career, 'maybe that was a message that I didn't really have a future at the club. When you are on loan, you think about playing for your future and impressing other suitors. My character is: I don't give up on anything until it is impossible. Even then, I don't think it is impossible.

'I came back from loan with Sheffield Wednesday and I found myself playing in the Cup against Cheltenham for Spurs. I came on for ten minutes. So that was a surprise. You never know when you are going to be called upon.

'I always had the hope that I was going to be a regular at Spurs and get a chance to show myself. I believe that, especially with my kind of game, my kind of style, when you play at a high level, it's more suited to my style. When you play in the lower leagues and you're trying to get on the ball and express yourself to get the team ticking, it's not really suited in those leagues. So I always felt like if I had the chance to play in the Premier League for Spurs I would have flourished.'

The way things worked out for Bostock at Spurs left him questioning whether professional football was for him. While the game offers no guarantees, he had been so far ahead of the curve in his mid-teens that few would have anticipated how badly the Spurs move would turn out. However, a devout Christian, he drew strength from his faith through this testing time.

'I grew up as a kid not knowing anything or believing in anything in terms of religion,' he says. 'I believed in myself, football and my dreams – that was it. But I went to church for the first time in my life and it was like what the guy at the front was saying was speaking directly to me and my life. From that day – I think I was 15 or 16 – I became a Christian. Being a Christian, having faith, it grounds you. You have a foundation that doesn't change. Football changes every week – you win, you lose, you get injured, you don't play – but my relationship with God doesn't change, and He doesn't change. Having that security and that foundation that my life is built upon – not just my career, but my life, my family – has been the biggest part of my life, my biggest strength. God is my rock.

'I think if I didn't have my faith, I'd be quick to compare myself to other people, maybe be disappointed or get disheartened, but I realise I'm on my own journey. All that happens to me happens for a reason. And nothing is wasted; every negative that happens to me can become a positive. I look at my life and I see it differently, and that's because of my relationship with God.'

Speaking to Bostock, his emotional intelligence is abundantly clear. While many young men in his situation during this period would have lost focus and sunk into patterns of negative thought, he remained positive.

'I think you have to because football, a bit like life, is not a destination: you are looking to be the best player you can be. Nobody knows what limit you have, so you have to keep going, keep grinding. That's how you fulfil your potential. That's how you learn what you are supposed to be. I have had a lot of ups and downs, but I think you learn more about yourself in the difficult times. I've been forced to see my development like that.'

In 2013, in a meeting with senior coaching staff members Tim Sherwood, Les Ferdinand and Chris Ramsey, Bostock was told the club would not be retaining his services when his contract expired that summer. Five years after signing for Spurs, with the world at his feet, the 21-year-old was a free agent.

'For a player who had been promised the world but hadn't been given the chance to show what he is capable of doing, to then be able to go on a free contract – it's difficult. In that moment you question your ability, you question whether the game is for you. You question a lot. But I realised there was nothing else in the world I'd rather be doing than playing football, so I had to get away from the pressure of the media and the voices. I just had to go and play and enjoy the game. The most games I had ever played in one season was maybe ten or 11. That's including substitute appearances. I'd never been given the chance to play and learn and express myself.'

Bostock's name, forever synonymous with his teenage ascent, still carried some weight. He had interest from 'one or two' English clubs, but offers from the likes of Manchester United and Chelsea were by now a distant memory.

Instead he elected for a move abroad, joining Royal Antwerp, managed by former Chelsea and Leeds United striker Jimmy Floyd Hasselbaink, in the Belgian Second Division.

'Hasselbaink was so keen to get his hands on me, to work with me and just let me grow. I had an option in the Belgian First Division but I felt like I couldn't miss out on working with Hasselbaink. And when a manager says, "Just come and play," that was music to my ears. I had to take a step back, a step down. Even though I knew it would be a bit embarrassing on paper, I knew it would do me good in the long run.'

* * *

19 May 2018. As the final whistle blows, bringing to a close Lens' 3-1 victory over Niort, the fans inside the Stade Bollaert-Delelis begin to celebrate their side's clinching of third place, thus setting a date for a promotion/relegation play-off with Lorient, who finished 18th in the French top tier. In one of the most unique and fascinating promotion races in recent memory, six clubs entered the final matchday of the 2016/17 Ligue 2 season separated by just three points, all battling to finish inside the top two places and earn an automatic spot in Ligue 1. The Lens fans deserve their victory. Only four clubs in the top tier had a higher average attendance than the *Sang et Or* throughout the campaign and many view Lens to have the best support in the country.

But the celebrations quickly fade, replaced by stunned silence as news from the Stade de Reims filters through. Thanks to a 96th-minute Emmanuel Bourgaud goal against Reims, Amiens jumped from sixth place into second, leapfrogging Troyes and pushing Lens out of the promotion play-off place in the most dramatic and heartbreaking fashion.

Bostock sits helplessly on the Lens bench, refreshing his phone for updates and informing his team-mates of the bad news. He'd been named Ligue 2 Player of the Season four days earlier but injury meant he could only watch on as events unfolded.

'Everyone was saying to me, "What's the score? What's the score?"' Bostock remembers. 'Until the last six seconds – because our game had finished and the other game still had time to play – I was saying, "We've made it. We've made third place." But then I looked at my phone and saw that Amiens had scored with the last kick of the game.

'I told them. I realised that all the fans got the same news on their phones. It was such a weird feeling, hearing 40,000 fans go silent.'

Bostock's form during his three seasons in Belgium had reignited interest in him. Under Hasselbaink at Antwerp, he showcased his creative skills and eye for a pass by assisting 16 goals, helping the club reach the play-offs. 'To work under Hasselbaink,' he reflects, 'was fundamental in my gaining confidence and enjoying the game again.'

After one season with Antwerp, he moved to OH Leuven in the summer of 2014, another second-tier Belgian side but one with serious designs on bouncing back up to the top flight, having just been relegated. With Bostock pulling the strings in midfield, scoring 13 goals and registering an incredible 19 assists, Leuven were promoted via the play-offs, with the Englishman named the Second Division's Player of the Season.

'I've always wanted to play in the first division somewhere. I've always wanted to play in the Premier League of a country. So to leave the second division in Belgium and to take your team to the first division, where you are going to play the Anderlechts, the Brugges, the Genks, it felt good. It was hard work and the sacrifice paid off.'

Leuven were relegated again from the Belgian Pro League the following season, but Bostock had impressed individually and would soon be on the move. Hasselbaink, now manager of

Queens Park Rangers, was keen to take his former charge back to England, but an offer from Lens, in France's Ligue 2, enchanted the former Spurs man.

'We had some interesting offers after that year. Lens came in. I didn't really want to play in France, to be honest with you. But when I came and saw the club and the stadium, I just thought, "Wow".

'I had offers in Serie A and in different countries, but [Lens] just felt right, so it was the choice that we made. They were in the Champions League ten or 15 years ago. They are a big club with big fans. We were in the Second Division last year and we were only one point away from winning promotion. We've got the fourth-highest attendance in France.'

Bostock needed no settling-in period in France, immediately becoming a key player for his new club, driving Lens' promotion push with five goals and four assists as a deep-lying playmaker in Alain Casanova's side. He was again named the division's Player of the Year, but promotion proved allusive. News of his European resurgence had evidently gotten as far as one of his former managers in England, though, with Harry Redknapp sufficiently impressed to try and sign the midfielder while in charge of Birmingham City in the Championship in 2017. 'Yeah, there was interest there,' Bostock says. 'I think it's definitely on the cards that we could return to England one day.'

Taylor Moore, a fellow former England youth captain, was a gifted young defender progressing through the ranks at Lens when Bostock arrived at the Stade Bollaert-Delelis. Moore now plays for Bristol City in the Championship, having left France shortly after Bostock joined the club, but he remembers being struck by his countryman's technical mastery and mental fortitude during early training sessions together.

'His left foot,' Moore enthuses. 'He's got a very, very good left foot. Also, his vision and the capability he has to pick a pass out that not many people on that pitch would see, even people in the stands sometimes wouldn't see. And his vision while he's playing is very, very good.

'His mental toughness – whether that's on or off the pitch – it was striking to see someone who had been so high and yet so low still have an approach to his everyday professional life like he did.

'The technical side of his game,' Moore continues, 'you realise, OK, there was a big hype about him when he was 15 – this is why.'

* * *

At the time we spoke, Bostock was in his second season with Lens and had six months remaining on his contract. Asked about the future, he was candid about keeping his options open and 'looking ahead', admitting, 'We'll see what will happen next, but I feel like I've built up some credit over the last few years. Hopefully I'll be able to be where I should be.'

It transpired that he was on the move just a few weeks after our interview, joining Bursaspor in the Turkish Süper Lig in January 2018, jumping at the opportunity to work under former Lyon coach Paul Le Guen.

He made his Bursaspor debut in February, playing the full 90 minutes in a 2-2 draw against champions Beşiktaş. But injuries limited him to just eight appearances in total for the Turkish side, and he was on the move again in the summer, back to France – but this time to Ligue 1, to sign for Toulouse. A decade after he joined Spurs as a 16-year-old, seemingly destined for stardom, Bostock has finally established himself as a key player for a club in one of Europe's major divisions.

European football journalist Andy Brassell has followed Bostock's career closely since he left English football as a 21-year-old and is quick to praise the midfielder's strength of will, having taken the long road to the top, both literally and metaphorically.

'Given the experience he had early on,' Brassell says, 'to go and do something else, to not quit, to have that sense of wanting to broaden your horizons, is really impressive. The pressure that he was under as a teenager would have crushed and finished a lot . of people. So, for him to go and find something else and mature as a player I think is amazing.

'The way he has developed as a player is not that surprising when you speak to him and you see how he is as a person. He's someone who always wants to grow. The fact that he has been able to do that and not take the baggage with him from what he went through as a teenager – which sounded really intense – is really impressive.'

Bostock's determination to succeed was strengthened in 2017 after he walked away unscathed from a serious car accident. He had been back in England during a break with Lens and collided head on at 70mph with a drunk driver coming down the wrong side of the road. The passenger in the other car was killed and pictures of Bostock's destroyed car show just how close he came to serious injury or worse.

'When you are involved in something like that, you are always thinking "What if? What if?" and sometimes you get flashbacks,' he told *The Guardian*. 'I couldn't sleep for a night, it has a big effect on your family but it also made me realise I have a destiny to achieve; I am here for a reason.'

Recently, Jadon Sancho has earned widespread praise for leaving Manchester City to test his skills and seek first-team opportunities abroad, signing for Borussia Dortmund. His boldness has been rewarded with regular minutes in the Bundesliga that he might not have gotten at talent-rich City and a senior England call-up. Talented British youngsters Marcus McGuane (Barcelona), Jonathan Panzo (Monaco), Chris Willock (Benfica) and others are hoping to tread a similar developmental path overseas.

When Bostock made his move to Antwerp in 2013, he did so under different circumstances to the above in-demand youngsters, but his subsequent success has blazed a trail for those who followed. And, enriched by his experiences, he would recommend that more young players do the same.

'I think a lot of players, if they don't make it at a big club, they just look down,' Bostock says. 'But you can look sideways, look at other options, look abroad. You would see there are a lot of clubs you could go and play for and develop.

'When I came over and left England, it was, "Yeah, he's from Spurs, but let's see if he can play." And when they saw that, there were no question marks from stuff they've heard before, they just judged me on my performances, which is what you want as a player. It was freeing to just get judged on how you play with no question marks around it.

'I feel like there's no blueprint for success or for a player's journey. Very rarely do you get a player come through a club who stays there their whole career. I think a lot of players, if they were in my situation when I was wondering if this game was still for me, they might not have taken that risk I took.

'The sacrifices you make, to be away from your family and out of the culture you know, it's paid off. Going abroad has been pivotal in my career. I felt like I proved to myself that I can play at a very high level. And I'm still getting better.

'It feels like a long time ago when I made my debut as a 15-year-old. I've had a lot of experiences, ups and downs. But,' he concludes, 'I've proven to myself that you just can't give up. You've just got to keep pressing and pushing, and you never know where you'll end up.

'That's my journey. It's been a bit unorthodox, but fruitful nonetheless.'

It's an ongoing journey, though. Still only 26, Bostock may yet have a decade left in the game, and there is one major ambition he is yet to realise, some unfinished business he intends to return to.

'The Premier League is the dream,' he admits. 'To watch *Match of the Day* every single week and to not be able to play on that platform would be disappointing. I'm confident I could play in the Premier League. I'm confident I can mix it with some of the best players. And I feel like, the journey I've been on, whatever opportunity I do get I'll take with both hands.

'Going through hard times makes you appreciate opportunities and success more than you usually would.'

The Weight

STANDING 6ft 3ins, hair shorn to the bone and nearly every visible inch of flesh from the neck down covered in tattoos, Martin Škrtel cuts an intimidating figure. What the Slovak lacked in subtlety and full cognisance of the art of defending's finer points during his eight years as a Liverpool regular, he made up for with brawn by the bucketload, all bludgeoning, ink-covered, sinuous limbs, power and prowess.

So Škrtel, as physically robust a defender as the Premier League had to offer, was quite a proposition for a scrawny, 19-year-old striker, whose exposure to competitive men's football up to that point numbered minutes in the low hundreds.

'He put Škrtel against me once in training,' Adam Morgan says, recalling a 2013 session at Liverpool's Melwood training ground, in which then-Reds manager Brendan Rodgers designed for the youngster to come in direct competition with the towering centre-half. 'And Škrtel absolutely battered me. Not nasty, but kicking me, moving me out the way.'

This was not some kind of punishment for an indiscretion, nor a case of a manager wanting to let a promising upstart know who's boss. This was, plain and simple, a test: Rodgers wanted to gauge Morgan's physical readiness for top-level football. '100 per cent,' Morgan agrees. But it was a test he stood no chance of passing. 'If I'd have bullied him, it wouldn't really have changed anything. I still would have been told I needed games. And I knew I needed games. It was frustrating me.'

These were the first months of friction for Morgan at Liverpool, having risen through the club's youth system, into the reserves and then the first-team set-up with relative ease –

always scoring, always ahead of the curve developmentally. Now, though, early in the 2013/14 season, which would eventually see Liverpool agonisingly miss out on a first league title in almost a quarter of a century, he could feel himself bumping against a glass ceiling.

'My head went a little bit. Nothing was happening. I'd had a year left on my contract, then it was six months. Brendan Rodgers said, "You need to go out and experience games. We've got [Luis] Suárez, [Daniel] Sturridge ... We're not going to offer you a new deal." My agent said we probably could have pushed for a new deal, another year, but we didn't want that.'

A lifelong Liverpool supporter who'd been on the club's books since the age of five and had regularly bundled inside Anfield to worship his heroes long before rubbing shoulders with them, the realisation that the ambition of emulating his idols had faded from view cut Morgan deep. After meeting with Rodgers, being told he wasn't ready, that his future lay elsewhere, Morgan made it back to his car before he could no longer brave-face the devastation. He sobbed inconsolably in the Melwood car park.

* * *

'As a young boy, I used to love Liverpool,' Morgan explains, nursing a glass of water as we sit in the restaurant area of a hotel a stone's throw from Liverpool's John Lennon airport. Over his shoulder, at the bar, sit two Irish Liverpool fans who've flown in for the night's Champions League game at Anfield. Little do they know, one of their beloved club's most promising home-grown talents of the last decade is sitting on the edge of earshot, cathartically unburdening himself by sharing his story, baring his soul, before dashing off to the gym, determined to maintain peak fitness in readiness of a testing season with Halifax Town in England's fifth tier. 'I'd go home and away every week with my dad,' he continues, pressing home his devotion to Liverpool FC – his club; his father's club; his father's father's club.

Morgan was first scouted by Liverpool at the preposterously young age of five, invited to train with the club once a week before eventually penning terms at nine, increasing contact with the club to two weekly sessions. His talent was no secret locally, and he had other offers, from Blackburn Rovers and Manchester United. But if Liverpool were an option, they were the only option.

While certainly a point of immense pride, representing the club he adored quickly became the norm for the young Morgan, who took elevation through the age groups in his stride, scoring freely. 'It was easy. Just doing what I do, enjoying myself. It was a natural progression all the way up. Then at 15, I started thinking, "Will I get a scholarship?"'

As the outstanding prodigies of their age group, Morgan and Raheem Sterling, the future £49m England international, were the first to be awarded scholarship deals by none other than club legend 'King' Kenny Dalglish, Morgan Sr's hero, who was first-team manager at the time.

A scholarship meant the chance to train every day at Melwood, with the first team training on an adjacent pitch, passing the likes of Steven Gerrard and Jamie Carragher in the corridor, exposure to the life, the lifestyle, the standards of elite-level pros.

'Looking back, I've had some unbelievable times over the years, but that was probably my most enjoyable,' Morgan remembers, coming over beatific as his mind's eye runs a halcyon slideshow, 'because it was full-time football at Liverpool – it was what I wanted to do.

'I was banging the goals in, everyone was talking about me. I think I scored 35 goals or something stupid like that.

'When you are a first-year scholar, you don't really play [for the academy side] every week because the second years are there, but I was playing every week, playing with some great players. Our starting team was: Jamie Stevens in goal, who's at Barnet now; "Flanno", Jon Flanagan, at right-back; Andre Wisdom, centre-half; Matty McGibbon, another local lad who was really good who doesn't play any more; Jack Robinson, left-back, QPR; Conor Coady, Wolves, centre-mid; Craig Roddan, who is at Sligo in Ireland; then we had Suso on the right, who's at AC Milan; Sterling on the left, who is obviously at Man City; Krisztián Adorján, who plays in Italy now; and then me up top. We had a really good team.

'We played in the Youth Cup that year, we beat Palace, Southend 8- or 9-0, and I scored five goals. Then we got Man United in the quarter-final, 20,000 people at Anfield.' This particular game, against the equally talent-packed under-18s side from Liverpool's bitter rivals, broadcast live on LFC TV, will for many fans be the moment Morgan came to their attention.

'I scored two. We were 2-0 up at half-time but ended up losing 3-2. Ravel Morrison scored two. I was heartbroken. [Paul] Pogba played, Jesse Lingard, Ravel Morrison, Will Keane, Michael Keane, and the goalie, Sam Johnstone. That was the final really, we were the best two teams. They played Sheffield United next and battered them something like 5-0.

'But we battered everyone, that was really enjoyable. We went close to winning the league. Loads of us had England commitments. I was playing for England as well. Everything was going well. Every time I played, I scored.

'The first age group I was called up for England was under-16s. Kenny Swain was the manager. I used to never get picked for the Victory Shield. I used to think, "What's going on here?" A few of the lads in my team were getting picked – "Why aren't I getting picked?"

'But then Kenny Swain came to one of our matches, and I knew who he was. I scored four against Derby, and we won 4-0. The next week I was in the England squad. And it just went from there, every England squad. I don't think I missed one for three years.'

Morgan shared with me a photograph from an England under-19s meet-up against Denmark at the Amex Stadium in 2011. Pictured were the 11 players chosen to start the game. Along with clubmates Flanagan and Coady, who captained the side, he was partnered in attack by Harry Kane. The two strikers have walked vastly divergent paths in the time since, with Kane now England captain at senior level and a World Cup Golden Boot winner, perhaps the finest No.9 in world football. But back then, Morgan and Kane were equals. In fact, there were doubts over Kane's top-line potential even beyond his initial breakthrough at Tottenham Hotspur, whereas few ever questioned Morgan's ability to score goals at any level.

The inevitable buzz began to grow louder. Liverpool, a club indelibly linked to its local community, had produced a slew of home-grown first-team stars in the 1990s, with the likes of Steve McManaman, Robbie Fowler and Jamie Carragher all breaking through to ensure Scouse representation in red. Yet, through many false dawns, Liverpool fans had been denied a local-lad-come-good to truly pin their hopes on since Steven Gerrard's emergence almost a decade and a half earlier. There was a desperation among fans for one of their own to make the grade. And there was no more fitting candidate than Morgan.

Liverpool fan Dan Fieldsend, author of *The European Game* – a triumphant close-up examination of elite continental clubs' best practices, with a particular focus on youth development – remembers this pining for a new Scouse superstar: 'When Adam Morgan was making this name for himself, around 2012, this was a time when we'd been starved of young players coming through for years. People were talking about Dani Pacheco as the next big thing. People were hoping that Adam Morgan coming through would be a bit of a lifeblood and inject that Scouse tradition that was being phased out at the time.

'I remember he did that celebration, the "five times" celebration, to the United fans [after scoring in the FA Youth Cup quarter-final]. I think, first and foremost, a player like that, who had a bit of edge and personality about them, was accepted first, and his talent and whatever he could do with the ball came second. The fans loved him for that. That was one of the first things I remember about Adam Morgan.

'From a fan's point of view, we were desperate for him to come through. We did the same thing with Jordan Rossiter. We built him up as this next big Scouse hope. Now we finally have a player in Trent Alexander-Arnold who has the quality. But for years we were desperate for Adam Morgan.'

And as a Liverpool-born-and-bred, left-footed striker with lethal finishing skills, comparisons to Anfield great Robbie Fowler – so adored on the Kop his nickname was, simply, 'God' – were unavoidable.

'Yeah, I could see that,' *Liverpool Echo* journalist James Pearce begins, remarking on Morgan's stylistic similarities with Fowler.

'He was that kind of natural finisher, the "fox in the box" kind of striker, as opposed to someone who was going to beat two or three players and bang one in the top corner. I could certainly see parallels to Fowler.

'But, even at that time,' Pearce adds cautiously, exposing how such comparisons can often do more harm than good, raising expectations too high, too early, 'you still tempered it, in the knowledge he still had so much left to learn and develop.'

That was the line of thought within the club, too, it seems. 'I don't think they'd ever put that pressure on a player,' Morgan suggests. 'I'd go up and train at Melwood with the first team sometimes, but the next day I'd go back down [to the youth team].' The hype train, as far as those within the club were concerned, was best left at the station. Departure was imminent, though.

* * *

Youth team, reserves – Morgan was scoring, scoring, scoring. 'It wasn't easy,' he protests, 'because I always put the work in, but it just came naturally. I loved it.'

Kenny Dalglish's romantic return to the Anfield helm in 2011 was only ever realistically a short-term measure. In May 2012, 'King' Kenny was sacked as Liverpool manager. His replacement, Brendan Rodgers, who had proven himself to be a modern, forward-thinking and bright coach with Swansea City, would oversee a pre-season tour of the United States and Canada as his first act as Liverpool boss. Morgan, as one of the club's outstanding young prospects, knew he stood a chance of being included in the touring party.

'No one said anything to me,' Morgan recalls. 'They just said the squad would be announced on the telly in the dressing room. The squad came up on there and my name was on it. Unbelievable. A lot of young lads were going and we were made up.

'We flew from Liverpool airport on a private plane, straight to America. You get there and you don't go through passport control or anything. You've got your own private one. I was just thinking, "What's going on?" I'd been away with Liverpool a hundred times, but always through the normal passport control. I was just loving it. I thought, "Here we go." I deserved a chance.

'We were training at Harvard University. Unbelievable. I've seen that film *The Social Network*, that's set in Harvard. It's the best university in the world and we were training there.'

The first game of the tour was against Toronto FC in Toronto. The squad flew north of the border for the match, and Rodgers pinned two team sheets up in the dressing room: one for the first half, and an entirely new XI for the second half. Morgan was named in the latter.

Tied 0-0 at half-time, Liverpool fell behind after the break, but Morgan pounced on a Sterling centre to tap home his first senior goal for the Reds. It was only a pre-season friendly, but for Morgan it might as well have been the World Cup Final. He sped off in jubilant celebration, as only a lifelong fan of the club would. This was fulfilment, the result of 15 years of hard work, the moment everything that had come before was leading up to. This was the beginning.

'Honest to God, it was the best feeling in the world. It was unbelievable. My dad had flown out that morning. I got a phone call to my room. It was Robbie Fowler. He said, "Come down here, I want to speak to you about the game tomorrow." "Alright, sound." I went down and my old man was standing there. He flew over and we got him tickets for the game.'

Morgan was again a second-half substitute in the next game, a 0-0 draw with Roma at Fenway Park, the home of the Boston Red Socks, the baseball team who share an ownership group with Liverpool. This time he was played out of position, wide on the right, but toiled away regardless. His endeavour was rewarded with a start in the final fixture against Tottenham Hotspur, another 0-0.

This whirlwind, whistle-stop, coming-of-age trip around the States had Morgan's head in a spin; his Twitter following quadrupled to 80,000 overnight; he was shaking hands with James Bond actor Daniel Craig in the changing room; he had scored a goal for his beloved Liverpool FC.

'I covered that pre-season tour in 2012,' James Pearce says, 'when Adam actually scored the first goal of Brendan Rodgers's managerial reign at Liverpool. Pre-season friendlies are usually pretty drab affairs – very stop-start and disjointed, not particularly enjoyable – but that was certainly one of the abiding memories of that tour: just how much that goal meant to Adam, because he celebrated like he'd scored the winner in the World Cup Final, rather than a goal in a pre-season friendly against Toronto.

'I remember interviewing his dad in the crowd afterwards,' Pearce continues. 'He was so deliriously happy, he was in tears. I thought it would be a lovely piece for the local newspaper. I kept asking him what it was like to see his lad score in front of what must have been 40-50,000. He talked about all the hours, and everything that goes into helping a kid get that far. It opens your eyes to what it means. In the grand scheme of things, it was a pretty meaningless game. But to Adam and his family, that day meant everything.'

Morgan picks up the story of his magical summer of 2012: 'On the way home, at the airport, they were giving all the young lads their passports back, but they hadn't given me mine. I said to the man, "Have you got my passport, please?" He said, "No, no, I need to keep it. You are going to travel to Gomel next week," where we played in the Europa League.'

He didn't play in the Europa League qualifier against the Belarussians. He was taken as the '19th man', a surplus player who'd travel with the team and fill in if a member of the 18-man matchday squad fell ill or got injured. And it was the same story for the return leg at Anfield. But he was overjoyed just to be involved, to be seen as a first-teamer.

'I had my own locker [at Melwood], my own suit. I don't think you can be called a first-team player until you play 50 games, but I was getting everything, all the perks of a first-team player – my own suit, suitcase, everything. I remember they came in and asked all the lads if we wanted the new iPhone, about two weeks before it came out. All the new boots, too – I had about six pairs.'

And his first taste of competitive action wasn't far away. Liverpool breezed past Gomel, 4-0 on aggregate, setting up a tie against Hearts in the third qualifying rounds. Morgan again travelled with the squad for the away leg and was this time brought on in place of Fabio Borini in stoppage time.

In the return leg, he started. At Anfield. On a European night, when the stadium takes on an extra electricity. At the home of the five-time champions of Europe – never mind that the opposition, hailing from Scotland, carried none of the mystery or exoticness of a Marseille, a Porto or an AC Milan – midweek evening games in continental competition are special. And Morgan was starting.

'On the Wednesday, we were training. And what [Rodgers] used to do was, the day before a game, we'd warm up and then [coach] Mike Marsh would give the bibs out. Normally, if you've got the same colour bib as Gerrard, you were starting. I was running with Jack Robbo, just doing circuits in the warm-up. Mike gave me a green bib and he gave Jack a red one. I looked at Suárez: he had a green bib. I thought, "What's going on here?"

'All of those in green walked over to the other pitch and I just stayed still. All the young lads and the lads who weren't starting went the other way. I'm just stood in the middle. Then Rodgers said to me, "Morgs, come on." Oh my God, I'm starting.

'I could not wait to get off the training pitch. I wanted to get inside and tell my dad. We were doing unopposed shape drills – out to the wide man, cross it in and then finish. The fences at Melwood are no higher than me. I was that nervous, when the ball came to me, unopposed on the penalty spot, I booted it right out of the training ground into some neighbour's garden. All of them, and the manager, started laughing – "You're going to play your way out of the team."

'I was starting on the right of midfield – well, right of a three, really. I'd have played left-back, I wouldn't have cared. I just wanted to play at Anfield.

'I'd played at Anfield 15 times, but in front of 100 people. This was the first team. I knew it was going to be full.'

A combination of nerves, anxiety and excitement made for a long day at the team hotel before the evening fixture. But, having sourced 46 tickets for friends, and with practically his entire family crammed into an executive box, Morgan played his first (and ultimately only) competitive senior game for Liverpool at Anfield, playing 65 minutes on the right wing in a 1-1 draw. 'I kept it simple,' begins Morgan's assessment. 'When I could get forward, I would. I did well. [Rodgers] praised me afterwards, said I'd done really well.'

With a competitive senior match at Anfield now ticked off his bucket list, Morgan next eyed a Premier League debut that was ultimately never to arrive. He was perhaps only denied this next milestone by a matter of mere inches, however.

'I scored in the game [against Hearts]. I put the ball in the net, but they said the ball had gone out of play. I buried it like normal and ran off, then saw the assistant with his flag up. If that would have counted,' Morgan posits, 'I probably would have been on the bench for the Saturday game. But I lived my dream there.'

* * *

Morgan made one more first-team appearance for Liverpool after the Hearts game, starting and playing 61 minutes of a Europa League defeat away to temporarily cash-rich Russian side Anzhi Makhachkala in October of 2012. By this point, he was training exclusively with the first team. But with competition for places unfeasibly stiff in the attacking positions at Liverpool, and question marks lingering over his physical readiness, Morgan played only for the reserves, occasionally selected for senior matchday squads but remaining unused by Rodgers.

A short loan spell with League Two's Rotherham United in January did little to persuade Rodgers to persevere, and Morgan was informed early the following season that his contract was not being renewed. It was time to find a new club. The Liverpool dream was over.

Morgan partly attributes his failure to truly grasp the few fleeting first-team opportunities that came his way to intimidation. He was a lifelong Liverpool fan and regular Anfield attendee who suddenly found himself a peer of his childhood idols. He never quite mastered how to reconcile the awe the likes of Gerrard and Carragher inspired within him with an acceptance that his heroes were now his colleagues, team-mates and competition.

'I found it easy going up [to train with the first team] when there was just a few of them, but when I went full time, I'd be nervous every single day. These were my heroes. If I was at

Everton I probably wouldn't have been as nervous – they'd just be players. But these were my heroes I was going in to work with.

'I look back now and think, "Should I have gone in and just thought, 'Fuck this, I deserve to be here'?" I'd be like, "That's Steven Gerrard!" I love him. But I don't love, like, Ashley Williams at Everton. I would have thought, "Fuck you, I'll get the ball before you."

'I never would have gone and smashed Steven Gerrard in a tackle. He would have nailed me first, mind. But I would just be thinking, "Whoa, hold off." And you shouldn't be in that mind-set.

'I was in awe, massively in awe. I've seen these players; I just want to do what they've done. I should have been like Gerrard when he said to Paul Ince, "I'm going to take your place." He just went in like a little Scouser and said that, but he meant it.

'Don't get me wrong, I was never going to play every week – I had Suárez, Sturridge, Borini ahead of me, and Andy Carroll, who was just leaving when I went up to the first team. It would have been very difficult for me, but you don't know what could happen.

'Jack Robinson is still one of my best friends. I speak to him almost every day. He would say the same: "Remember how nervous we used to be going into that dressing room at Melwood?" For me, I never felt fully like I belonged there. That wasn't because people didn't make me feel welcome; everyone always made me feel welcome. It's just that when you're training with them and they are calling you by your name ... I've loved [Gerrard] since I was this big, and he knows me. It's just like you are one of the lads.'

* * *

'I needed a new challenge,' Morgan says, picking up his story at the point we began: after being told by Brendan Rodgers that he didn't have a future at Liverpool. 'After a few days of being upset, the loan window was shutting. Yeovil, Leicester and Carlisle came in for me, with [permanent contract] offers as well.'

Wanting to remain at as high a level as possible, League One's (soon to be League Two's) Carlisle United were ruled out.

Championship clubs Yeovil Town and Leicester City had made identical offers: a three-year contract at the end of the season-long loan; same money. Feeling a need to put distance between himself and Liverpool – the football club and the city – Morgan plumped for Yeovil, a full 234 miles south of Liverpool.

In addition to an immediate starting berth, which Leicester couldn't guarantee, Yeovil offered Morgan the chance to start afresh, forget about how things had ended at Liverpool and build himself back up. An eventual return to Premier League football was well within the realm of possibility should he perform well in the second tier.

But the change of scenery only brought fresh problems. With Morgan keen to impress and manager Gary Johnson eager to throw his new signing straight into the fray, the still-teenage striker played through a niggling ankle injury he'd taken with him to Somerset, playing 85 minutes against Watford, days after signing for Yeovil.

'My ankle was sore, but I thought it was better not to say anything. So I started and we won 3-0. My ankle was sore still, but I played against Blackburn on the Tuesday, we won 1-0 and I'm thinking, "Fucking hell, this is easy." I hadn't scored but I'd been doing well.

'Then we drew 2-2 with Charlton the next Saturday. I'd played three games in a week and my ankle was killing me. I told the manager. I was on the bench for a little while and he was telling me, "You're not fit enough." I said, "I told you my ankle was sore." I need four full 90-minute games, then I'm ready. I know my body. I was telling him this, but he wasn't having it.'

Out of the team, his relationship with his new manager already beginning to deteriorate and increasingly feeling alone and out of place in Yeovil, the distance from Liverpool Morgan had craved quickly became a source of despair.

'I'm a bit homesick,' Morgan looks down at his empty glass as he pulls up memories of his darkest period. 'I started to bet, which is something I never should do. I was just occupying myself with whatever I could. Always betting.

'I was living in a hotel on my own, nothing to do, no mates, no family around me. The manager was on my back and it was making me worse. I was going to the bookies.' I'd never even been a bettor, really, but it was getting hold of me. I hated it down there. Hated it.'

Yeovil were relegated to League One at the end of the season. Morgan ended the campaign with just three starts to his name – the first three games after he joined – and no goals, his commitment and fitness questioned despite, he felt, evidence to the contrary, having passed every fitness test he was given and moving out of the hotel, into a flat in the town, which he still owns.

'I remember going home for the summer, driving back. I was driving up the M6, crying, thinking, "I just don't want to go back there." I was getting good money, but I didn't want to go back.'

'I went back for the first day of pre-season. All the lads were running, but I had to train on my own, go to the gym on my own. I was on my own again, playing poker on my laptop. Being a slob. But I was training like mad, fit as anything. But when I was home I had nothing to do. I liked doing two sessions a day because it would keep me occupied.'

Yeovil began the 2014/15 season in rotten form, winning just two of their first 17 fixtures in the third tier. They slipped into the relegation places in October and never got their heads back above water. Morgan had been sent on loan to St Johnston in the Scottish Premiership for the first half of the season, but the Scottish side cut the deal short, with the striker returning to Yeovil in December having made just five appearances.

Yeovil's one saving grace was a decent FA Cup run, taking them into the third round where they were to face Manchester United, the 20-time champions of England, at Huish Park. While all around the club relished the escapism the glamorous cup fixture brought, United's imminent arrival provided another regrettable milestone in the strained-to-breaking relationship between Morgan and his under-pressure boss.

'[Johnson] pulled me in his office,' Morgan remembers. 'I hadn't been speaking to him for months, aside from a few words. He said, "I want you to go home." This was on 16 December [the day Yeovil beat Accrington Stanley in a second-round replay to confirm their meeting with United on 4 January], "and don't come back until 16 January. I don't want you around the place when we're playing Man United. And we're going to sack you when you come back."

'Sack me? My head was spinning all over the place – what's going on with this footy? It was going so well and then like that I'm forgotten about. We were in League One – what was I doing there? Not that I was too good for the standard, but you're not even giving me a chance, you're saying I'm not fit.'

Upon returning from banishment, Morgan met with Johnson in his office. Yeovil had lost 2-0 to United. The cup distraction was over and the reality of the club's plight, rock bottom of League One, was biting hard. The tense meeting quickly grew heated. Morgan's efforts to 'kill him with kindness', presenting faux deference, aiming to glean answers for his treatment, appeared only to irk Johnson.

'Don't forget, at this time I'm 19 years old. I'd just been in this bubble at Liverpool. I didn't know how to deal with these things. That's why my head was gone. I said, "Alright, I'm going to go." He stood up and followed me to the door. I was thinking he was going to slam the door behind me, then he starts pushing into me. He said, "You're going to get it one day." "Not off you, I'm not."

'His office was by the tunnel, so I walked out and all the lads were there. I said, "Go on, do it in front of them." He was giving me shit in my face, but I was just smiling. I said to the lads, "Look, I'm just standing here. Who's the one being aggressive?"

'As he was walking off, I said to him, "I'm not worried anyway, you're going to get sacked before me." And he turned around and ran at me. I shouldn't have said it. He was trying to get at me. I said to him, "See you later," and went home.'

Johnson was sacked on 4 February.

* * *

Assistant manager Terry Skiverton took the reins after Johnson's sacking and he brought Morgan in from the cold, with the former Liverpool striker scoring his first and only Yeovil goal via a 94th-minute penalty to earn a 2-2 draw with Gillingham in February. Morgan couldn't prevent Yeovil from a second successive relegation, though, as they once again finished bottom of the league.

'We got relegated again and because my money didn't go down they said, "It's nothing personal, but we cannot play you." I was getting a big appearance fee. I wanted out of there anyway. They offered me a nice payoff and I took it.

'All I've ever said is I need a chance to play football. At this time, I hated football. I loved the [Yeovil] fans. I was just out of my comfort zone.'

* * *

Morgan signed for League Two's Accrington after leaving Yeovil, a move that brought him much closer to home. But by this point, his passion for the game and desire to continue a top-level football career had waned. From being heralded as one of Liverpool and England's top prospects at 21, he was now struggling to break into the Accrington first team.

'I was hating it. I didn't like getting up in the morning because of this experience I'd had [at Yeovil]. That scarred me,' Morgan attests.

Released mid-season, he turned his back on the game. He continued to play at local level, because football was all he knew, but he'd reached a nadir.

'I thought, "That's me done now." I tried to get into League clubs that summer but no one would take a chance. I went on trial to York and, again, I had a dodgy time with an agent – they wanted to sign me, but the agent was asking for stupid money for himself.

'My mate was at Curzon Ashton [in the National League North]. He messaged to ask if I was playing for anyone. I said, "I'm swerving it, lad." My head had just gone. I couldn't be bothered. But then I thought, "All those years my mum and dad took me to and from football ... I've got to give it a go." So I went there.

'The first game there I was on the bench – FA Cup first round. We were 1-0 down to Westfields, four leagues below us. I came on and scored the equaliser. That feeling was just as good as scoring for Liverpool. No joke, honestly. It finished 1-1. We beat them 3-0 in the replay – I scored two. I scored in the league for them, too. I was just scoring, scoring, scoring.'

His spark reignited, the second round of the FA Cup brought Morgan the opportunity to showcase the skills he still harboured, to remind the football world he was still here and he still knew how to locate the back of the net. Curzon drew AFC Wimbledon, a game broadcast live on the BBC. Morgan says, 'I thought, "This is my chance to show everyone what I can do."'

And he got swiftly to work in front of the cameras, lashing a 30-yard effort into the top corner, just 28 seconds after kick-off. A close-range header doubled his tally and Curzon's lead 20 minutes later, and a tidy finish completed his hat-trick just after the hour mark.

Curzon's League One opponents would fight back to snatch victory thanks to four goals in the final ten minutes, but, on an individual note, Morgan couldn't have dreamed of a better afternoon's work.

'I honestly had ten agents phone me the next day saying they could get me a move. I met a couple of them, and I've heard it all before: "I can do this for you, I can do that for you." Bollocks.'

Of the offers that came his way, Morgan chose to sign for Halifax Town, the club he still played for at the time of our interview. His nine goals from 19 games helped the Yorkshire side earn promotion to the National League in his first season, leaving him one step away from the Football League return he still has designs on.

* * *

At the time of writing, Morgan is still only 24 years old, the youngest player to feature in this book. Since we met, he has spent a short time with Sligo Rovers in the League of Ireland Premier Division before returning to Curzon Ashton. This is not, surely, where he imagined he'd be at this stage of his career, the victim of cascading fortunes as issues of competition, injuries, mismanaged relationships and isolation have taken their toll, both personally and professionally.

But Morgan remains admirably honest and optimistic. He credits the PFA with helping him overcome the gambling addiction and anxiety that took hold while in Yeovil, and he continues to look upwards, with his best years still conceivably ahead of him.

'Now I feel like a man again, I feel confident. I want to help people now. I want to make it to the top still. I'm not realistically aiming for the Premier League at the minute, but I can still make a living out of this game, because I'll always play – I'll play five-a-side with my mates when I'm 40.

'Football has been the best and worst times of my life, but I'm prepared to open my heart again and try, because I know I've got the ability.

'I could play in the Championship. I've seen some players in the Championship and I know I'm better than them. I just want the opportunity to show everyone what I can do. If you score 30 goals in League One, you're going to the Championship; then if you score 20 goals in the Championship, you're going to the Premier League. All the same people who said, "He's finished ... He was always shite," would be saying, "He's the best," – that's how fickle football is, and I know that, I don't let it affect me.

'I know I've got the ability. And I've got the will to keep doing it now. But now is the first time I'm starting to think, "Is that too big of a jump?" I don't want to think that it is, but I've just got to keep working hard. I don't know.'

As we finish up, before he heads to the gym to keep himself in peak fitness should opportunity come knocking, a wave of catharsis hits Morgan.

'I feel like a weight has just come off my shoulders.'

Epilogue

FOOTBALL offers no guarantees. Not to clubs, not to fans and not to players. As the stories in this book illustrate, there are many crossroads in a footballer's career at which the right path must be chosen every time in order to progress further. And there are rarely signposts pointing the way.

There always have and will always be stories such as these. Opportunities are in short supply and, no matter how talented or dedicated the individual, pitfalls await. Football's randomness is part of what makes the beautiful game so attractive; the most considered tactical plan can be undone by a divot in the turf; seasons can spiral downwards off the back of slips, slices and ricochets. Likewise, a sudden change of direction to avoid a tackle can cause a devastating injury, or a change of manager can see a star player become an outcast. Hearts can, and will, be broken.

The players featured in this book have all dealt admirably with their setbacks and struggles, coming out the other side with a healthy perspective on their experiences. That's not to say that it's been easy for them, though, or that others in similar situations don't fare much, much worse.

There will always be gifted footballers who slip through the net, but can the game do better by its lost boys? Colin Gordon certainly thinks so. And he is well placed to comment, having played professionally for Fulham, Birmingham City and Leicester City, been an agent, a manager and a club chairman.

I went to see Gordon at Aggborough Stadium, home of Kidderminster Harriers, where he is chairman and majority shareholder. A co-founder of football agency Key Sports, he specialised in the identification and handling of talented young players, looking after Theo Walcott, Phil Jones and Ravel Morrison among others. I asked him what duty of care agents and clubs owe to their young players.

'Everything,' came his firm reply. 'From emotional, tactical, physical. You have to understand their games, understand their potential, understand what they could go on to achieve and therefore plot a career and be patient.

'When we go and recruit players at that level, we might not get paid for three or four years. But now, that doesn't happen, because any kid produced at a decent side lower down, one of the big clubs will want to take them and the agent is holding his hands out for a huge fee. And therein lies a problem.'

Having seen the often murky world of the football agent from the inside, Gordon is distrustful and disdainful of the industry and its infiltration by unscrupulous individuals.

'The PFA should police the whole industry,' he says, 'because at the end of the day it's the welfare of their members. They should give a kite mark to every agent who conducts themselves properly, and they should take their kite mark away from people who don't. And football should adhere to the fact that if they haven't got a kite mark, you can't deal with them. Then maybe we'll get some common sense and decency back in the industry.'

He is also damning of the disposable nature with which top-level clubs treat their young players. With patience thin at the highest level, clubs increasingly look to import ready-made yet often sub-standard players from overseas rather than blood their own academy-bred youngsters.

'There is an issue with pathways at the clubs, because of the young talent they are stockpiling. And even in the rest of the Premier League, because of the overseas players we sign who are no better than what we've already got.

'Every young player should aspire to breaking into the first team he's at, and then have choices. But agents can give the dad a job or a lot of money or a nice new Range Rover, and the FA bury their head in the sand. We are losing talent galore. The kind of talent that could have brought us back the World Cup rather than having a glorious failure. And we are ignoring it.

'Regulations should be [tightened up], but the authorities involved don't know what they're looking at. They are well-meaning amateurs. It's only people who have been in the industry and really understand how it works who should be able to police it.'

I asked Stefan Moore (Chapter 10) whether there was anything he feels could have helped prevent his rapid slide from the Premier League to non-league football. 'Guidance,' came his instant reply. 'I needed someone questioning me. There was no one who really did that. My agent wasn't really that sort of guy. With managers, I'd just think, "You're only moaning because we've lost or we've not won." Guidance is a good thing.'

It's a sentiment Gordon appreciates, feeling many players aren't getting sound advice from the people they trust. 'For all the hard-luck stories you've got, there's a common theme: poor choices, poor decisions,' he says, 'And [the agent's] job is to help make good, informed decisions. Parents: just be parents; step away from their career, let good people manage and let your boy progress, develop, prosper at the rate he was meant to develop at. Every player that you've mentioned to me will have a sob story, but it will be based around a poor decision.

'I think some of the young footballers now, the money they earn is obscene. I think that money should be invested in a trust fund for them, for if they don't make it as players, or for when they leave the game,' Gordon suggests, advocating the kind of arrangement Tottenham Hotspur put in place for Ally Dick (Chapter 1) back in the 1980s. In a meeting with Greg Dyke, FA chairman from 2013 to 2016, Gordon presented the trust fund idea as a way of combating the too-much-too-young culture and protecting those who slide from the game's upper echelons from a hard landing. 'Brilliant. Fantastic idea,' enthused Dyke. But 'I didn't hear back from him,' Gordon says. 'Then I got told by the FA he only works three days a week.'

In 2012 the Premier League moved to address growing concerns over the amount and quality of young players its clubs were producing by initiating the Elite Player Performance Plan (EPPP), which has also been adopted by the 72 Football League clubs. 'The plan,' claims the Premier League's official website, 'promotes the empowerment of each individual player through a player-led approach.'

EPPP has received criticism from many quarters, largely for its perceived enabling of the biggest clubs to hoover up the best talent from smaller teams, and with players from the age of nine given a fixed valuation. Gordon, for one, is not a fan: 'The whole EPPP is shambolic; if you give a player a value at nine years of age, you better be careful what you wish for.'

The Premier League reported in 2015 that 65 per cent of the 18-year-olds within the EPPP structure were awarded professional contracts, a relatively high uptake. But with around 12,000 kids on the books of the top 92 clubs, this means an awful lot will continue to fall through the net. EPPP ensures any player aged 16-18 taken on for a scholarship will continue to receive a high-quality education even if they are released by their club, with courses ranging from recognised qualifications, vocational training and courses on wellbeing. But there are concerns that the education on offer is not being taken seriously enough by young men whose focus is trained on a professional football career, while there are fewer provisions in place for players released by academies before the age of 16. A 2015 study by Dr David Blakelock of Teesside University discovered that 55 per cent of players let go by professional clubs' academies suffer 'clinical levels of psychological distress' within 21 days of their release. In 2013 a 26-year-old man committed suicide after years of battling depression triggered by his release from a Premier League club at 16.

Mental health and wellbeing is a subject football is finally beginning to take seriously, following the tragedy of Gary Speed's suicide in 2011 and Clarke Carlisle's brave openness about his own struggles with depression. The PFA now has a wellbeing arm with a 24/7 helpline and dedicated support network, while individual clubs, the FA, EFL and Premier League are all investing in this previously neglected area. But Kevin George, a former footballer who now works as a 'human performance consultant', delivering talks to clubs and players of all ages on 'emotional literacy', believes more can and must be done, with empathy and more-specific education the key.

'We see it all the time with players: people will say, "They've got a bad attitude" or "They can't even get fit, they're not serious", but we don't understand what they've been through or how they've been affected,' George says.

'The game can do better by its young players by educating them. By educating them on mental health, about things like anxiety. And I say that because it's the most common experience with mental health people will have throughout their lives, regardless of what they do. Talking about anxiety in terms of how unique it is to who we are – it turns up in different ways, like my anxiety will come up different to your anxiety. And not all anxiety is bad – there might be times when I have a level of nerves before a game, but that keeps me on my toes. When it gets too much, that's a problem. It's being aware of self and how little things play out.

'You can't take away the pressure,' George continues. 'It's such a big thing that these players are doing – they're playing an elite sport. But providing the education and providing staff that have therapeutic training, that would have a massive difference.

'Mental health is a tick-box. Clubs miss the point that it's in their best interest to get wellbeing and welfare, because from a business perspective it makes sense. There are players right now who are at under-21 level, England players, who should be worth £50m but they're on the verge of getting released by their clubs. It's because of personal issues, or issues the clubs don't know how to manage, or issues with the club.

'What we need to do is better prepare them, in terms of the tools we give them.'

Colin Gordon is succinct in his summation of how clubs and the footballing authorities can take better care of the young players the game casts aside. 'Look after the majority: that would be my position on it,' he says, suggesting concern should be spread more evenly among aspiring footballers, rather than focusing on the few deemed the most valuable.

There is no easy path to the top. Any player playing at the highest level has gotten there by surmounting innumerable obstacles, passing through endless selection processes while also making sound decision after sound decision, learning quickly from mistakes and benefitting from more than a little good fortune. The rewards are high and so are the risks. The stars simply can't always align for the many, even the outrageously talented. It is what comes next, though, that must be better understood.